MW00635917

REBELS WITH A CAUSE

REBELS WITH A CAUSE

Reimagining Boys, Ourselves, and Our Culture

NIOBE WAY

DUTTON

DUTTON
An imprint of Penguin Random House LLC
penguinrandomhouse.com

LIBRARY OF CONGRESS CATALOGING-IN-PUBLICATION DATA

Names: Way, Niobe, 1963– author.
Title: Rebels with a cause: reimagining boys, ourselves, and our culture / Niobe Way.
Description: [New York]: Dutton, [2024] | Includes bibliographical references and index.
Identifiers: LCCN 2024012610 (print) | LCCN 2024012611 (ebook) |
ISBN 9780593184264 (hardcover) | ISBN 9780593184271 (ebook)
Subjects: LCSH: Boys—Psychology. | Boys—Mental health. |
Masculinity. | Male friendship.
Classification: LCC HQ775 .W339 2024 (print) |
LCC HQ775 (ebook) | DDC 649/.132—dc23/eng/20240419
LC record available at https://lccn.loc.gov/2024012610
LC ebook record available at https://lccn.loc.gov/2024012611

Printed in the United States of America

1st Printing

BOOK DESIGN BY DANIEL BROUNT

To the rebels and their cause

It isn't the rebels who cause the troubles of the world,
it's the troubles that cause the rebels.

—CARL OGLESBY[1]

Contents

REBELS WITH A CAUSE

THIN AND THICK STORIES[1]

Many stories matter. Stories have been used to dispossess and to malign, but stories can also be used to empower and to humanize. Stories can break the dignity of a people, but stories can also repair that broken dignity.

—CHIMAMANDA NGOZI ADICHIE[2]

THERE IS A SCENE in the 1955 movie *Rebel Without a Cause*[3] in which the protagonist, Jim Stark, is begging his father to allow him to go to the police station to report that a boy has died due to a dare gone wrong. His parents don't want him to go because they know it will ruin his life if he reveals that he was part of this deadly game. With tears in his eyes, Jim shouts to his dad: "You are not listening to me! . . . I am involved! We are all involved. Mom, a boy—*a kid*—was killed tonight!"[4] suggesting that there is collective blame to go around. The synopsis of the movie on the internet is: "high school students who should lead idyllic lives in their stable, comfortable suburban families explode with violence that their parents cannot understand." According to Jim, however, the problem is not just the violence, about which his parents do not seem to care and for which they take no responsibility. It's also that they believe he lives an "idyllic" life and thus has no cause.

Listening to boys and young men in my research and in the schools in which I have worked mostly but not exclusively in the

United States over the past four decades, I have come to understand the cause not only of this iconic rebel but also of all others like him. It is simple. They want us—the adults in the room—to listen, care, and take responsibility. They also want us to value friendships and recognize that these are key to their and our mental health. Not having friendships can even make them and us go "wacko." In Jim's case, his desperation to find a close friend leads him to engage in the risky behavior that results in the death of a peer. The fact that his parents do not understand why he is upset and do not want to help him deal responsibly with the devastating consequences of his actions lead him to erupt. His actions and subsequent anger stem not, however, from his hormones, having an adolescent or male brain, or simply being a bad person. They come from living in a culture that doesn't listen, care, or take individual or collective responsibility.

Evidence of such a "boy" culture, one in which the goal is to have a lot of money so as to have a lot of toys, is seen in recent books such as *The Subtle Art of Not Giving a F*ck* and in the widely shared slogan "Just Do It," which means do what you want and don't think about how it may affect others. It is also a culture that doesn't value friendships and tells thin stories about boys, men, humans, and our culture as reflected in our modern definitions of manhood, maturity, and success, with their emphasis on the stereotypically "hard" sides of ourselves and their mocking of our "soft" sides. One of the best-known of these types of stories is that bad behavior among boys and men is inevitable, as "boys will be boys," suggesting that their actions reflect their biology rather than a culture that promotes violence or at least doesn't do much to prevent it. The danger of this story is that if we think it's biology, we don't think we can change it, and thus we don't try. But if we understand that their behavior is a product of a culture that values the so-called masculine sides of ourselves over the so-called feminine sides, we can prevent the violence that stems from such a culture by valuing both sides of our humanity and thus join the rebels whose cause is the focus of this book.

My aim in sharing what boys and young men have taught me about them and about us is to reveal the nature of their and our problems and the solutions. They teach us about who we are as humans and how the culture we have created for them gets in the way and leads to a crisis of connection, as suggested by rising rates of depression, anxiety, loneliness, and suicide, as well as partisan divides, hate crimes, and mass violence. They also teach us about the solutions to the crisis that are rooted in our nature but that aren't reflected in our culture. Not only do their thick stories open our eyes to see the elephant in the room, they also empower and humanize them and us, and repair our broken dignity, as argued by Chimamanda Ngozi Adichie, by reminding us that our future is not in the hands of fate or artificial intelligence but in us humans who already know naturally how to create a world in which we listen, care, and take individual and collective responsibility.

1.

From the time I was a child, I have had a type of double consciousness and thus have understood that there are at least two stories to everything and everyone. The first story, the one that most people share, is considered common knowledge. The second story, the one less often shared, is more difficult to hear given the volume of the first one. We need to listen more closely and with curiosity to hear the second story. We can think of the first story as analogous to a tree as a young child would draw it: with roots, a trunk, branches, and leaves. It's not necessarily false, but it represents nothing more than the image of a tree. The second story reflects more than just its image. It considers where the tree grows, how it nourishes other trees around it, what types of diseases kill it, and why trees are necessary for human survival. I have always been fascinated by why we are more likely to tell the first type of story rather than the second.

Thin stories, or the first type, are not inert. Rather, they work as culturally dominant forces determining how we live, think, feel, and behave. They provide the model by which we raise and educate our children; treat one another; and act at home, in school, and in the workplace. They determine what our goals and aspirations are, and how we interact with technology and the natural world around us. They form our ideas about what it means to be a boy, a girl, a man, a woman, an adult, and a human and what it means to develop over time.

Those of us living in Western society have been telling thin stories for centuries, guided by the philosophies of Descartes, Locke, Hobbes, and Rousseau. These stories split reason from emotion, give human capacities and desires a gender in their references to "man," make culture into nature, and have no heart.[5] In these distinctly European stories told by white and economically privileged men, the men are separated from the women and children, thinking is separated from feeling, the self from the other, the mind from the body, and nature from culture. They are more than just separated, however; they are also placed on a hierarchy. Men (especially those who are white, rich, and straight) and their so-called masculine qualities are placed at the top, while women and children (especially those of color and those who are from poor and working-class communities) and their so-called feminine qualities are put at the bottom. Evidence of the hierarchy of human qualities is in our definitions of manhood, maturity, success, modernity, and even science, with its privileging of our "hard" qualities and capacities such as stoicism, independence, assertiveness, thinking, and crunching numbers over the "soft" ones such as vulnerability, dependency, sensitivity, feeling, and the analyses of words and language. The mainstream definitions of manhood, maturity, and success are premised on the capacity for self-sufficiency and independence and don't include the ability to be interdependent or to sustain mutually supportive relationships in which no one gets sacrificed over another person. The open expression of vulnerability and sensitivity, especially by boys and men, is considered not only lame but also immature, girlie, and gay, which is an insult in a culture that places girls, women, and gay people at the bottom of the hierarchy. Similarly, modernity and science emphasize money over people or numbers over words, with the "soft" qualities on the bottom being considered "traditional" and thus inconsistent with advancement or not based on a "rigorous" scientific method and thus not science.

We know these ideologically driven stories about humans and human qualities are problematic because they often contradict how we really think and feel, especially when we are young; but we share them as we grow older out of fear that we won't be able to get or stay at the top of the hierarchy of humans if we don't believe in them and act accordingly. We also fear we will be even more alone than we are if we are stuck at or demoted to the bottom. With much help from our family, friends, colleagues, and the media, we convince ourselves, especially those who identify as male, that if we emphasize the "hard" parts of ourselves and diminish or outright deny the "soft" parts, we will ultimately attain what we want in life and our children will, too. While it rarely turns out that way, our fear of being or staying at the bottom drives us to believe in stories that we know are not true.

Our culture, with its privileging of all people and things considered "hard" over those deemed "soft," is reflective of a "boy" culture that doesn't actually characterize boys, as will be evident throughout this book, but is a *caricature*, or a stereotype, of a boy. It is also not a "man" culture, however, as it is immature in its privileging of the me over the we, retribution over restoration, money over people, and having fun over taking responsibility. Such a culture reifies itself and thus is perceived to be the natural order rather than the cultural disorder of things. It determines how we treat ourselves and one another, and even how we understand our own problems and go about trying to solve them. We see our mental health crisis, for example, as being about the individual—thus offering therapy and medication to those who suffer—rather than also about a culture that is depressing, anxiety-provoking, and lonely to live in, to which the appropriate response would be changing the culture so that it aligns better with our human needs and our social nature.[6]

I am not claiming—nor are the boys and young men I include in this book—that the hierarchy of humanness and human qualities should be flipped so that those at the bottom would be on top and those on top would be put at the bottom. Men and adults are as human as women and children. Stoicism and vulnerability are equally worthy of celebration; without vulnerability, we would have a hard time connecting to others, and without stoicism, we would have a hard time supporting others. Feeling is an important human skill, but so, too, is thinking. According to Antonio Damasio, a world-renowned neuroscientist, only patients who have suffered severe brain trauma can think without feeling. In addition, friendships are as important as romantic relationships, and research suggests that they are, in fact, even more important for our health and well-being.[7] No humans, human qualities, or relationships should be sacrificed in the name of exhibiting maturity, becoming a man, or being successful. It is the sacrificing of one type of human, one type of relationship, and one side of ourselves over the other that leads to our crisis of connection. The solution to the crisis, therefore, is to create a culture that disrupts rather than flips the hierarchies so that no one ends up at the top or the bottom, but all are seen as equally human, with both sides of their humanity equally valued.

How "boy" culture gets injected into our psyches is through thin stories, with one of the most insidious being about gender differences. The story goes something like this: Boys and men roam the earth with little to no feelings of vulnerability, at least in comparison to girls and women. Driven mostly by their desire for sex and money, they don't want or need emotional intimacy or deep connection, especially with other boys or men, or at least less so than with girls and women; are less emotionally sensitive or astute than girls and women; and certainly are more rational and intelligent, especially in the areas of math and science. They want independence, autonomy, and freedom above everything else. Teenage boys are "rebels *without* a cause," making trouble just because they are stuck in their emotional and social immaturity. If they are acting "like a girl," they are not a man, and most certainly not a straight one. And finally, they are naturally interested, or at least should be, in the "hard" professions—for example, investment banking and anything connected to STEM fields—and are naturally not cut out to do the "softer" careers such as teaching or caring for others.

Girls and women, in contrast, roam the earth with few thoughts, except perhaps those related to makeup, fashion, food, boyfriends, husbands, and children. They have little to no sexual desire, or at least less than boys and men; want nothing but emotional intimacy, especially with boys and men; compete with other girls and women; are untrustworthy; and most of all want to get married and have children and don't value their intellectual sides as much as boys and men do. If they are intelligent, it is simply in the areas of emotions and relationships, both considered less impressive than the "real" intelligence evident in the STEM fields. If they want power and don't want children and/or marriage, they are acting like a man or "a bitch" and thus are not really women at all—or at least not very nice ones. Teenage girls are considered queen bees or wannabes, and thus their rebellious attitudes are often seen as evidence of their immaturity. And just as boys and men are not made for "soft" professions, girls and women are assumed not to be made for the "hard" ones, especially those that involve crunching a lot of numbers. The assumptions that males and females come from different planets and thus have more differences than similarities and that our gender stereotypical behavior (and yes, many of us do act like stereotypes) reflects biological facts rather than cultural fiction are all part of the ideology of "boy" culture.

The hard data suggest that gender and sex (the chromosomal type) are not the same thing. A study by Bobbi J. Carothers and Harry T. Reis of more than 13,000 individuals[8] finds that men and women do not fall into different groups: "Thus, contrary to the assertions of pop psychology . . . it is untrue that men and women think about their relationships in qualitatively different ways." Lise Eliot, a social neuroscientist, has written *Pink Brain, Blue Brain,* a book about how "infant brains are so malleable that what begin as small differences at birth become amplified over time, as parents and teachers—and the culture at large—unwittingly reinforce gender stereotypes."[9] Revealing how cultural beliefs and practices create gender differences, she states:

> Boys and girls are identified in utero and the nurseries painted to match months before birth. From girls' preschool ballet lessons and makeovers to boys' peewee football, hockey, and baseball league, our world is in many ways more gender divided than ever . . . The more we parents hear about hard-wiring and biological programming, the less we bother tempering our pink or blue fantasies and start attributing every skill or deficit to innate sex differences . . . Even teachers are now preaching the gospel of sex differences, goaded by bad in-service seminars, by so-called brain-based learning theories . . . And fueling it further is the massive pink-versus-blue marketing of dolls with ever thinner waists and action figures with ever broader shoulders. While some parents still fight valiantly to avoid stereotyping, the larger culture has embraced it with a vengeance.[10]

If you think these gender stereotypes are outdated, log on to the internet, check out Netflix and TikTok, read postings on Instagram, or walk into any toy or clothing store or bookshop and you will see ample evidence of gender stereotypes that don't sound much different from those prevalent when my eighty-year-old parents were young. Products now appear to be driven by such stereotypes even more than before, with a "pink tax" on products aimed at girls and women, which means that these products cost more than the exact same ones for boys and men.[11] Minda Belete, a student who investigated this topic for his senior thesis at NYU Abu Dhabi, told me: "It's expensive to be on the bottom of the hierarchy."

The data also suggest an intensification of gender stereotypes over time. Sociologist Lloyd Lueptow found that students in the 1990s were significantly more likely to report greater differences than those in the 1970s, especially when it came to qualities such as "sympathetic," "talkative," "friendly," and "affectionate," which were seen as typical of women; whereas qualities such as "aggressive," "self-confident," "decisive," and "adventurous" were seen as typical of men.[12] In *Pink Brain, Blue Brain,* Eliot states that while the data have indicated consistently that there are more differences among males or among females than between the two sexes, our gender stereotyping appears to have only gotten worse. She blames this pattern on difference equality, which is the belief that the qualities associated with Mars (masculinity) or Venus (femininity) are equal in value and should be nurtured only according to the planet to which one belongs. Following this line of argument, writers such as Michael Gurian, Leonard Sax, and Simon Baron-Cohen proselytize on the "essential" sex differences and ignore the hard data that suggest otherwise.

One can also hear evidence of the widespread belief in gender stereotypes in the stories told by our colleagues, friends, and family members, with boys and men being described as "emotional idiots" compared to girls and women, and girls and women as untrustworthy or "needy" compared to boys and men. My female students apologize for speaking in class and taking up too much space or don't speak at all. Then there is the conflation of stereotypically feminine behavior with being a transgender female or gay, such as the story about the woman who told her partner that he must be a trans *woman* given that he is so emotional and sensitive, or the one about the nephew who must be "gay" because he gets his feelings hurt easily and values his male friendships. We are so stuck in our stereotypes that we think that a dean at a university who chooses to paint her office pink is being a feminist rather than just painting her office in the color that she thinks would be nice with her furniture. Even the Oscar-nominated movie *Close,* which is about the friendship between two thirteen-year-old boys, is interpreted as a "gay relationship drama" rather than as a tale about how boys desire close male friendships and what the consequences are of not having them. While we think we have progressed in terms of our gender stereotypes, we haven't; and in fact, we may even be going backward.

I asked a classroom of forty undergraduates in the fall semester of 2022 to write down the words that they associate with masculinity. They wrote down "tough," "stoic," "intelligent," "strong," "independent," "rational," "logical," "hard worker," "productive," "determined," "ambitious," "confident," "competitive," "toxic," "unemotional," "dominant," "aggressive," and "warlike." When they were asked to write down words associated with femininity, they wrote "kind," "gentle," "family-oriented," "pretty," "caring," "sensitive," "emotional," "lazy," "weak," "materialistic," and "calculating." Although both sets of words included negative and positive connotations, the masculine words were more likely to be positive, with only eleven of the fifty-two (21 percent) words suggesting a negative quality, whereas eleven of the thirty-eight (29 percent) feminine words had negative connotations. Our thin stories about the social construct of gender appear to be getting even thinner, and the explicit hierarchy in them remains firm.

In a recent article in *The Guardian,* a journalist explores why he and his male peers have such a hard time developing close male friendships. He initially entertains my empirically grounded thesis, quoting me directly, that such difficulty is a product of a "boy" culture that pathologizes such relationships for boys and men. Then he switches to what he perceives to be the more valid reason, which is that men are biologically wired not to want emotionally intimate friendships. He quotes "the godfather of friendship research," Dr. Robin Dunbar, who "argues that men don't become less likely to have intimate friendships: they are born that way . . . [Dunbar says,] 'What's become very clear in the last decade . . . is the completely different way the social world of men and women works.'"[13]

A journalist for *The New York Times* also sided recently with this naturalized argument in an article about why marriage is becoming less attractive for heterosexual women.[14] She explains that the reason such women are having such a hard time finding emotionally sensitive partners is that men are "limited in their ability" to be emotionally expressive and "some" do not naturally have the emotional sensitivity necessary for romantic relationships with women. Not only are these views inconsistent with my data and data collected over the twentieth century and into the twenty-first, but they confound what may be true within a particular cultural and historical context with what is biological. Had the journalists and the scholars looked at friendship in and outside of the United States over the past few centuries, they would have seen that the desire for intimate friendships, including those between two people of the same sex, and the capacity to be emotionally sensitive are not reflective of a gender or sexual identity. These are simply human desires, capacities, and needs.

The persistence of our gender stereotypes and hierarchies is also found in a recent United Nations survey, which indicated that nine out of ten people have a bias against women, believing them to be less competent than men and, according to some 25 percent of the respondents, "deserving of being beaten."[15] Additional evidence of our male biases intensifying can be found in data that indicate that there are significantly more biological females identifying as male these days than vice versa. Only a decade ago, the opposite was true. In a society that increasingly idealizes all things deemed male and masculine and mocks most if not all things deemed female and feminine, these trends are not surprising.

While the possibility of alternative gender pronouns or having a nonbinary gender identity has made us believe that we have moved past old-fashioned gender binaries, stereotypes, and hierarchies, it appears to be having the unintended consequence of reifying them for those who reject such gender fluidity. Those who *don't* identify as "they," and in some cases are even irritated by those who do, appear to be more rigidly aligned to the gender binary of "he" or "she" than ever before. By focusing on changing pronouns as the only solution to the rigidity of our social constructs of gender, we are not addressing why some of us want to challenge the gender binary in the first place. Maia Kobabe, the author of *Gender Queer,* one of the most frequently banned books in the United States, describes not wanting to engage in stereotypically gendered behavior as one of the reasons for rejecting the "she" or "he" identities because, as Kobabe once wrote as a teen, "I don't want to be a girl. I don't want to be a boy either. I just want to be myself."[16]

In a classroom on the campus of NYU in Abu Dhabi, I ask my students, most of whom are from the continents of Europe, Asia, and Africa, how they would describe their identities. They respond with the following: "I love god," "I am an introverted person," "I want to change the world to make it a better place," "I want to help challenge child marriage laws in my country." Their responses stand in stark contrast to those in my New York classrooms, where most students start with their gender or non-gender binary pronoun, reflecting the distinctly U.S. version of "boy" culture in that it's both progressive in challenging the binary in the first place and yet at the same time leads to a backlash where the binary becomes even more reified by those who adhere to it.

2.

In contrast to a thin story, which is not necessarily false but when seen as a product of nature rather than of culture becomes misleading, a thick story doesn't stand isolated from its context. It has depth and nuance and may even feel intuitive. When you hear such a story, it often makes your skin tingle because it resonates but is rarely spoken out loud. It reflects what you know to be true but think that you are the only one for whom it is true. Because if it were true for everyone, you reason, it would be better known and more widely shared. To hear them, you must pay attention and listen closely and with curiosity.

There are three thick stories in my life that have nurtured my ability to hear other ones. The first one has to do with my name, Niobe. My mother gave me my name, which comes from a Greek mythological character who was the queen of Thebes and had seven sons and seven daughters. According to Homer's *Iliad*, written in the eighth century BC, Niobe boasted about the beauty and number of her fourteen children to the goddess Leto, who had only two children, Apollo and Artemis. As punishment for her hubris—a Greek-derived word that means "arrogance"—Apollo killed Niobe's sons and Artemis killed her daughters, although some versions of the myth describe how one daughter escaped the slaughter. Upon discovering her dead children, Niobe wept until she turned into a pillar of salt. The weeping rock of Niobe, according to the myth, sits quietly on Mount Sipylus in the modern state of Turkey. She is the symbol of tragedy throughout Western literature, with Shakespeare referring to "Niobe, all tears" in his *Hamlet.*[17] The myth is considered a warning by the gods to arrogant mortals who disrespect their authority. Throughout my childhood and into adulthood, I thought this story was the only one that existed. It was *the* myth of Niobe. I was even hesitant to show pride of any sort, as I thought it might come back to haunt me.

In my midtwenties, I was lying on a massage table when the masseuse told me of the existence of an alternative story of Niobe—a feminist version—and she asked whether I knew it. I was shocked, as it had never occurred to me that there could be another version of a story I knew so well. I discovered that the feminist version was also rooted in antiquity. Ovid's *Metamorphoses,* a poem written in the eighth century AD, a thousand years after Homer's version of the story, suggests that Niobe's children were murdered by Artemis and Apollo because she refused to worship the gods and mocked those who did. In Ovid's poem, Niobe says to the people of Thebes: "What madness it is to prefer the gods in heaven, whom you only hear about, over those that you can see . . . Go home! Enough of holy sacrifice! And get those laurel wreaths out of your hair."[18] Like the little boy who proclaims that the emperor is not wearing any clothes, Niobe, in Ovid's version, questions why gods should be listened to over mortals. While Homer tells the story from the gods'-eye view, Ovid tells it from the human perspective and thus disrupts the story that suggests that humans are less worthy than their gods. Ovid's version of the story makes Niobe into a hero, in other words, who suffered because she spoke truth to power, rather than an antihero whose hubris underestimated the power of the gods. Yet despite the fact that Ovid's version is a more modern interpretation of what went down between Niobe and the gods, it is Homer's version that continues to be told, with the exception of the character named Niobe in three of the *Matrix* films, who is played by the actress Jada Pinkett Smith in a very Ovidian manner. Since it is a mythological story, it is not a matter of which story is true or more complete, but of which we tell and why.

The second story that helped me hear other thick stories has to do with the era in which I was born. The 1960s are often considered a period of significant progress in social justice, a time most people are proud of. Then and in the decade following, we saw the passing of the Civil Rights Act of 1964, Title IX in 1972, and the Equal Credit Opportunity Act of 1974, which made it possible for women to get credit cards without their husbands' approval. In 1973, *Roe v. Wade* legalized abortion, allowing women to determine their own reproductive desires. My parents and their friends made protest signs and headed out with me and my siblings to the streets to demonstrate for women's rights and civil rights. In the spring of 1968, I remember watching my father in his boxer shorts sitting on the edge of the bathtub in our house on West 105th Street in New York City and cleaning his wounds after returning from a protest at Columbia University during which the police had become violent.

As I grew older, however, I began to hear another story. The Equal Rights Amendment (ERA) for women's equality was and remains unratified even today.[19] Students across the United States continue to be segregated by race and class, and even more so than in the 1950s, despite the decision in *Brown v. Board of Education* that it is unconstitutional. Voter suppression, especially in poor communities and communities of color, continues to be rampant despite the Voting Rights Act of 1965, as well as amendments to the act in 1970, 1975, 1982, 1992, and 2006.[20] While the story of progress during the 1960s is not untrue, it captures only part of what happened and thus is inherently thin in its suggestion that we have arrived in terms of civil rights.

The third thick story that has increased my ability to hear the stories that I tell in this book has to do with the town I grew up in, Oberlin, Ohio. The story of the college where my mother taught from the late 1960s to the mid-1970s that is familiar to most is that it was the first college to admit Black students and women, in 1835 and 1837, respectively. The town had and continues to have a population of about 8,000 and was station 99 on the Underground Railroad in the nineteenth century. If you lived in the town of Oberlin in the mid-nineteenth century, you would have seen Black and white children in school together and Black and white people attending church together. Some of the bigger houses in Oberlin during that era belonged to Black families, including the attorney John Mercer Langston, who was the first Black lawyer in the United States. Langston provided scholarships for Black students at Oberlin College and housed both Black and white students from the college. Oberlin College was also the place where Martin Luther King Jr. and Malcolm X gave well-known speeches in the 1960s.

I grew up with these stories. Oberlin College was clearly ahead of its time during the nineteenth and twentieth centuries and in many ways continues to be so. Yet I also know from firsthand experience that while Oberlin College was the first to accept women, my mother was one of only a few women on the faculty in the 1970s over a hundred years after the first woman was accepted into the college. The Black students who attended my elementary, middle, and high school in the 1970s lived on the outskirts of Oberlin, while the white students, many of whom had parents who were affiliated with the college, lived closer to downtown. The white people who worked in the town but who weren't affiliated with the college lived farther from town than the Oberlin faculty, but not as far out as the Black families. Even though my high school was diverse, with an equal proportion of Black and white students, and with students from both working-class and middle-class families, racial and social class tensions were present everywhere. The white students in my high school who were affiliated with the college via their parents, for example, often looked down on their nonaffiliated peers, and they, in turn, disliked the arrogance of their college-affiliated peers. Such a pecking order was evident in terms of who was friends with and who dated whom. Even today, Oberlin appears to be rife with racial and social class tensions, as reflected in the Gibson's Bakery fiasco, in which the white owners of the bakery and the Oberlin college community fought each other over accusations of racism.[21] At the same time, Oberlin College continues to be perceived as a liberal bastion among American towns and colleges. It's not that the progressive story of Oberlin College is false; it just doesn't fully reflect the lived experiences of many of those who know the town more intimately.

3.

Thin and thick stories are not just present in our personal lives. They are also found in our academic disciplines and even in our science, including in my field of developmental psychology. The thin ones are shared mostly in the handbooks of child and human development and the pamphlets in pediatricians' offices. The thick ones are usually taught outside of undergraduate psychology classrooms and are known by therapists and clinicians who hear them from their clients and by pediatricians who listen to their patients.

One of the most widely shared thin stories evident in my field is that humans develop in stages (i.e., infancy, childhood, adolescence) and grow from simplicity to complexity. Replicating our linear and progressive theories of human evolution and human history, the dominant theories in my field believe that we only get better as we get older. While stage theories such as Erik Erikson's eight stages of man and Jean Piaget's stages of cognitive development are now considered outdated in my field, the beliefs that child development is an orderly, linear, and stagelike process and that children are less intelligent than adults are still common, especially among those who are not developmental researchers, including a journalist who recently asked me, "So what are the stages of adolescence?" Most people, furthermore, respond to the probing and brilliant questions asked by five-year-old children by saying, "That's so cute," thereby diminishing their intelligence.

Implicit in this thin story of development is that it happens outside of a cultural context. While beliefs and practices specific to any one culture may shape development, the basic processes of development are assumed to be the same under "normal" circumstances, with the definition of "normal" almost always being the experiences of white middle- and upper-class families living in American culture. The low number of studies of culture that focus on this demographic suggests that my field believes that culture is relevant only for those who are from cultures different from white middle- and upper-class families living in American culture. When culture is studied, however, the story often remains thin, with the definition of culture being the beliefs and practices within a particular context and rarely including the macro ideologies that determine the shape and volume of those beliefs and practices. While developmental psychologists have indeed created ecological models and conducted empirical research that includes examining the impact of cultural ideologies on families and child development, research on the topic continues to be rare in comparison to, for example, the study of self-regulation. And when it is done, the empirical work is often ignored in the textbooks on child or human development.

Another thin story that continues to permeate my field is that gender is a natural rather than a cultural category. While most social science disciplines believe that gender is a social construct, whereas sex is a biological one, developmental psychologists still seem to believe gender and sex are the same thing and that gender development reflects a natural rather than a cultural process. Textbooks on human development continue to assert that boys and men are naturally dominant, assertive, activity-oriented, independent, competitive, and less empathic, sensitive, emotional, and interested in intimate same-sex friendships than girls and women; while girls and women are naturally more empathic, relational, emotional, cooperative, and interested in intimate same-sex friendships than boys and men. They also continue to focus on gender differences rather than on the wide variation evident in the research among boys and men or among girls and women.[22]

But my field doesn't just tell thin stories. It also tells thick stories. One of the most well-known tellers of thick stories is Carol Gilligan, who was listed in 1996 by *Time* magazine as one of that year's twenty-five most influential Americans. In her classic book *In a Different Voice,* she revealed the male bias in studies of human development and the tendency to privilege male voices over female voices, as well as what is deemed "masculine," with its focus on autonomy, separation, and justice, over what is deemed "feminine," such as relationships, connection, and care. Countering the stage theory of Lawrence Kohlberg, who placed the voice of care or a relationship orientation as a lower form of moral decision-making than the voice of justice or an individual rights orientation, Gilligan finds in her research with college-aged women considering an abortion that the "different voice" is one that is both caring about relationships and concerned about individual responsibilities.[23] Her work suggests that the voice of care and responsibility is not a sign of moral weakness but of moral courage. She writes:

> The inclusion of women's experience brings to developmental understanding a new perspective on relationships that changes the basic constructs of interpretation. The concept of identity expands to include the experience of interconnection. The moral domain is similarly enlarged by the inclusion of responsibility and care in relationships. And the underlying epistemology correspondingly shifts from the Greek ideal of knowledge as a correspondence between mind and form to the Biblical [and Koranic] conception of knowing as a process of human relationship.[24]

Gilligan not only situates relationships and responsibility at the center of human experience but also embeds the self *in* relationship and thus resists the Western philosophical impulse to split them.

Other tellers of thick stories in my field of developmental psychology include Margaret Beale Spencer and Cynthia García Coll and their colleagues.[25] These scholars have grounded their work in an understanding of context and culture that underscores rather than ignores the hierarchy of humans where certain people (i.e., those who are rich, white, and/or male) are considered more human than others and thus more deserving of the basic necessities of life. They reveal in their well-cited research articles that such a hierarchy makes it almost impossible to thrive, let alone survive, for those children and families who are considered less deserving than others based on their race, ethnicity, social class, and gender. Spencer and her students also underscore that it is the perception or meaning-making by those who are oppressed that determines the impact of the context, not simply the context itself. All humans, in other words, have agency in their own development and often figure out strategies for short-term survival and long-term liberation. The research carried out by these scholars not only reveals the damaging effects of a culture that is premised on a hierarchy of humans but also challenges the thin story that those perceived to be at the bottom have no voice or capacity to challenge the power structure and thereby solve their own problems as long as those in power don't prevent them from doing so.

Thick stories about human development have also been offered by those outside my field. Anthropologist Margaret Mead finds in her studies of different cultures around the world that no one "sex difference" is true for all cultures. In *Sex and Temperament,* Mead writes:

> While every culture has in some way institutionalized the roles of men and women, it has not necessarily been in terms of contrast between the prescribed personalities of the two sexes, nor

> in terms of dominance or submission . . . No culture has failed to seize upon the conspicuous facts of age and sex in some way, whether it be the convention of one Philippine tribe that no man can keep a secret, the Manus assumption that only men enjoy playing with babies, the Toda prescription of almost all domestic work as too sacred for women, or the Arapesh insistence that women's heads are stronger than men's.[26]
>
> . . . The Arapesh believe that painting in color is appropriate only to men, and the Mundugumor consider fishing an essentially feminine task. But any idea that temperamental traits of the order of dominance, bravery, aggressiveness, objectivity, malleability, are inalienably associated with one sex (as opposed to the other) is entirely lacking.[27]

While Gilligan, Spencer, and García Coll tell a thicker story of those from their own cultures, Mead, drawing on her anthropological training, saw a thicker story by looking outside of her own culture.

When I was a teenager and wanted to investigate what it means to be an American teenager, my father told me that I should "go live in China," as only by understanding the experience of non-American teenagers could I fully understand myself. When through my longitudinal and mixed-methods research, I did listen to those who do not identify as the same gender, ethnicity, or social class as I do to learn about friendships, I not only more fully understood my own friendships and those of my brothers but I also learned a story different from the one I had been taught in my graduate-level classes on human development. I learned that boys were not simply "activity oriented" or interested only in having male "buddies" who didn't care about emotional intimacy. The boys and young men in my studies who were primarily of color and from working-class communities expressed their desires for male friends with whom they could share their "deep secrets" and with whom their vulnerability wouldn't be the source of jokes. They also spoke about the essential nature of these relationships for their mental health. What I learned over the course of my almost four decades of research and in my work in middle and high schools over the past decade is that these themes were true not only for the boys in my studies but also for many others as well.

When asked to describe his best friend, Justin, a fifteen-year-old boy in one of my studies, said: "My best friend and I love each other . . . that's it . . . You have this thing that is deep, so deep, it's within you, you can't explain it . . . I guess in life, sometimes two people can really, really understand each other and really have a trust, respect, and love for each other. It just happens. It's human nature." At the age of fifteen, Jason said: "My ideal best friend is a close, close friend who I could say anything to . . . 'cause sometimes you need to spill your heart out to somebody, and if there's nobody there, then you gonna keep it inside, then you will have anger. So you need somebody to talk to always." As fourteen-year-old Juan put it: "I've got two best friends—Willy and Brian. Like sometimes when me and Willy argue, me and Brian are real close. Then when me and Brian are not doing so good, me and Willy are real close. It's like circles of love. Sometimes we're all close."[28] The boys and young men in my studies also emphasized needing such friendships so that they don't go "wacko." They suggested that they do not simply accommodate to "boy" culture in their "cool poses" that suggest they don't care but also resist it by speaking what they feel and know despite a culture that makes such expressions "girlie and gay."

Yet as the boys in my longitudinal studies became men, they began to sound like masculine stereotypes with their "I don't care" and "whatever" responses to the very same questions concerning friendships about which only a year earlier they had cared deeply. Using phrases such as "no homo" in their responses to our questions about their male friends for the first time thus suggested that this transition from "soft" to "hard" language is not reflective of their nature but of a culture that equates intimate male friendships with a gender and a sexuality.

When asked what had changed about his friendships since his freshman year in high school, Justin, who only a few years earlier had maintained that "my best friend and I love each other," said in his senior year:

> I don't know, maybe, not a lot, but I guess that best friends become close friends. So that's basically the only thing that changed. It's like best friends become close friends, close friends become general friends, and then general friends become acquaintances. So they just . . . if there's distance whether it's, I don't know, natural or whatever. You can say that, but it just happens that way.[29]

When asked whether he still has a best friend like the one he had in the previous year, Marco said:

> No. I don't say I do, 'cause I feel that a friend is going to be there for you and he'll support you and stuff like that. Whether they're good and bad times, you can share with him, you could share your feelings with him, your true feelings . . . Yeah.

> Basically, I hate it, I hate it, 'cause you know I wouldn't mind talking to somebody my age that I can relate to him on a different basis.[30]

By middle to late adolescence, the boys and young men in my studies seemed to face a crisis of connection in which they found it increasingly difficult to find or maintain "deep depth" male friendships. Their crisis was evident not only in their struggle to find friendships but also in their depressed affect and their attempts to sound like they didn't care when they clearly did. Evidence that "boy" culture is at the root of their struggles was in the response of one young man who said, "It might be nice to be a girl because then I wouldn't have to be emotionless."

Rebels with a Cause does not, however, simply retell the story I told in *Deep Secrets,* my previous book about boys' friendships and their crisis of connection. In this book, I reveal what boys and young men teach us about ourselves and the culture in which we live, why most of us are having a crisis of connection, and the solutions to the crisis that is not only specific to them but includes all those who live in "boy" culture and who are struggling with such a crisis. My focus on boys and young men in this book is not because I believe their stories are more important than those of girls and women or non-gender binary people but because what we believe about ourselves is often the same as what we believe about boys and men. Even the word "man" continues to be the default reference to all humans.[31] And if we are going to prevent the violence committed almost exclusively by boys and men, including those who are white and socioeconomically privileged—the demographic of many mass shooters—we must understand why it is happening in the first place.

To share what I have learned from boys and young men, I draw from my own research, as well as from the research of others carried out over the past century, and from teaching students at NYU on the New York, Abu Dhabi, and Shanghai campuses and co-teaching middle and high school students across New York City. In addition, I draw from novels, movies, and the mainstream media, including the articles about boys who commit violence and the manifestos they have written, as they inevitably capture a part of reality not present in studies or in classrooms. I quote extensively from boys and young men because it is necessary to hear what they have to say directly, without the constant interjection of an adult voice interpreting what they have said. By sharing their stories, I encourage the reader to listen with curiosity, care not only about boys and young men but also about everyone else who is suffering, albeit to different degrees, and take responsibility for the ways each of us perpetuate "boy" culture and thus are part of the problem—and of course a fundamental part of the solution.

Part One

BOYS' NATURE

The truth we do not tell is that men are longing for love.

—bell hooks[1]

1.

Human Nature

WHEN MY SON WAS five years old, his father and I got divorced. I didn't want our home to be filled with sadness, so when I came home from work, I tried to look happy. One evening as I walked in the front door and gave my son a big smile, he said, "Mama, why do you smile when you are feeling sad?" I was startled. How did he know that I was faking my happiness? I didn't know what to say, so like most adults when asked uncomfortable questions by children, I changed the topic. Recently, a friend shared a story of her son at five years old, who asked her in a matter-of-fact voice, "Are you yelling at me, Mommy, because your mommy yelled at you?" Another mother told me that her eight-year-old son said, "It makes sense why you would be upset about spills. Your dad used to scream at you for spilling milk. I get it, Mom."[1] Rather than taking graduate-level courses in psychology, perhaps we just need to listen to children.

Such extraordinary capacities to read the social and emotional world among boys and girls have been noted by parents and researchers alike for over a century.[2] Evolutionary biologist Charles Darwin kept a journal of his children in their first years of life and noted their keen emotional observations and deeply caring nature. In March 1842, Darwin noted about his two-year-old son, Doddy:

> On my return from Shrewsbury after 10 days absence, Doddy appeared slightly shy,—I can hardly describe how this was shewn, except by his eyes being slightly averted from mine. He almost immediately came & sat on my knee, kissed me, & was then much excited . . . Doddy's observant nature is shewn by his *daily* telling . . . everyone, without omission, to have pudding, when their meat was finished, & to take a crust, when their pudding was finished.—Elizabeth remarked [about his] careful politeness at meals towards his guests, was like his granpapa the Doctor.[3]

Darwin was particularly impressed by his son's ability to read the emotions of others. On March 23, he noted: "Doddy looking at full-face likeness of Isaac Walton in frontispiece of the Angler said 'like papa looking at Doddy' & then changed it into 'like papa laughing at Doddy.'—The plate [picture] is not at all like me, but it has the faintest smile about the eyes & is a full face." On March 26, Darwin writes: "Doddy was generous enough to give Anny [his little sister] the last mouthful of his gingerbread & today he again put his last crumb on the sofa for Anny to run to & then cried in rather a vainglorious tone 'oh kind Doddy' 'kind Doddy.'"[4]

Darwin also commented on the caring nature of his four-year-old son, Willy:

> Annie 3 years and ½ was looking at a print of a girl weeping at her mother's grave . . . Willy then seemed to find it rather melancholy & sad. Is her Mamma really dead? Has she got no nurse? . . . About 3 months ago . . . when he went with me to Etruria as soon as his things were putting on to go, he began the most bitter cry for fear Annie should be unhappy without him, & when we were set out he began crying again anxiously enquiring whether she would be unhappy.

Darwin's beliefs about our social and moral nature likely stem from his observations of his own children, including his sons.

Judy Chu's developmental research with four- and five-year-old boys finds that boys are often "very aware" and "tuned into how things affect [others]."[5] Jake's mom recounted how her son said to her: "Mom, your voice sounds kind of happy and it also sounds like you're kind of worried about something," and she responded: "'Well, I'm happy that it is a beautiful day today, but you're right, I'm worried because I know it's going to be a really busy day for me' . . . Jake is just, like, clued in. It's like, 'Mom, why did you kind of use that kind of angry voice with me?' . . . He's constantly decoding me."[6] Mike's mom described her son in a similar way: "Yeah, and it's almost half conscious for me that I'm feeling tense or stressed and Mike will say, 'Mom, why are you sounding angry?' or 'Why are you, or are you tired?'"[7] Min-Haeng's mom also remarked on his ability to notice how she is feeling. While moments of emotional attunement are evident in older boys, the early years appear to be a time in which boys feel particularly free to be expressive.

As parents, we are not surprised by such stories, as we know them from listening to own children and to the friends of our children. Every year during their childhood and early adolescence, Amine, one of my son's close friends, made elaborate birthday cards for my son. These cards contained hand-drawn pictures and expressed how much their friendship made him happy. His mother told me that her son would spend hours creating them not only for my son but for all of his close friends. Parents of boys and girls often share stories of their children's sensitivity and emotional acuity. Yet developmental theories suggest that children don't yet have the social or emotional intelligence to understand or reflect on the actions and emotions of others with such sensitivity, or to recognize that people can sound both happy and worried at the same time and that people can fake emotions. Even the topic of social and emotional acuity or attunement is not given as much attention in the study of children relative to that given to their cognitive capacities, even though the former capacities are clearly a component of the latter ones. Reading recent textbooks on human development,[8] one would think that emotional acuity, attunement, and sensitivity, which both Darwin and Chu underscored in their observations of children, are in fact tangential to child development. Why has my field overlooked or downplayed the significance of a set of qualities that parents already know are important and that are fundamental to building human connection?

Carol Gilligan provides the answer in her book *In a Different Voice*.[9] Describing Lawrence Kohlberg's stages of moral development, in which justice-oriented responses to moral dilemmas are considered the highest form of morality and care-oriented responses a lower form, she reveals a male bias in our stories of child development, including the ones we continue to share in the offices of our pediatricians. Such a bias privileges human qualities associated with masculinity, such as thinking, over human qualities associated with femininity, such as feelings. Primatologist and ethologist Frans de Waal agrees with Gilligan, claiming that we have "macho origin myths" that downplay our human capacities for empathy and care and emphasize our competitive and aggressive sides in our theories of human nature. When discussing human nature in our textbooks, we even compare ourselves with our more aggressive cousins, the chimpanzees, rather than with our more peace-loving ones, the bonobos, even though the latter apes share the same genetic similarity with humans as the former. In her book *Mothers and Others,* evolutionary anthropologist Sarah Hrdy also suggests a male bias in our theories not only of human nature but also of human evolution by exposing the absence of any discussion of child-rearing strategies and practices in our understanding of how we evolved. If we didn't raise our children, she maintains wisely, we wouldn't be here at all. She also underscores that our evolutionary history of "cooperative breeding" involves all members of the community regardless of their gender identities. Only in a culture that gives a gender and sexuality to core human capacities and needs and puts them in a hierarchy, with the so-called masculine activities over the purportedly feminine ones, would we end up neglecting an obvious and fundamental aspect of our human story.

STARTING IN THE MIDDLE of the twentieth century, however, some storytellers in the field of developmental psychology have, in fact, resisted such a male bias in their research and told a "different story" about who we are as humans and what shapes how we develop and who we become. During the 1940s and '50s, child psychiatrist John

Bowlby observed the distress young children exhibited at the loss of a primary caretaker and identified a trajectory of responses that began with protest and, when such protest was ineffective, led to despair and ultimately to detachment. His work, which sparked almost a century of research, was in response to a general downplaying of the significance of real-life events. Bowlby chose to focus on the impact of separation from the primary caretaker, as he was convinced it had negative effects. James Robertson, one of Bowlby's research assistants, began to observe children's behavior as they were separated from parents in three institutional settings, as well as when they were at home with their parents prior to the separation and after they were reunited with them. His observations suggested that children need to "experience a warm, intimate, and continuous relationship" with their mother or primary caretaker, and if they didn't, they were likely to show signs of severe emotional distress.[10]

In the 1950s, Robertson made a film called *A Two-Year-Old Goes to Hospital* that illustrates the distress that children experience from even a short separation from their parents. The film records the emotional deterioration of Laura, aged two, while she is in the hospital for eight days to have a minor operation without the comfort of her mother. According to a description of the film, "because her mother is not there and the nurses change frequently, she must face the fears, frights, and hurts with no familiar person to cling to. She is extremely upset by a rectal anesthetic. Then she becomes quiet and 'settles.' But at the end of her stay, she is withdrawn from her mother, shaken in her trust."[11] As a result of the film, significant changes were made in hospitals so that caretakers could stay with their children when they were hospitalized. It is considered a "seminal influence on the development of hospital care for children."[12]

While Bowlby initiated the investigation of early attachment processes and Robertson took the research into the mainstream, it was Mary Ainsworth and her research with babies and mothers in Uganda that led to the well-known typologies of secure and insecure attachment, and to decades of longitudinal research on the ways in which such typologies were found to be associated with social and emotional well-being. Working as a research assistant to Bowlby, Ainsworth began her study of attachment by spending time in several villages near Kampala, Uganda, and visiting homes of babies and mothers over a period of nine months. She and her interpreter interviewed the mother and observed the interactions of the mother and the baby and with the rest of the family. What she saw did not support the view at that time that infants were passive recipients of socialization. Rather, her research suggested that babies actively sought out their mothers, particularly when they were alarmed or hurt. She concluded that babies use their mothers as a secure base from which to explore and rely on their mothers to decrease their anxiety when they are in distress. This "safety regulating system," she maintained along with Bowlby, serves an evolutionary function, as it provides protection from predators and thus ensures survival.

Yet Ainsworth also noted variation in the quality of the attachment among the babies, leading her to characterize attachment as secure or insecure (avoidant or ambivalent). According to Ainsworth: "Insecurely attached babies cried a lot even when the mother was present, whereas securely attached babies cried little unless mothers were absent or seemed about to leave."[13] Securely attached children appeared to have confidence that their mothers would soothe them in times of distress or anxiety, be emotionally sensitive, and protect them when their safety was threatened; whereas insecurely attached children did not appear to have such confidence. Securely attached children, she theorized at the time, would be more likely to freely explore their environments; whereas insecurely attached children would be more clingy or ambivalent (flipping between turning toward and turning away) with their mothers and less likely to explore their environments.

To empirically assess these patterns after she returned home from Uganda, Ainsworth created an observational research procedure called the "strange situation," which entails a child playing with toys for twenty-one minutes in a laboratory while caregivers and strangers enter and leave the lab at different times. During the strange situation, the child experiences being left entirely alone, alone with a stranger, together with a stranger and caretaker, and just with a caretaker. The intent of such a procedure is to create stress for the child with a stranger as well as comfort with the caretaker. The researcher observes through a one-way mirror how the child responds to the departure of the caretaker as well as to her return. From these observations, Ainsworth and her team determined the reaction of the child to the return of the caretaker was a better marker of attachment style than their reaction to the departure. While most children were distressed by the departure of their caretakers, their responses to their return varied greatly and predicted the extent to which a child was willing to freely explore their environment. When the child responds positively to the return of the caretaker, reaching out and/or running over to her to greet her, and returns to play with the toys in the room, the child is coded as securely attached. When the child is more cautious, wary, ambivalent, or avoidant of the caretaker when she returns to the room and has difficulty returning to play with the toys in the room, the child is coded as insecurely attached.

Secure attachment of children with their primary caretaker has been repeatedly found to predict better psychological and social outcomes in longitudinal studies over the life course; whereas insecure attachment has been found to be associated with more negative social and emotional outcomes in later life.[14]

What is most striking about Ainsworth and Bowlby's theory of attachment, given that it was developed in a mid-twentieth century that was most assuredly infused with a male bias, is that it is inclusive of both autonomy and connection in its definition of attachment. Not only do babies seek out their primary caretakers especially in times of distress, but this confidence that their caretakers will take care of them when needed enables those who are securely attached to be autonomous and freely explore their environment. Neither connection nor autonomy, in the theory of attachment, is privileged over the other; both are seen as equally important developmental goals and, in fact, are dependent on each other. When children feel confident that their primary caretakers will protect them from danger, will be sensitive to their feelings, and are emotionally attuned to their needs, they have the courage to explore the world and to take risks that may even increase their anxiety, but they are willing to do so, knowing that they have caretakers who will provide a safe space for them to return. When they do not feel such confidence, they will be less likely to take such risks or will take risks that may be damaging to themselves and others instead of those that are potentially growth producing.[15]

To explain the mechanisms by which attachment styles lead to social and emotional adjustment, developmental psychologist Inge Bretherton and her colleagues describe the ways in which children internalize the messages communicated to them by their primary caretakers.[16] Children, according to attachment theory, create a mental model of whether they are worthy of love and care based on how attuned or sensitive primary caretakers are toward them, especially during times of distress. If they are consistently unavailable, children internalize that they are not worthy of attention or love. If they are more available than not, children internalize that they are indeed worthy of such attention. This internalized mental model gets transferred to other relationships throughout life, and that is why securely attached children appear to have more satisfying and long-lasting relationships over the life course than those who are insecurely attached.[17] Attachment theorists are quick to point out, however, that healthy or mutually supportive relationships later in life can repair any damage done in the early years. Thus, your early relationships with caretakers do not function as a type of fate later in life. Experiences with loving relationships, including friendships, throughout life have been found to enhance one's ability to have mutually supportive relationships that are necessary for health and well-being.[18]

Following the work of Bowlby and Ainsworth and other attachment researchers, developmental psychologist Edward Tronick began exploring the process of emotional attunement between mother and baby that he defined as a state of recognizing and engaging with another person's emotional state. He believed, along with his colleague Beatrice Beebe, that "trust comes not from the goodness of the attachment or of the mother per se, but rather from the ability of the infant and mother to mend the inevitable breaks in their relationship—to connect to one another following periods of disconnection."[19] Emotional attunement is the way that the mother and the baby repair the break, "the glue that bonds."

To examine this process of attunement, Tronick devised the Still Face Experiment, which involves the creation of a break between mother and child followed by a repair.[20] The experiment involves a mother and her baby in a lab setting engaging with each other as they would at home. The baby is sitting in an infant seat and smiling and cooing with the mother as she speaks in a joyful tone to the baby. When the baby points to something in the room, the mother looks to see where the baby is pointing. They are matching each other's internal states and engaging in what my field calls "joint attention." The mother is then instructed by the experimenter not to respond to her infant's gestures, smiles, and coos (to keep a "still face"). Immediately the baby picks up the break in connection and becomes upset. When the baby's repeated efforts to reengage are ignored by the mother, the baby becomes even more distressed and starts crying. The mother is then told to return to attuning to her baby's emotions, and they go back to smiling and cooing together. Tracy Dennis-Tiwary and her colleagues conducted a version of this experiment but had mothers look at their cell phones rather than become still-faced. The researchers found that infants responded similarly with signs of distress at the absence of their mothers' attention.[21] When I show the two-minute video of Tronick's Still Face Experiment to my NYU students, they often tear up. They tell me that they see themselves in the baby and know how the baby feels after the mother becomes unresponsive. They report often experiencing such emotional mismatches in school and out between how they feel and how the other person responds to them.

Responding to the almost exclusive focus on children and their caretakers in the study of relationships, Harry Stack Sullivan turned his attention to the peers of children and adolescents at around the same time that Bowlby and Ainsworth were getting attention for their attachment theory. In his classic book *The Interpersonal Theory of Psychiatry,* he uses clinical cases with boys to argue that humans have a need for interpersonal intimacy or love with a peer, particularly during early adolescence. Such a need is not just focused on finding a playmate; it is an interest in being emotionally intimate with another person who inevitably becomes a chum or close friend. Sullivan describes how this change from a childhood interest in similarity to an adolescent interest in same-sex intimacy "represents the beginning of something very like full-blown . . . love."[22]

> The other fellow [the recipient of love] takes on a perfectly novel relationship with the person concerned; he becomes of practically equal importance in all fields of value. Nothing remotely like that has ever appeared before . . . Your child begins to develop a real sensitivity to what matters to another person. And this is not in the sense of "what should I do to get what I want," but instead "what should I do to contribute to the happiness or to support the prestige and feeling of worthwhileness of my chum."[23]

Researchers studying friendships continue to draw on Sullivan's theory of interpersonal psychiatry and consistently find that those who have mutually supportive friends are less likely to be depressed, anxious, and suicidal, abuse drugs and alcohol, or engage in other forms of high-risk behavior, and are more likely to do well in school.[24] Joseph Allen, a professor of developmental psychology at the University of Virginia and a teller of thick stories in my field, found in his longitudinal study of adolescents from age thirteen to twenty-four that the quality of close friendship during adolescence significantly predicted better social and emotional adjustment later in life, including lower levels of depressive symptoms and better work performance, and was a better predictor of such outcomes when compared with parental reports of the parent and teen relationships. He and his colleagues also found that the quality of close friendships early in adolescence predicts academic achievement many years later.[25] Another report[26] indicated that while about 44 percent of high school students had experienced persistent feelings of sadness or hopelessness in the previous year, and almost 20 percent had seriously considered suicide, the teens who felt close to their peers at school fared better on all mental health measures. Friendships also appear to serve an evolutionary function, as they foster cooperation and the ability to care for others.[27] Evolutionary biologist George C. Williams writes: "[An] individual who maximizes his friendships and minimizes his antagonisms will have an evolutionary advantage, and selection should favor those characters that promote the optimization of personal relationships."[28]

A 2016 study from the University of North Carolina[29] found that while friendship quality was associated with a lower risk of physiological problems, the more friends one had, the lower one's risk of such problems. They also found that the number of friends a person had in middle age had much less of an impact on the risk of physiological problems than did the quality of the friendships. My guess, however, is that this pattern is a matter of difference in the context, as quantity is more possible when one is younger than when one is older. Quality of relationships always trumps quantity in the research on friendships regardless of the age of the respondent. Psychologist William Chopik found that those who valued friendships were more likely to report higher levels of health and well-being and that this association grew with age.[30] The association between the valuing of friendships and health was even greater than the association between the valuing of family and health. He also found that having mutually supportive friendships among older adults is associated with less cognitive decline.

Researchers have found that perceptions of the difficulty of a task are shaped by the proximity of a close friend.[31] In an experimental design, researchers at the University of Virginia asked college students carrying a weighted backpack to stand at the base of a hill and estimate the steepness of the hill. Some participants stood next to close friends, people they had known for a long time; some stood next to friends they had not known for long; some stood next to strangers; and the rest stood alone. The students who stood with close friends gave significantly lower estimates of the steepness of the hill than those who stood alone, next to strangers, or next to new friends. The longer the close friends had known each other, the less steep the hill appeared. In the same study, college students were asked to recall a positive social relationship, a neutral one, or a negative one immediately before estimating the steepness of a hill.[32] They found that those who recalled a positive social relationship estimated the hill to be less steep than those who recalled a neutral or negative one. In addition, the closer the participants felt to the person they were recalling, the less steep the hill appeared to be. The world seems less stressful, in other words, the more one thinks about or is physically proximal to a loved one.

When developmental psychologist George Vaillant was asked recently what he learned from his fifty-year longitudinal study of men originally recruited from Harvard College,[33] he said, as Carol Gilligan had already concluded from her studies many decades earlier, that "the only thing that really matters in life are your relationships to other people."[34] Similarly, in the early 1990s, developmental psychologist Roy Baumeister argued that we have not only a desire for relationships, including friendships, but also a fundamental need to belong: "Human beings have a pervasive drive to form and maintain at least a minimum quantity of lasting, positive, and significant interpersonal relationships."[35] Challenging Maslow's (1968) hierarchy of needs, which puts love and belonging in the middle of the pyramid of human needs, Baumeister puts belongingness at the bottom. A feeling of belongingness with others is necessary to satisfy all other needs. Drawing from decades of his own experimental research at the Max Planck Institute on empathy and altruism among children, developmental psychologist Michael Tomasello also concludes that humans are "ultra-social" animals.[36]

AS A RESULT OF this mostly mid- to late-twentieth-century developmental research, a paradigm shift in the sciences began in the early 1990s regarding how we understand human nature, with a focus on our social and emotional nature and needs. Books with titles such as *The Social Animal,* by *New York Times* columnist David Brooks, and *The Age of Empathy,* by Frans de Waal, started to appear in bookstores. Led by social psychologist John Cacioppo at the University of Chicago, researchers who were a part of the emerging field of social neuroscience in the early 1990s began to use MRI technology to investigate the human brain and drew the same conclusion as Bowlby, Ainsworth, Tronick, Sullivan, Gilligan, Vaillant, Allen, Baumeister, and Tomasello. Namely, that we are social and emotional animals who need one another to survive and to thrive psychologically and physically.[37]

In his book *Social: Why Our Brains Are Wired to Connect,* neuroscientist Matthew Lieberman writes: "[We] are wired to be social. We are driven by deep motivations to stay connected with friends and family. We are naturally curious about what is going on in the minds of other people . . . We will spend our entire lives motivated by social connection."[38] When we are not engaged otherwise, we "think about other people like a reflex, suggesting that our brains are actively promoting cooperation, empathy, and understanding even during 'down time.'"[39] Our brains are in "social default mode" for approximately 70 percent of our time, according to Lieberman, which means we spend most of our lives thinking about the thoughts and feelings of others. One study that he cites in his book examined the brain regions of two-week-old babies and found that they were engaged in "highly coordinated activity" with others.[40] Researchers have even found such activity in two-day-old infants. Such sensitivity, according to an ever-growing body of research, is critical for anticipating the needs and wants of others and thus coordinating and cooperating with them, as well as building meaningful relationships.

Working with his wife and colleague Naomi Eisenberger, Lieberman also finds that social pain and physical pain are experienced similarly according to what lights up on brain scans when subjects experience each kind of pain. Such synchronicity suggests that they are activating the same neural circuitry. Various types of social pain were studied, including breaking up with someone. They found that the area of the brain that is activated was the same area that is activated when you are experiencing physical pain such as breaking a leg. They further explored whether taking aspirin would help not only with a headache but also with a heartache. They found that taking Tylenol (versus a placebo) over a period of three weeks helped to diminish feelings of social pain.[41] Eisenberger and Lieberman argue that the link between social and physical pain is adaptive, evolutionarily speaking, as it ensures that we stay close to each other.

In *The Age of Empathy,* Frans de Waal underscores our social nature and our capacity to empathize with one another and to attune to others' thoughts and feelings. He argues we are "highly cooperative, sensitive to injustice, sometimes warmongering, but mostly peace loving."[42] We even synchronize our bodies, "running when others run, laughing when others laugh, crying when others cry, or yawning when others yawn" so that "their movements and emotions echo within us as if they're our own."[43] The capacity to engage in such "embodied cognition," according to De Waal, is due to our mirror neurons, which lead us to be able to attune to others' emotional states.

Evolutionary anthropologist Sarah Blaffer Hrdy draws a similar conclusion from her studies of ancient cultures: "From a tender age and without special training, modern humans identify with the plights of others and, without being asked, volunteer to help and share, even with strangers. In these respects, our line of apes is a class by itself."[44] This ability to identify with others and vicariously experience their suffering is not simply learned; it is part of us. She centers the evolutionary story on child-rearing and alloparenting, or raising children cooperatively, a practice that entails an entire community's being involved in the process, not simply the children's biological parents.[45] In her book *Mothers and Others,* Hrdy describes a tribe in southern Africa's Kalahari Desert with an extensive exchange network that shares items such as utensils, beads, and cloth, which are given and then passed on to others. Such exchanges let each partner know that they "'hold each other in their hearts' and can be called on in times of need."[46] Trading partners can be acquired at birth or passed on as a heritable legacy when one of the partners dies. Partners are built up over a lifetime, and children inherit the deceased parent's exchange parents, as well as kinship networks, and "gifts were often given at that time to reinforce the continuity, since to give, share, and reciprocate was to survive."[47] From this example and others throughout her book, Hrdy concludes:

> Were it not for the peculiar combination of empathy and mind reading, we would not have evolved to be humans at all . . . Without the capacity to put ourselves cognitively and emotionally in someone else's shoes to feel what they feel, to be interested in their fears and motives, longings, griefs, vanities and other details of their existing, without this mixture of curiosity about and emotional identification with others, a combination that adds up to mutual understanding and sometimes compassion, *Homo sapiens* would never have evolved at all.[48]

Popular essayist Malcolm Gladwell tells a similar story in his book *Outliers*.[49] It concerns Roseto, Pennsylvania, a tight-knit community of Italian immigrants. A physician became fascinated by the low rates of suicide, drug addiction, alcoholism, and crime in the town, compared with those in the rest of the state and nation. He and his team wanted to know the reasons for such healthy outcomes. They examined the nutrition and genetics of the people who lived in the town, as well as the environment in which they lived. None of these factors appeared to explain the low levels of problems. Finally, after years of investigation, they realized that the answer lay in the social connections of the community, the sharing of stories between neighbors, the familiarity in stores, the feelings within the community of belonging to a greater whole. The researchers called for the entire field of medicine to reorient toward understanding the social context of their patients. Instead of limiting themselves to questioning their patients about behaviors such as smoking or drinking, healthcare practitioners should also be asking questions about the quality of their relationships and offering resources for finding supportive communities. Similarly, in research carried out in Chicago during an extreme heat wave in the 1990s, sociologist Eric Klinenberg found that social isolation increased the risk of death and that "a close connection to another person, even to a pet, made people far more likely to survive."[50] He also found that women fared better than men, which he says was because "they have stronger ties to friends and family."[51] He notes further that "Latinos [from low-income neighborhoods] had an easier time than other ethnic groups in Chicago . . . as they tend to live in crowded apartments and densely populated neighborhoods where dying alone is impossible."[52]

WHILE WE HAVE HAD a fundamental paradigm shift in the sciences sparked by the tellers of thick stories in my field, we have yet to incorporate into our story the research of those who reveal the ideological belief systems that get in the way of our social and emotional nature and needs and often lead to a crisis of connection. In his classic book *Childhood and Society,* which was originally published in 1950, Erik Erikson argues that the study of development must explore the historical, social, and political context of the society in which the child was born and raised, as it is this context that fundamentally determines the social, emotional, and cognitive aspects of human experience or, to put it in layperson language, whether we can or want to live a long life. In his work, he draws from his studies of those living on Native American reservations to make his point that a study of humans out of context is not able to comprehend human thoughts, feelings, or behaviors, as the cultural context, or story that describes such context, reveals the meanings. In his later work, he also describes the ways in which the identity development of youth during the 1960s and '70s was shaped by the Vietnam War and the civil rights movement, underscoring the role of the cultural ideologies in such development.

Following Erikson, Urie Bronfenbrenner presents his own model for understanding the impact of society on the child, which he calls the ecological model of human development.[53] In his model, the individual is at the center of an onion-like set of circles within circles, with the innermost ring being the micro context (e.g., home and school environment, peers), the next the meso context (e.g., the interactions of the micro contexts), and the next moving outward being the exo context (e.g., national policies). The outermost circle of his model is the macro context (e.g., widespread cultural beliefs and practices including ideological ones). Drawing from various empirical studies across the twentieth century, Bronfenbrenner makes the case that each layer of context is equally important to understanding why humans think, feel, and do as they do within and across generations.[54]

After the passing of *Roe v. Wade* by the Supreme Court, Carol Gilligan, who was a teaching fellow for Erik Erikson, began studying the moral decision-making of women who were pregnant and considering an abortion. She heard a tension in the narratives of the women in her studies between caring for or taking responsibility for self and caring for or taking responsibility for others, with the former deemed selfish and the latter equated with feminine goodness. Women in her studies struggled to resolve the tension as they understood that taking care of themselves would be frowned upon by those around them, but taking care of others and ignoring their own needs would lead them to disconnect from their own needs and would thus feel morally problematic. Her research underscores how the ideology of patriarchy, with its construct of a "good woman," leads women to experience a crisis of connection where their options are either to take themselves out of the relationship for the sake of a relationship that is not authentic because it doesn't include their own needs or to lose relationships entirely for the sake of holding on to and listening to their own needs and thus being alone.

Developmental psychologist Lyn Mikel Brown finds in her research with Gilligan and others that girls, too, face a crisis of connection, in which the pressure to be a "perfect girl" who doesn't speak what she knows and feels when it makes others uncomfortable or angry intensifies as they become young women in a patriarchal culture. An eight-year-old girl in their study of girls from early to late adolescence makes explicit this process of unknowing as one grows older: "I think young children have a mind much more than anyone else because, I don't know, they don't have much of a brain. And I think that after a while you just sort of forget your mind because everything is being shoved at you in your brain."[55] Gilligan and Brown reveal the ways that a cultural ideology that is premised on the silencing of girls and women is not good for girls or women, or for anyone else.

In the 1970s, Margaret Beale Spencer began to investigate Black preschool children with an observation similar to the one that Gilligan was making at that time regarding girls and women. Spencer noted that Black children had been left out of the study of human development and that the field of developmental psychology didn't investigate the impact of cultural ideologies such as white supremacy (or the hierarchy of humans with whiteness being at the top) on child development. What Spencer found in her early studies is that while the Black children did prefer the white dolls, thus confirming the classic doll studies Kenneth and Mamie Clark carried out in the 1940s, they did not turn that bias against themselves and reported feeling very good about themselves. Her early discovery of this cognitive dissonance in children underscored not only the effects of cultural ideology on children' preferences (e.g., preferring white dolls) but also the ways that children negotiated or interpreted their contexts for the purposes of identity development. She found, in other words, that children were not simply passive recipients of cultural socialization but actively engaged with and interpreted the meanings of their context in ways that made sense to them. Her subsequent research and the research of her students over many decades ultimately led her to develop an ecological model of human development called the Phenomenological Variant of Ecological Systems Theory (PVEST), which underscores the ways that macro-level forces interact with individual-level risk and protective factors to shape how children make sense of their worlds, including their identities and relationships.[56]

Cynthia García Coll, another teller of thick stories in my field, and her colleagues extended Bronfenbrenner's ecological model by revealing the impact of social stratification or hierarchies based on race, ethnicity, and social class on families and children. She and her colleagues bring social positioning, which is one's location in the hierarchy of humans, into the center of their studies rather than leave it at the periphery.[57] Drawing from their own research, they critique the thin stories that offer explanations for poor school performance or for high-risk behaviors among students of color—the stories, for example, that focus on genetic and/or environmental deficiencies rather than on ideological structures that make it virtually impossible to succeed. Their research reveals the way that discrimination and residential and economic segregation lead to social and psychological segregation in which "families and children of color are not given access to the necessary social and emotional resources to do well because of social stratification mechanisms."[58]

WHAT IS MOST STRIKING about this large body of research I have reviewed in this chapter, is that we continue to ignore the findings of this research in the past century in our everyday lives. Evidence of such a pattern is everywhere, starting with the fact that we continue to have to prove in our research and in our daily lives that feelings and relationships matter, and we never have to prove that thinking, or the individual, matters. We continue to maintain gender stereotypes, knowing intuitively and empirically that such stereotypes can lead not only to mental health problems but also to violence. We also continue to believe that emotionally intimate friendships are necessary mainly for teenage girls and gay boys and not so much for men and not fundamental for physical or mental health, as the data suggest they are. Evidence of our ongoing belief in our thin stories includes bestselling books, such as Richard Reeves's *Of Boys and Men:*

Why the Modern Male Is Struggling, Why It Matters, and What to Do About It,[59] that make natural what is cultural according to the data, including from the mouths of boys and young men themselves.[60] Articles in the newspaper, furthermore, continue to make claims that reify gender stereotypes.[61] If we begin to listen with curiosity, however, to the very group that is deemed biologically inept both socially and emotionally and also is most likely to commit suicide and homicide, we begin to see not only the thinness of our stories about them and about us but also the way to solve our own problems.

2.

Boys' Friendships[1]

IN THIRD GRADE, MY son was bullied by his peers. He didn't tell me for many months, until one night at dinner he broke down and gave me the details. I was consumed with sadness and anger at his teacher and his peers. When his father and I went to discuss the issue with an administrator at his school, we were told to read a well-known book about boys that suggested that what was happening to my son was "normal," as "boys will be boys." I was shocked that this corrosive stereotype was shaping a school with a 1,200-person student body. Even with our numerous anti-bullying efforts in schools, we continue to think that boys are driven solely by the need for dominance and that boys should just suck it up when they are at the losing end.

A thicker story about boys and young men became obvious to me when I was a volunteer counselor as part of my doctoral training at an urban high school in the late 1980s. In my sessions with boys and young men, I heard story after story of boys wanting friends with whom they could share "deep secrets." I became fascinated with why we knew so little about boys' friendships, why we assume they weren't interested in these types of friendships, why I had forgotten that my two younger brothers also spent much of their younger years yearning for such friendships, and why we knew almost nothing about the kinds of friendships boys had during adolescence. I wondered if other boys' stories sounded like what I heard in my counseling sessions and from my brothers.

I have spent my career investigating such questions via mixed-method (using both questionnaires and semi-structured interviews) and longitudinal research with students, following them from early to late adolescence. My samples, which are mostly from urban and public schools, are primarily from poor and working-class communities and from a wide array of racial and ethnic identities, including African American, Puerto Rican, Dominican American, Chinese American, and European American. It is these boys and young men who taught me what it means to be a boy and to be human, and how our culture gets in the way of their and our ability to thrive and even to survive. It is a story that was not being presented in developmental textbooks or in the culture at large when I began my research almost four decades ago and still to this day continues to be mostly absent from both contexts.

The semi-structured research interviews my team and I conducted with approximately 140 boys (who are the focus of my previous book *Deep Secrets*) when they were freshmen in high school and following them longitudinally for three to four years suggested four overarching patterns: (1) Boys want male friends with whom they can share their "deep secrets" and are particularly likely to express such a desire during early and middle adolescence. (2) Boys know that emotionally intimate friendships are critical for their mental health and speak directly about the potential mental health problems that would result from not having such friendships. (3) As they reach middle to late adolescence, boys struggle to find and maintain such close male friendships and thus experience a crisis of connection. (4) Boys suggest that the cultural pressures to "act like a man"—that is to say, not behave in a manner others would consider "girlie and gay"—and to "mature" by becoming more stoic and less emotional, are the culprits behind their struggles to find and maintain male friendships during middle and late adolescence. Such a "boy" culture, they suggest, leads to their crisis of connection, and their subsequent mental health problems, just as they predicted they would in early adolescence.

1. Deep Secrets

The boys in my studies defined a best friend during early and middle adolescence as someone with whom they could share secrets, and betrayal of this confidence was often the cause for terminating a friendship. Alejandro,[2] a fifteen-year-old, put it this way: "I trust my friends. Like if I have a deep secret, I don't want to tell anybody. I tell one of my friends that I know won't tell anybody else unless I give them permission to tell somebody else." When asked if friends are important, Lucas replied, "You can't just do everything yourself or tell your problems to yourself. You can't, like, just talk to yourself. It's good to have someone to talk to and tell your secrets to."

Marcus described his "ideal best friend" as "a close, close friend who I could say anything to . . . 'cause sometimes you need to spill you heart out to somebody, and if there's nobody there, then you gonna keep it inside, then you will have anger. So you need somebody to talk to always." When asked to explain why he feels close to his friends, he responded: "If I'm having problems at home, they'll like counsel me, I just trust them with anything, like deep secrets, anything." When asked the same question, Eddie said, "It's like a bond, we keep secrets, like if there is something that's important to me, like I could tell him and he won't go and make fun of it. Like if my family is having problems or something." Carlos described his best friendship: "Like we could express our feelings or whatever. And tell each other how we feel. Like if I feel bad one day, I tell him why . . . We show each other love. I know the kid inside of him . . . 'Cause I, I grew up with that kid, you understand? I know who he really is." Jin Long says that he is close to his best friend because he can "talk about stuff like deep deep. Our feelings and stuff, like what we talked about today [in the interview]."

Charles said that what he most likes about his friendships is "I don't know. Like my friends . . . They are honest, like they tell me things, like they tell me their secrets." When asked what he likes most, Omar said, "Me and [my best friend] can talk about real serious stuff that I wouldn't even talk to my mom about." Doug's response to the same question was: "[My best friend] could just tell me anything and I could tell him anything. Like I always know everything about him . . . We always chill, like we don't hide secrets from each other . . . If I have a problem, I can go tell him. If he has a problem, he can go tell me." For Will, "a friend . . . is a person that would be your friend no matter what, who will be there through thick and thin, you know, someone to talk to about everything, you know, just basically a true friend." When Eric was asked why sharing secrets is so important, he responded: "It's that you get a closer relationship. You feel for each other more. Like we see what we like and how we are alike and, you know, like we're close to each other, real close, so nothing would get like in between us."

Xinyin said that the intimacy is so strong between him and his best friend that it feels as if they have known each other in a past life. He explained: "Oh, um, when we talk, we keep telling each other secrets, and he trusts me and I trust him, so we [developed] that kind of friendship . . . [My best friend] is kind of an open man. His feelings are open. And he, he knows a lot about how someone's feeling—how they feel." In his sophomore year, he said that what he likes most about his friendship is that "you could tell him your feelings, and we could discuss together our feelings and how they are alike." Even in his junior-year interview, he stated that feelings were critical to how he experiences his friendships: "My best friend feels the same way I do, we know the way each other feels." When asked how he knows this, he claimed to "just know it." When his friend's father went to Hong Kong to look for a job, "he was having a hard time and he didn't tell me. But I looked at him and I said, 'Is something happening to your family?' He was like, 'Yeah, it is my father in Hong Kong and stuff.' I could tell his feelings."

The boys in my research repeatedly indicated that the intimacy or sharing of secrets is what they *liked most* about their friendships. Junot said, "We always tell each other everything. And, um, like, about something happens and I save it for [my best friend]." During his junior-year interview, he elaborated: "[What I like most about my best friendship] is the connection. It's like, you know how you know somebody for so long you could talk about anything, and you won't even think, I mean you won't even think about . . . 'Oh, what are they thinking?' You just talk." Kevin described in his interview the type of friendship he would like to have: "I could tell them everything . . . Like if I'm like having serious problems in my family, if I could tell them like without them trying to cheat or tease me or something like that. That's it." Henry said that what he likes most is "just basically I can just tell them everything, pretty much like, they won't make fun of me, like they won't laugh or anything, like if I told them something, you know, embarrassing."

The content of boys' secrets varied considerably, and the term "secrets" was often used interchangeably with "problems." Problems were always secrets, but secrets weren't necessarily problems. In his sophomore year, Amir said that he shares secrets with lots of his friends but keeps the "really, really big" secrets for his best friend: "If I have like problems at home and I can't tell anybody, then I would tell my best friend, but if it's just a regular secret about girls, then I will tell my other friends as well." Andy made distinctions between types of secrets when talking about the friends whom he doesn't trust:

> I mean I can like joke around with them and like if I'm like having trouble in my classes, like if somebody knows the subject better than me, like I'll ask them. Like yeah, it's pretty much like that, not too deep, though . . . I wouldn't tell them like my too secretest things, not too secretive . . . Yeah. Like about a girl or something. I mean that's the deepest, nothing deeper than that, though.

The content of "regular" or "not too deep" secrets was typically about crushes on girls. Really, really big secrets or "secretest things" were related to conflicts at home or, often, coping with disabilities or drug or alcohol abuse of a family member. Paul indicated that he shares secrets with his best friends "all the time" and admits that it is good to have a best friend, because "sometimes, like you don't want to tell your family members 'cause it's probably about them and you just tell your friend and they'll keep a secret and help you." Family-related problems or secrets were considered the deepest secrets of all.

Boys' worries about being betrayed by their friends were also deep secrets. Ronan explained: "Nobody would like a friend betraying you. You would feel hurt about that, and I don't want to feel hurt, so that's why trust is important." Tony said that with his friends, he "feels safe and comfortable," because they "don't play around or joke around that much." William maintained that he trusts his friends because "I know none of my friends would do anything to hurt me . . . These are people I could depend on or call my friends because we've been through thick and thin together. We've had arguments, we are still friends." Ethan explained why trust is so important: "Once you have trust with your friends, then everything else is all right. 'Cause nobody would like somebody, like your friend, doing something bad back to you. You would feel hurt about that, and I don't want to feel hurt. So that's why trust is important."

In response to their fears of betrayal, boys spoke about creating trust tests, which entailed a boy making up a secret and seeing whether word of this false secret got out. If the friend did not share the boy's faux secrets, the friend passed the trust test. Francisco explained:

> Well . . . I started off with, um, oh, I don't—like I'd tell him, "Oh, I hate this girl, she's really stupid." So he'd be like, "Oh, okay." And then I'd see the next day if he told anyone, and if he didn't, then I'd go like even further into like secrets, and it all depends

> on the severity of it, I guess. It would just get, it would just get more and more severe, until like I'd see when he would just start blurting it out.

When Thomas was asked how he knows whether he can trust his friends, he said, "With certain people you tell like maybe a lie or something to see if they're gonna go around [and tell others]. It's like a test. Like you test certain people and some of them do tell. Then you don't tell that person stuff that you don't want around school." When Miguel wanted to know if he could trust his friends, he would tell them "like a thing, like a bad thing. And I wanna see if they tell anybody, especially my girl. So I tell them a lie, but then I see if they tell my girl. And some of them, some of them don't, so now I know who not to trust and who to trust." Carl and his best friend didn't use trust tests, they simply built their trust over time:

> When we first met each other, I wanted to like—when I first noticed that me and him were hanging out a lot, I wanted it to be a carefree relationship. I wanted him to be able to come over to my house and like I made sure that he trusted me. The way I did that was by showing him that I had trust for him first, and . . . that way he opened up to me . . . I think like everybody should have a relationship like me and [my friend], 'cause if he walked in this door right now, he would have such the biggest smile on his face.

In their stories during early to middle adolescence, the boys express explicit vulnerability. Felix reflected: "My best friend thinks physical pain is worse than emotional pain, and I don't think that's true, 'cause physical pain could last but for so long, but when it's in the mind, it doesn't go away." Acutely attuned to the nuances of the emotional world, Felix was typical of the boys in my studies. Keith described his close friends during his sophomore year: "When I need help, they're there for me. When I'm hungry, they buy junk food and give it to me. When I feel lonely, they comfort me." Using the language of romance, Mike described his best friends: "You could tell them anything, you could give them anything. It's like you're giving yourself to them."

When considering whether he would like to be closer to his male friends, Justin said:

> I think so. But I don't really know if they're gonna stay here for four years. So I feel like I can't get too attached, 'cause then if they leave, I still get attached to them even though 'cause a friend, he, he could come and go, even though I really don't want it to happen. But it could come and go. I could make new friends or whatever. So it doesn't matter if I get attached to them or not. I don't know . . . I don't want to [become attached], because if they leave I really don't, I never really got emotional for a guy before, but I don't know if I would or if I wouldn't.

Benjamin made his vulnerability explicit while explaining what he likes about his best friend: "Mmm, most everything. His kindness. Everything. I know, I know he, you know, he cares for people, me, you know. He's not like that, you see him in the street, he's not [just walking] by . . . You know, he talks to you . . . he won't, you know, like just see you and just don't say anything. He'll talk to you." Describing what he likes about his best friend, David said:

> I think our relationship is wonderful. Because we like, I can't explain. The feelings that I have for him . . . if something would happen to him, I probably won't feel right . . . Like when he was sick and I hadn't seen him for like a week and I went to his house . . . and I asked his grandmother what was wrong with him and he was in the room like he couldn't move. So I went in there. I sat in his house for the whole day talking to him. And like the next day he got up and he felt better.

Paul explained: "Yeah, 'cause [my best friend] is like a second person you could speak to . . . It's like see how the kids carry a little teddy bear or whatever, and when they cry, they'll hold it and stuff. So when like you get upset or something, you just walk over to them and they'll loosen, they'll loosen up whatever. They'll be like, 'Yeah, it's all right,' even though it's not." Paul recognized both the safety that a friend provides and the ways boys cover up and tell stories that they know are not true.

2. Mental Health

The boys in my research also made explicit the links between their mental health and close friendships, suggesting that not having emotionally intimate male friendships may lead to poor mental health, and not the other way around. During his freshman year, Steve described why he thinks friendships are important: "Because without friendships, you know, you won't get along with anybody and it's harder in life . . . it's someone to comfort you when you are feeling down, and without a friendship, then life is not worth living." He gave an example of a time when his goldfish died:

> I lost, um, maybe I had a goldfish and I had it for a long time. I won it at the fair. I haven't had that in a long time because every time I had goldfishes, they often die fast. But I had this goldfish for a long time, and it died, so I started crying and crying. I don't know why, but I went to, um, a friend, a sister—well, actually I went to Thomas and . . . I was crying and he just told me to stop crying, and you know he comforted me, he talked to me, telling me about him losing a hamster.

During his sophomore year, Steve stated in a matter-of-fact voice: "You need friends to talk to sometimes, you know like you have nobody to talk to, you don't have a friend, it's hard. You got to keep things bottled up inside, you might just . . . [start] crying or whatever. Like if a family member is beating on you or something and you can't tell a friend, you might just go out [and] do drugs, sell drugs, whatever." When asked why his friendships are important, one young man said:

> P: If you don't have friends, no, you got no one to tell secrets to.
> I: And so what happens then?
> P: Then it's like you need to keep all the secrets to yourself.
> I: What do you think it'd be like if you didn't have someone?
> P: Then it's like, I always like think bad stuff in my brain, 'cause like no one's helping me and I just need to keep all the secrets to myself.

Xinyin said that he needs "someone to talk to, like you have problems with something, you go talk to him. You know, if you keep all the stuff to yourself, you go crazy. Try to take it out on someone else."[3] Albert concurred: "Without friends you will go crazy or mad or you'll be lonely all of the time, be depressed."[4] Kai explained that his "friendships are important 'cause you need a friend or else you would be depressed, you won't be happy, you would try to kill yourself, 'cause then you'll be all alone and have no one to talk to." Augustus, who had recently lost his grandmother, responded to his interviewer's question by posing his own question: "What if you have no family, let's say you have no family, your family passes away. Who can you go to? Who you're gonna talk to? Might as well be dead or something. I don't mean to put it in a negative way, but I am just saying—it's like not a good feeling to be alone." Another boy said, "If you don't have any friends, you'd be lonely, depressed, . . . you gotta talk to somebody. You can't just be by yourself all day." Ronan stated bluntly: "That I'm not alone by myself. Everybody needs somebody to like talk to . . . besides your parents and your family."

When asked about an ideal friendship, Danny said:

> Be like I could trust them, or he could trust me or we could play together, and he wouldn't get mad at everything. And then he could trust me when I do get mad [at him] . . . 'Cause like, it's like having a second, second voice from yourself. Friends, you can talk to them about a lot of things that you would normally talk about only to yourself. So having a friend is like, um, when you're in trouble you can talk to them about things. They could help you, so you don't have to worry about yourself.

Sharing secrets, however, was necessary not only to avoid losing your mind but also to learn problem-solving strategies. When Tony was asked by his interviewer about his best friend, he responded: "I feel very happy, 'cause like when I talk to him about secrets, right, he mostly like helps me—like answers some of my questions and stuff. And sometimes when someone tells him some secrets about me, right, he mostly tells me, 'cause we are like best friends." Although Tony was uncertain of his friend's reliability (e.g., "sometimes" and "mostly"), he was nonetheless appreciative of his friend's help. When Jerome was asked in his freshman year to describe his best friend, he responded: "He's like a brother . . . When I talk about problems, he'll tell me or give me ideas or things to do."

Boys had emotionally intimate friendships to gain not only emotional support but also guidance on how to handle difficult situations. This theme is a critical part of boys' thick stories, as it explicitly counters the story that mental health problems are the cause of friendship difficulties rather than the other way around. If the primary problem is framed as a mental health issue rather than a crisis of connection, the solutions to address the problem remain focused on the therapy and medication rather than on helping boys find the friendships that they want and need.

3. A Crisis of Connection

As the boys in my studies reached middle to late adolescence, their language in their interviews began to shift from love and desire to frustration, anger, sadness, and/or simply indifference. When asked in his senior year how his friendships have changed since he was a freshman, Michael said: "Like my friendship with my best friend is fading . . . I'm saying it's still there but . . . It's sad, 'cause he lives only one block away from me . . . It's like a DJ used his crossfader and started fading it slowly and slowly, and now I'm like halfway through the cross-fade." During his senior year, Guillermo replied to the same question in this way:

> Not really. I think myself. The friend I had, I lost it . . . That was the only person that I could trust, and we talked about everything. When I was down, he used to help me feel better. The same I did to him. So I feel pretty lonely and sometimes depressed . . . because I don't have no one to go out with, no one to speak [to] on the phone, no one to tell my secrets or to help me solve my problems. [Why don't you think you have someone?] Because I think that it will never be the same . . . I think that when you have a real friend and you lost it, I don't think you find another one like him. That's the point of view I have . . . I tried to look for a person, you know, but it's not that easy.

Anthony, who when he was a freshman spoke at length about the importance of close male friendships, said in his sophomore-year interview: "People don't need friends. They don't. There's a lot of things people could do on their own." His interviewer followed up with asking him: "Do you think people need friends once in a while?" To which he responded: "Yeah, once in a while if something happens, you could talk about it. No, I really don't care. If something happens, then it doesn't matter. I'll just be like, 'Forget you.'" Omar also affected a masculine pose when asked a similar question: "I don't feel anything. [My friends] don't tell me anything, they don't put me down or nothing. Everything is cool." Not all boys sounded so hard, but most of them appeared to be struggling to maintain or find meaningful male friendships.

When Henry was asked about his friendships in his freshman year, he used words such as "safe" and "comfortable" to describe how he felt when he spent time with his friends. He said that he liked his best friend because he was "serious and honest" and did not "lie about personal things." He also indicated that his best friend was trustworthy and would keep his secrets. When asked about the fact that he speaks Chinese with his best friend, he noted that "friendship is not the way you speak. It's the way you feel for each other, the way you care about each other and all that stuff, and not the way you talk—doesn't matter the way you talk."

Friendships were important for Henry, "because you won't be that lonely, people care about you more and you really care about them." By his junior year, however, Henry had changed his tune. The content of his interview was full of stories of betrayals by his male peers. He had a close friend (who he says is not a best friend), and when asked why this boy is only a close friend, not a best friend, Henry struggled to respond: "I don't know . . . I'm used to being alone." He answered many of the interviewer's questions with "I don't know, I don't care," the mantra of mainstream masculinity. When the interviewer asked him why he was saying "I don't care," Henry responded: "Probably I don't like my friends that much." Revealing an astute understanding of himself, Henry linked his anger at his friends with his desire not to care. The reason he didn't like his friends his junior year? "It is probably the communication . . . and we hardly communicate with each other . . . I don't know." While he claimed not to know, Henry knew precisely why he was no longer close to his friends.

By his senior year, Henry seemed entirely alone, and his ability to talk about his feelings seemed almost nonexistent. When asked by his interviewer if he has a close or best friend, he said, "I vote no one." He spoke of not being able to communicate with his friends about things that are important to him, and he maintained that the process of friendships during high school has been one of "more to less." When asked why he doesn't have a best friend, he repeated his masculine mantra: "I don't know, and I DON'T CARE." Like Pierre in Maurice Sendak's classic children's book about the boy who didn't care until a lion eats him up, Henry didn't want to care and added, "I just want to be alone." But then he admitted in a quiet tone of voice: "Sometimes, sometimes I don't want to be alone . . . Probably [I would like to have a best friend] . . . I don't know, have that friend who you could talk to them and have them be there."

Michael, who during his freshman and sophomore years passionately discussed the intimacy he had with his male best friend, said in his senior-year interview: "[long pause] Hmm, [we don't have disagreements about] nothing about nothing, really, we don't argue, and so I can't say no, can't say that, so I don't know, not much, I don't feel anything." Sounding confused, he seemed to shift from not knowing to not feeling. He confided to his interviewer that he and his best friend no longer shared much personal information because he does not trust his friend as much as he did before. When asked in his senior year why he is no longer close with his best friend, Michael countered that while he still is close, "I would consider myself more [of a best friend] because I put me first now in a way, and then like friends, family, so I had to check for me first instead of [him] as like a best friend, because without me, I can't have any friends." Taking the privileging of autonomy over relationships literally, he stated that *he* was his best friend. By making such a move, he revealed the choice made by many boys, which is that they would prefer isolating themselves or "finding a girlfriend" over continuing their search for closeness with other boys.

When Adrian was asked in his first-year interview whether friendships are important, he replied, "Yeah, you need people to talk to. You stay alone, you get lonely." In his sophomore year, he said, "If you didn't have any friends, you'd be lonely. You know? You don't have anyone else to talk to or hang out with. You'd be lonely." Asked to define a best friend, he responded: "A best friend? Somebody who's there for you. Somebody that'll listen to your problems and understand what you are talking about. That kind of friend." By his junior and senior year, however, Adrian no longer sounded vulnerable; instead, his responses were stoic. In his junior year, he explained that "you need to have friends to have fun with, to talk to, to hang out with. If you don't have any, you'd be bored for the rest of your life." Adrian's use of the word "bored" was drained of any feelings. By the fourth year of his involvement in our study, he simply said: "You know what I'm saying. If you don't have friends, you're gonna be bored for the rest of your life. You know? You need friends to hang out with." His answer when asked why he doesn't have a best friend in his senior year is: "I don't know, I really don't care if I have a best friend as long as I have friends." In other words, he had given up on having the type of friendships that so many boys expressed the desire for during early and middle adolescence.

Tyrone also spoke about the loss of his friendships, but he did so in a more muted tone than many of the other boys in my studies. When asked whether he has a best friend, he reported:

> No, nah, it's like everybody I get close to, they either go away or, you know, so it's just like, nah, . . . and you know I have a friend

> that I chill with, you know, hang out with from time to time. But not one that I usually do everything with. You know, how like you just have that best friend and it's always like—say it's like you and him? Stuff like that. Nah. I did, I really did, but you know . . . me and this other kid took up for each other, everything just came together, like, you know, it was like it was made to be . . . If I had a problem, I could always talk to him 'cause he knew mostly all my family. I knew mostly all his family, and everything just worked . . . and they moved, and you know. Ever since then, it's just like nobody . . . I don't want to get too close to somebody because I fear when I get close to people—the people I love have been taken away from me. And I just say, "Hey, I don't want to get too close to anybody 'cause I don't want to lose them."

Juan, the boy who in his freshman year referred to "circles of love" between him and his two best friends, discussed the loss of his friendships by his third year of high school with a similar degree of vulnerability. He felt angry and betrayed because he had been teased by his "best friends" for his beliefs (he goes to church) and believed his friends had not been there for him when he was having problems, although he did not provide specifics in his interview. Shawn, at the age of eighteen, also wore his heart on his sleeve: "I've got like a brick wall around me . . . gonna take a lot just to get inside me . . . 'cause I see many people out here, they be open [with each other] and many people could find a way to break them apart. But I don't want nobody knowing me and being able to break me apart and do anything they want with me." He admitted, however, that he was struggling to get rid of his "suit of armor" so that he could have "real friendships." Straddling the line between what he knew and what he was supposed to know, he understood the consequences of giving up on the former and giving into the latter.

Looking directly at the person who was interviewing him during his junior year, Jamal said, "I don't label people as like my best friend, you know. I don't put, you know faith in people 'cause I don't wanna suffer." Similarly, Perry said that while he feels very close to his cousin, he is cautious with his peers. "I try not to be too attached to anybody when I first meet them. Let the relationship build on what we do and the way they conduct themselves. I try not to, because if you start liking the person before you know who they are, then maybe they could turn on you." Fernando, who has a girlfriend, said, "I feel a little more trust in girls than guys 'cause I find . . . guys a little snaky. I don't know. Like, um, like they'll sit there and tell you lies and say it's true." Interviews with boys in late adolescence had a remarkably different tone from those of only a few years earlier.

4. "Boy" Culture

The fourth theme evident in my studies and in the applied work I currently do in schools across New York City offers insight into the reasons why boys and young men struggle to hold on to or find male friendships during middle to late adolescence. What they suggest is that their crisis of connection is rooted in a culture that doesn't value the relationships that they want and need for their mental health and, in fact, believes it's not "normal" for boys to want or have such relationships in the first place. Evidence of such a "boy" culture was found in the homophobic language that they used, with phrases such as "no homo" popping up for the first time in their interviews during middle to late adolescence, suggesting that what was a human desire in early adolescence becomes a desire linked with a sexuality.

Boys and young men began to make it explicit, in other words, that having or even desiring emotionally intimate male friendships is a "girlie and gay" thing, and thus, in a homophobic and sexist culture, lame. One boy even challenged his interviewer who was asking about his close male friendships—the same questions that he so eloquently answered only a year earlier—by asking: "Why are you asking me so many questions about my friendships? I am not gay!" When asked about what it would be like to be a girl, one sixteen-year-old boy said, "It might be nice to be a girl, because then I wouldn't have to be emotionless," suggesting that having emotions, which is essential for having "deep secrets" friendships, is a girlie thing, not a "guy" thing. Boys knew that becoming a man meant giving up on their desires for emotionally intimate male friendships and stifling the emotions that were so easily expressed in their interviews only a year or two earlier.

Boys also knew that *maturing* in "boy" culture meant becoming stoic and not needing relationships anymore. In his sophomore year, Mohammed stated that "trust means you can really, you know, keep things with him, you know what I'm saying? Like secrets, whatever. It's like a bank, you keep money and it's like a safe. Like trust is that thing. You could put your words to somebody, or he would really understand, you know, things." When asked if friends are important, he responded: "Yes, because, um, . . . you don't want to be alone, you know . . . let's say you have a problem, and you can't face it yourself and at the same time you don't have anyone to ask for help to, and you don't want to get into problems like that and if you have a friend that can help you, they can help you . . . Somebody who knows you well, who understands you." By his junior year, however, Mohammed sounded more like a stereotypical boy: "I could tell [my friend], but you know I wouldn't feel that comfortable to tell him. [Why not?] Me, personally, . . . I think like it's none of his business to get into it. You know, I don't see why I should tell him . . . And I'm just not that comfortable . . . if I had problems with my family or problems with anybody, I'm the kind of person that would keep it to myself." His hardened self had even infiltrated his relationship with his mother: "I have gotten more mature, so I trust [my mother] with less things. I tell her less than I used to in junior high school because I feel like I could take care of it myself." In his conflation of manhood and maturity, Mohammed underscores the insidious nature of "boy" culture, which demands that boys deny their "soft" side to be real men *and* to be mature.

Mohammed seems to know, however, that what is implicitly being asked of him is problematic: "I feel that, you know, . . . a best friend, you know, is someone you could trust and someone you could, you know, tell all your personal things to—that's a best friend, I think. But I don't think I have a need to tell somebody all my personal things or whatever it is. You know. I could keep it to myself." His repeated use of the phrase "you know" and "I think" followed by "I don't think" suggests a struggle to know what he knows and feel what he feels. Most boys during middle to late adolescence sounded like Mohammed. Yet he continued in his junior-year interview to reveal his vulnerability: "My [former best friend] used to be my best friend, but . . . something changed . . . I think like I don't really have a best friend right now . . . Yes, I wouldn't mind having a best friend, but well, not really, but I wouldn't mind." Mohammed also admitted to feeling "so depressed." The following year, he told his interviewer that he does not "have time" to do his senior-year interview. "Boy" culture had seemingly taken hold of his heart, and thus he was unwilling to share what he thinks and feels any longer even with his interviewer.

The boys and young men in my studies remind us not only about the importance of friendships for health and well-being but also about our human desire for attachment and our natural capacity for emotional sensitivity and attuning to the thoughts and feelings of others. A patriarchal culture that feminizes such things and thus demeans them gets in the way of our capacity not only to feel but even to think and will inevitably lead to a crisis of connection in which we disconnect from our own humanity—which is rooted in our "hard" and "soft" sides—and from the humanity of others. What is particularly striking in my research is that boys and young men already know this thick story, and they tell it as if they assume we already know it, too. What they suggest is that if we raise them to go against their nature by not valuing what they want and need, they will struggle to find what they want and need, and the consequences will likely be dire not only for them but for everyone else as well.

3.

The Story of Nick[1]

LOOKING LIKE A TYPICAL American teenager, wearing loose, low-riding long shorts and a New York Knicks sleeveless jersey, Nick, at fourteen years old, is the youngest of five children. Nick had a medium build, with large brown eyes and dark brown hair cut short and close to his head. He lived with an older brother, two older sisters, and his mother, who was from Puerto Rico, in an apartment building near his high school. His father had left the family soon after Nick was born and hadn't had contact with them since. Born and raised in New York City, Nick was an avid basketball player, often carried a basketball around in school, and wanted to be a professional basketball player when he grew up. He proudly told the interviewer in his freshman year: "No kids for my weight can do things that I can do. Like, I play more sports, they call me the boss down my block. We have a boss down for each block, and I'm the boss down for my block. I play handball, basketball, football. I play all sports." In his freshman year of high school, Nick looked and acted like a stereotypical boy. But he did not speak like one.

Freshman Year: Staying Close to Mom and Noel

When asked about why his relationship with his mother was close:

> I get a lot of attention from her. Like, just, I'm the baby. She always spends time with me, like she'll take out all her time just to spend with me, like whatever I need, like she'll, she'll be kinda a friend, if I really need her. Let's say, I just broke up with my girlfriend, and I really liked her, and I was with tears, she'll come and say, "It's okay, it's okay." Um, you know, I'll cry on her shoulder, and we'll stay, laying down in the bed, and like we'll stay, and we'll talk for a long time and finally we'll just fall asleep . . . and when I wake up, I won't feel the same. I will feel better.

Nick's mother had recently been diagnosed with ovarian cancer, so he had been trying to spend more time with her. Nick described himself as a friendly and very funny person who "loves to joke around with friends." "If I meet a person, I'll try to give my best impression so that they can say hello the next time and not be like wave their hand [clears throat] or be shy. I'll try to give a good impression so I can make that person feel comfortable, like whether it's a new student or a new kid on the block." From his interactions with his schoolmates in the hallways, it was clear Nick was well liked by his peers. His social network consisted exclusively of boys from the neighborhood whom he had known from a very early age and who mostly attended his school.

Nick's best friend, Noel, who was also Puerto Rican and whom he had known since he was three, lived below him in the same apartment building. His friendship with Noel, like many of his close friendships, was remarkable in its depth and intimacy. Even during the latter years of high school, when Nick was increasingly distrustful of other boys, he continued to describe his love for Noel and the ways Noel had helped him through many difficult times.

When asked about his friendships at the beginning of his freshman year, Nick initially sounded like a gender stereotype:

> [With my friends] we talk about basketball and sports mostly, and girls, so there's never like any problem between us, so, it's pretty good, our relationship. It's real good . . . You know, I don't have any problems with them, never have problems, and if we do, you know, it's like little things, like little problems . . . like we argue about sports, about sports players, how good they are. Little problems, but not that bad.

Yet as Nick began to lay out the details of his friendship, a different voice emerged:

> [What I like about my friendships] is that like, if I'm in a fight, they'll jump in. If I'm having a problem, they'll be like, "What's wrong?" and then, "Would you wanna talk to me about the problem?" . . . When I was feeling down, when my mother went to the hospital . . . they saw it on my face and they was like, "Yo, what's going on, dude, what happened?" And I was like, "Nothing, my mom's in the hospital," and later, all my friends was coming up to me, asking me the same question, and they were like, "You wanna talk?"

Physical toughness framed a more vulnerable side and became the theme for his first interview. While couched in masculine terms

("Yo, what's going on, dude?"), the language of sensitivity repeatedly came to the surface ("You wanna talk?").

Nick explained that he and his friends do everything together and "talk to each other about serious things, share some deep secrets":

> Noel and I are close and everything, like I sleep over at his house, he sleeps at my house; I call his mom "Moms," he calls my mom "Mom." We're serious, like his family is real close to me, like my second family, like as if they were my first. [His family] has a room [for me] to stay in, 'cause I stay there any time I want. If I wanna talk, anybody's open ears are there. If I wanna cry there, they'll show that they're there for me.

Nick believed that his friendship with Noel has only gotten better over time:

> It changed a lot. Just like my other friends, changed a lot. When we were younger, it used to be like not so tight, not so tight as we are now. Not like, if something goes wrong, like one of us will shed a tear, the other one'll cry. When we were younger like, one of us, it was just like fun and games, but now we're serious, 'cause we're growing up and life got serious.

At the age of fourteen, Nick understood the importance of emotional expression in his "serious life" and his "tighter" relationships.

Nick defined "serious" as "like, um, when it's time to get down, like when one of us is in trouble and the other one needs help, we both stick together and be there for each other." Revealing the intimacy that ran throughout his discussions, Nick drew attention to the mutually supportive nature of his friendships. Yet he also wavered at times, moving back into stereotypically tough-guy language when asked about "sticking together." "Let's see, if one person is in trouble with another guy, and he might get killed and everybody else could stick to each other so that that one person won't kill him, we'll get, we'll get help for that one person." Although he admitted that this scenario has never happened to him, he used a scene from what sounds like a gangster movie to make his friendship with Noel seem normal.

Like so many of his male peers, Nick saw girls as an impediment to his intimacy with his male friends:

> Like my best friend's girlfriends are like trying to take him away from me, 'cause they know I'm spending a lot of time with him, and he won't let that happen. Now he has a girlfriend and he's real serious with her, and no matter what, he'll always spend time with me. No matter what, I'm serious with my girlfriends or my family or he's serious with his girls or his family, we'll always spend time or make time to see each other, at least hanging out to say, "What's up?" or to talk on the phone at least.

Nick worried that girls, especially those with whom the boys were "real serious," would steal his closest friends. He hoped Noel's loyalty would continue in the years to come.

Sophomore Year: With a Basketball in His Hand

When Nick was interviewed during his sophomore year, his interviewer already knew that his mother had died over the summer. The interviewer wrote a note to our team at the end of her conversation with Nick:

> Nick seemed to be compensating for a lot of things by having fun and being silly and I've seen him in the hallways a lot and he does make a lot of jokes. I think that keeps him in bright spirits, but when he does talk about his mom, it's like a cloud rolled over his face . . . I mean he just becomes totally solemn when he talks about his mom. It's like a happy/sad feeling you get from him: happy because he has great memories of her and their relationship, and just sad because of what's happened. In addition, the whole time he had a basketball in his hand, and every time I've seen him, he walks around school with this basketball in his hand.

Nick's interview that year was focused on his sadness regarding his mother, his struggles with Noel, and his confession that he no longer went to church ("I don't have time"). His basketball seemed to offer a secure base from which he could be vulnerable without seeming to be girlie.

Now living with his sisters and his stepfather, he moved back and forth in his descriptions of friendships between a "hard" and a "soft" voice. When asked about how he and his friends were like "brothers," he said: "Like we give each other advice or they'll give advice, like if I have problems with a girl, have fights, Latino fights." Yet he followed up by saying:

> My friends relate to most of the things I have to deal with. Like if they lost somebody in the family they love, they understand

> how it is to work that out . . . They understand what you want to do. Because it happened to me and it really hurts. [My friends say] "you just got to deal with it, and I know it's hard, but if you loved her, she loved you, too." They'll be like, like sometimes they be telling me: "You got us now, we are like your brothers." And that really helps me.

Nick revealed not only his own emotional depth but that of his friends (e.g., "if you loved her, she loved you, too"). He did not try to cover over his hurt and insecurity, and they seemed to return the favor by showing understanding and care. He said, "I trust my friends to respect my feelings . . . If I tell them something and tell them not to tell nobody they will keep my secrets, even to my other friends."

When asked about his best friend Noel, Nick sounded ambivalent:

> Actually, I have two best friends. One is Marcus, he's eighteen and he goes to college, and Noel, he's fifteen, *he wants to let me go* [italics mine]. So he's like really my best friend, but like he don't, he's not my friend, like he don't want to hang out no more because he's always with his girlfriend. So it's like he's still my best friend, he is still down [with] me, but like Marcus is the one I hang out with.

Like the loyal friend he wanted Noel to be, Nick was still loyal to Noel. Describing his new friends: "I trust them with mostly everything . . . [For me to trust them] they got to show me what they are about first. I have to know where they come from, how they really are. I want to know, you know, not just the basketball you, or just hanging out. You know, like how you are when you go home, you know, how you act when you are at home." He wanted what many boys want, which is to know how someone is "at home" as well on the literal and metaphoric court.

Wondering aloud, his interviewer asked Nick: "How do you do it? What keeps you yourself?" Nick responded with emotional clarity:

> Because I feel I have a lot of sorrow, you know, like a lot of pain inside, since my mother's loss . . . you know, and like it hurts, so I don't want to walk around frowning and all sad and everything, all mad and taking it out, because I want to be happy, you know. I want to enjoy my life, you know, I don't want to walk around, you know, depressed—no, I'm not really depressed, you know. I'm happy right now, because I have friends, I have a family still here, and I know that my mother is, you know, resting in peace. So right now I'm kinda happy. So I'm not going to walk around crying and weeping and feeling sorry for myself. I'm going to go on living and doing what I got to do . . . Stay happy, and I'm not going to show the sad side.

While his loss afforded him an expressive language, it also demanded stoicism. He knew he was fortunate in many ways but still felt sad and vulnerable.

Asked about the details of his friendship with Noel, Nick described the changes:

> We just grew farther and farther apart instead of closer and closer. We were so close, best friends. It was so close, like real,

> real close. But like as soon as this girl came in, he just let me go, and it really hurt. You know, it's like, you know, I understand you have a girl, you know, you have to spend time with your girl, you know, this time for me because, you know, I'm not saying you have to spend time with me. But, you know, as a best friend, you just can't, you know, you are just going to let me go like that? How do you think I'm going to react? How am I going to feel?

Using the language of romantic love, Nick asked the question that boys often want to ask after they have been betrayed by others.

Nick spent most of his time that year with Marcus:

> I mean, he's a best friend . . . While Noel is pushing me away, Marcus is trying to, you know, he wants me to be his friend. Marcus needs a best friend. You know, he's the type of person that I can get along with, you know, like he needs somebody just like me. You know, he has problems at home, so he wants to share with somebody, somebody close that he could trust and will understand.

Nick's ability not only to take care of himself ("while Noel is pushing me away") but also to take care of others was likely why boys liked to spend time with Nick. As to his relationship with Marcus, Nick said, "Yeah, [he] tells me everything that I want to know when we talk. I mean I don't feel right, you know [his] mother's getting mad at home. I don't know what to do . . . That's just how close we are. He tells me how he is feeling." When asked about why Marcus was closer to him than others, he explained that Marcus understands him and "knows his problems" and "he knows that I don't get that much love from my brother and sisters, so he's kind of being, you know, helping me, be here for both of us." At the end of the interview, Nick admitted he missed Noel and hoped that he would come back to him soon.

Junior Year: Finding Noel

In his junior year, Nick continued to live with his sisters and stepfather, with whom he'd had a contentious relationship since his mother died. Nick had a girlfriend that year, with whom he hoped to eventually "settle down" and be a better father to his kids ("if I have kids") than his biological father was to him. Wearing his heart on his sleeve, Nick said he "wants to have a mother—I want to have a wife—that is like my mother was." His sadness over the loss remained palpable. Nick continued to be an avid basketball player and spent most of his free time playing the game and talking with his friends about "sports, girls, and family issues." As in each of his interviews, he moved back and forth between adhering to and resisting the language of tough guys. Describing his best friends, he reminded his interviewer that even if you are not with people anymore, you still have them in your memories: "Best friends don't come and go. You know, best friends are for life. You know you're with—even though that best friend may be gone and goes and forgets about you and never comes back, you know? You are always gonna remember that friend because it's a best friend and you shared things that you wouldn't share with like a friend in school."

Sounding like so many of the boys during late adolescence in my studies, Nick spoke about the "inevitable loss" that happened as he grew up: "Friendships were actually more important when I was a kid because I always needed friends. You can't really be in an environment by yourself, that's not really that good. So as a kid, I depended on having friends more when I was younger. [Now] we are just going to school, going to work, and we sort of separated." Yet during this response, he revealed a contradiction between what he knew inside and what he was supposed to know as a boy becoming a man:

> Like I really, really care, like my friends—you can't say to my friends that have gone, like you know, "Come [back]." Um, I feel sort of sad that they are gone. But the friends that I have now, you know, we try to make the best of it. You know, like I said, friends do come and go, but the friends that you have now, you try to make the best of it . . . I still do tell them secrets like about my family. Like my mother, I miss her and [they will say,] "I understand what you're feeling" . . . They will just be there.

Nick and Noel were best friends again that year, and Nick referred to Noel as "like a brother" because of "all the things we have been through and shared." Noel had promised never "to leave" him again:

> I lost my mother, it was like him losing his. He was there at the funeral. He was there and he cried. And I told him, he hugged—I cried. He was really there for me. Even now, the conversation comes up and I come in tears, he'll say, "It's all right," and he'll give me a hug. He'll say, "I'll be there for you, you know, I've always been there for you, eleven years." That's a long time . . . You feel special. That person makes you feel special. And you try a lot to make that person feel special. To let that person

> know what—what he's been doing for you . . . he knows that I'm his best friend. So he knows that I'll be there a lot for him. I spend time with him, you know. There's times that he'll need me or want to hang out, help, need my help for something, and I'll be there for him and I will say, "Noel, you know, if you ever need anything, I'm here." Or "If you need help with this, I'm here." I was there for him when he had a fight with his stepfather. He was like really emotional, you know. I say, you know, "I'm always gonna be there. If you need anything, I'm here, you know. If you want to come stay in my house." And he's done the same for me.

His repeated "you knows" contained an implicit question about whether the listener knows what he is talking about. As if to clarify, Nick added: "A friendship means that the person makes you feel special and you make that person feel special. You give a little, get a little . . . Give love. You give a lot. You give yourself. Um, you give—you give time to that person . . . you are there for that person." While his response may have suggested a desire to distance himself from these feelings of mutual love, it also suggested that he knew what all boys know about friendships.

Senior Year: Protecting His Heart

Nick continued to live with his sisters and his stepfather during his senior year. He was still with the same girlfriend from the previous year, but he spent little time during his final interview talking about her, suggesting that their relationship is not close. Most of his interview was focused on his friendships, his desire to try to improve his school performance, his passion for basketball, and his arguments with his stepfather. When he went to college, he planned to try to make it on the college basketball team and hoped to major in music technology, as he wanted to work in a recording studio. Nick exuded hope about his future and his friendship with Noel: "Noel has always been my best friend. It's like even though we went to different schools, we will always see each other either after school or on the weekends." Nick claimed that the reason he broke off from Noel for a while was that he spent too much time with his girlfriend and Nick spent too much time "on the courts." Protecting his manly cover, he gave equal weight to them both in their difficulties. He thought that they "work hard" to stay together and are each committed to "trying to do things to stay together . . . we don't want to grow further apart." About his friends more generally, Nick said that he trusts them with "anything . . . I trust them a lot. They won't hurt my feelings, and they will respect what I have to say if I told them something. I trust that they're gonna give me good advice, that they'll be there for me, that they'll always love me. I will love them, too." Sounding like the Nick from earlier interviews, he relied on emotional language to describe his friendships.

During his senior-year interview, Nick provided details about why he had a falling-out with Noel during his sophomore year. Marcus had tried to "break [them] up" by spreading rumors that Nick had said negative things about Noel and his girlfriend. As a result, Nick dropped Marcus as a best friend following his sophomore year, even though he felt frustrated with Noel's girlfriend at that time:

> I felt like she was taking him away from me. And it's like I would hang with her [and Noel], she would want to only hang

> out with him. So it's like, you know, we were pulling him by one arm and the other and he didn't want to split apart, so basically what happened was, with the rumors that Marcus spread, Noel just moved more toward her way.

Resisting gender stereotypes, Nick explained in detail how hard his sophomore year was without Noel: "That was hard when Noel left me in my sophomore year because my best friend's leaving me, you know. That's somebody that I love, you know. It was hard for me to hang out with Noel because he . . . Noel didn't want me around. And that really hurt, because your best friend, or somebody that you love, they don't want you around. You know. You feel hurt." Wanting his interviewer to know how he felt, he repeated "you know" as if asking her to confirm that she understood what he feels.

Yet because of his experience with Noel, Nick had learned to be cautious:

> I don't give—I don't give my heart out to too many people, you know, especially when it could get broken or hurt easily. I've been through too many times of that. So it's like I don't have any room—I have to recuperate from my broken heart. There's been death in my family, girlfriends, you know, guy friends. I don't have any more [room] for my heart to get stepped on. So I've picked myself up for a while. I'm walking. But you know, you never know when you fall down again. So I'm trying to just keep my eye out.

His caution was also evident when he spoke of his other friends:

> They are pretty cool. Just don't trust anybody, 'cause nearly everybody talks trash behind your back . . . A lot of them are dishonest in some ways. Like you can't trust them. I thought I could trust them before, but they're dishonest . . . I learned not to trust . . . If I tell them, like, secrets, like if someone in my family was dying, that's none of your business. 'Cause if I tell them, I know they'd tell everybody and spread the word.

Yet his emotional distance from his friends did not make him any less emotionally astute:

> If you don't come [to where we are supposed to meet], I'm gonna get mad. I'm not gonna get mad 'cause you dissed me, I'm gonna get mad 'cause I missed you. But I'll probably show it to you like I'm gonna get mad 'cause you dissed me. But it's really, I'm gonna get mad 'cause I love you and I miss you. That's what it is.

When asked how his friendships had changed over time, he said at the end of his interview:

> I don't know. You could say that they grew but then they didn't grow. Meaning that it grew that like you know more people—we started hanging out together more, but then it didn't grow in the sense that when they started smoking and drinking as we got older, we grew further apart because . . . that's not what I'm about . . . [I: How has it changed since middle school?] Just like I said, you know, it went downhill. It's like we were tight, you know, we were close. And then you know, like I said, it just grew

> further apart as we got older . . . Some people, they got further apart. Some other people got closer . . . For me, so while I got closer to some people in the group, I got further apart from some of the others. And now it's just like, I'm not close to anybody now.

Reflecting on the distance with his friends, Nick added:

> That's been like the biggest, like the biggest change. Like, I don't know. I can't explain it . . . Yeah, we just go out, hang out, have fun. That's that. Now it's different, you know . . . things are always gonna change, you know. So we knew—we knew it was gonna come, but you know, it's like we could have prevented it, but we just let it happen. And I'm not saying I wanted it that way, the change. And I'm not saying that I didn't want it. But you know, things change. That's the way it has to be . . . A best friend is someone you can talk to, share your inner thoughts with, and they could do the same as well. Someone, you know, to have a shoulder to cry on. Someone that you could be a shoulder to cry on for them, just share, share things and different experiences with each other and have fun basically. Just be like a family.

No longer looking for reassurance from his interviewer with "you know," he spoke about the changes in his friendships as inevitable and repeated clichés that he didn't appear to believe in. He had become "a man" who understood the losses that this requires in "boy" culture.

Nick's story and all of the stories told by the boys in my studies suggest that boys and young men are extraordinarily socially, emotionally, and cognitively intelligent. They understand their own emotions and the nuances of their relationships at a depth that adults, especially men, often forget that they once had and that all humans have according to a century of developmental research. They recognize that anger can cover over sadness and that sometimes you need to just cry on someone's shoulder and share feelings together. They have a desire for close friendships in which they are seen and heard and in which both friends are attuned to each other even if they don't agree.

They also know that friendships are critical to their mental health and there can be serious psychological and behavior consequences of not having them. Indeed, right at the age when boys begin to struggle to hold on to or find close male friendships, their rates of suicide go up dramatically, from three times the rates of girls to five times more likely than girls, although girls are more likely to attempt suicide. While boys don't necessarily blame the culture directly for their problems, they do so indirectly in their descriptions of the need to shut down emotionally in the name of maturity and manhood and in their use of homophobic language equating a human desire with what they now perceive to be a lame one. But what is "boy" culture exactly? It's not just believing that only females or feminized men have feelings, and it doesn't just influence boys and men.

Part Two

"BOY" CULTURE

There comes a point where we need to stop just pulling people out of the river. We need to go upstream and find out why they are falling in.

—BISHOP DESMOND TUTU

4.

Adherence[1]

When my daughter was nine years old, I told her that boys are often stereotyped as naturally better at math than girls. Since she excels in math, she immediately asked, "Who believes that?" When I told her, "Most people," she responded incredulously: "Why do we believe in things that we know aren't true?" Kate Stone Lombardi, the author of *The Mama's Boy Myth,* asked a similar question when she discovered that the hundreds of mothers whom she interviewed told her that while their own sons were sensitive, empathic, and emotional, they knew that other boys were not.[2] They believed a stereotype about boys, even though it wasn't true for their own sons. The answer to my daughter's question appears to be that we think our thin stories about boys (and everyone else) are biological facts rather than cultural fiction and thus unchangeable.

This "boy" culture of ours—in which human capacities such as thinking and feeling are split and given a gender and sexuality so that boys and men, especially those who are white, rich, and heterosexual, are considered to be the thinkers and thus are put at the top of the hierarchy and girls and women and everyone else are the feelers who are put at the bottom—is not about real boys, as indicated by almost a century of data, but about our stereotypes of them. "Boy" culture is rooted in ideologies that intersect with one another, including but not limited to patriarchy, capitalism, white supremacy, homophobia, and transphobia. Each of these ideologies is premised on a hierarchy of humans in which some humans are considered more human than others and, in the case of capitalism and patriarchy, some human capacities, qualities, and needs are valued more than others. It is a culture that pits us against one another, with each side trying to stay or get on top, and interferes with our abilities not only to be happy or to find satisfying relationships but also simply to cope. Although this culture has a distinctly American flavor in its "I can do it by myself" rugged individualist mentality, it is shared around the world given the American technology created by our "boys" at the top.

"Boy" culture splits rationality from emotionality, the mind from the body, and encourages us not to care about what others think and feel. It values the me over the we, the individual over the collective, and adults over children, thinking the former is intelligent and the latter is innocent. The only type of relationship valued in this culture is the romantic and heterosexual type, but that's only because children are necessary, and thus if you choose not to have them within a heterosexual relationship, something is considered to be wrong with you. And if you choose to have them within a homosexual relationship, something is also considered to be wrong with you. Friendships in such a culture are deemed necessary only when one doesn't have a romantic partner and as extraneous to what really matters, which is making sure the economic market stays stable. It is a culture that turns *social* media into me media, where the objective is to get the most likes rather than to be liked or to like others, and where "connection" is based on self-disclosure rather than on being curious about and sensitive to the thoughts and feelings of others. It is a culture that doesn't value curiosity, especially the interpersonal type, and thinks it kills cats. It believes, furthermore, that girls and women are "nosy" (the slur word for curious) and too sensitive. Hooking up at the expense of emotional connection is considered a sign of liberation for girls and women, and a healthy sign of manhood for boys and men. Because "boy" culture is in bed with capitalism, money is valued over love and quantity is valued over quality, with numbers suggesting objectivity and words suggesting subjectivity. The latter elements—love, quality, and subjectivity—are perceived to be, in fact, for sissies who can't make real money or who are afraid of numbers. When such a culture does value our softer sides, the focus is on emotional regulation rather than emotional sensitivity and on intellectual curiosity rather than interpersonal curiosity.

Collective problems in such a culture are treated as individual ones; mothers are blamed for the problems of their children, and wives for the failures of their (often ex) husbands. Excelling in the STEM fields is the ultimate sign of intelligence, while doing well in the arts or humanities is considered wasting one's time, as it won't lead to making money. Going to college is also a waste of time unless you major in a STEM field or make worthwhile connections. Getting into an *elite* college, however, is more important than friendships, kindness, caring, happiness, sleeping, and eating. But these colleges are valued not so much for the quality of their education as for their networking possibilities. Emotional intelligence and intellectual intelligence are seen as opposites, with the latter being a genuine sign of smartness, while the former is the equivalent of being nice, which is assumed not to really be a skill. Relational intelligence in "boy" culture isn't a thing, underscoring its individual orientation; the field of child development doesn't even study it.

Extroverted people are considered socially skilled, and introverted people are considered unskilled and lacking desire for social connection rather than just confused by the so-called skills necessary to be liked in "boy" culture.[3] Vulnerability is perceived as embarrassing, weak, and immature, while maturity is defined as being invulnerable and thus often requires faking it. Biology is privileged over culture, with the assumption that the former is "hard" and thus more reliable, and the latter is "soft" and thus not scientific. Humans are privileged over the natural environment, with the former being perceived as "hard" and the latter being seen as "soft" and thus for tree huggers rather than for serious people. Morality is perceived to be old-fashioned, and immoral behavior and even war are considered justified when one's manhood is threatened. "Boy" culture believes that an "eye for an eye" and even a people for an eye prevent further violence. In sum, it is a culture that tells thin stories that are antisocial, anti-intellectual, anti-emotional, anti-relational, immature, and immoral, and that often lead to violence. Ironically, it is boys and young men who teach us about this culture and are also the ones deeply suffering from it, as suggested by their suicide and homicide rates. And since they are suffering, we are all suffering, too.

Such a culture is so effective in disconnecting us from ourselves and one another because it undermines the very capacities to think and feel that are necessary to make moral decisions, especially complex ones, and to maintain connections with other people. The ability five-year-olds exhibit for interpersonal curiosity, for example, allows them to see and understand other people and why they think and feel and behave as they do.[4] An average child asks 107 questions per hour.[5] When Albina, a former student of mine at NYU Abu Dhabi, was five years old, she bet her older sister that she could come up with at least a hundred questions in one go. She stayed up doing this all night with her older sister, who tried to answer all of them in the same night as well. While she doesn't remember all the questions, she knows they were about people and not just about things in the world.

Our capacity for curiosity allows us to see our common humanity, as once we begin to ask questions of one another, we see that our stereotypes are not true and that we humans are more similar than different in spite of the fact that the hierarchy of humanness means we also have a lot of different experiences depending on where we are situated in the hierarchy. Yet "boy" culture considers interpersonal curiosity and the recognition of our common humanity as "soft" and thus relegates it to the bottom of the hierarchy of things to value and thus nourish in our children. "How am I going to pay my bills with curiosity and common humanity?" the voice says in our heads. But the reason we can't pay our bills is that those at the top don't see our common humanity and don't want to be demoted to the bottom of the hierarchy.[6]

Our "boy" culture has intensified to such a degree over the past few decades that we have even feminized doing well in school and going to college. I have been told by boys and young men that reading is a girlie activity. The feminization of academic achievement, except as it applies to the STEM fields, leads to women being more likely to do well academically than men in college, and more likely to apply to and stay in college. Men's overall college completion rates in the United States have fallen behind women's for every generation born since the 1960s, with men now dropping out of college in dramatic numbers.[7] Among working-class men, the numbers are even greater, with fewer than one in five[8] now completing college. In the academic literature, it's called the "male drift," which is defined as men not going to college, not finding a job, and not looking out for their mental or physical health.

The fault for this pattern is often placed on women teachers, on feminism, and on the level of "wokeness" on college campuses. According to boys and young men, however, the fault lies entirely with a culture that has gendered and sexualized human capacities, interests, and careers and thus made academic achievement, including going to college, a feminized activity. We think that wanting to follow a career in which one takes care of others or teaches people is part of a *pink*-collar economy.[9] "Be a man and get a real job," one that is *blue*-collar, is the message directed at young men, especially for those at the bottom of the hierarchy socioeconomically. For these young men, going to college will likely not help them put food on the table or a home to live in, especially if it means incurring a lot of debt.

The relevant data that support what boys and young men teach us about the insidious nature of "boy" culture are found in the statistics on gay men, who are bucking the male drift trend. In his analysis of U.S. household surveys, Joel Mittleman finds that while 36 percent of adults in the United States have bachelor's degrees, 52 percent of gay men do:[10] "If America's gay men formed their own country, it would be the world's most highly educated by far . . . Growing up, boys and young men who identify as gay often feel like outsiders to the culture of masculinity enforced by their straight peers. Although that status can create vulnerabilities in the schoolyard and at home, it also seems to lead to tremendous liberation in the classroom."[11] In his analysis of 7,000 student survey items, Mittleman finds that the attributes most associated with "being a boy" across his entire sample include playing video games and being an athlete and do not include doing well in school. However, gay boys consistently described "being a boy" as being academically successful. He even finds that gay men do better than women because, he claims, they are constantly having to prove themselves in a culture that doesn't see them as "real men."[12] American boyhood, according to Mittleman, "feels like a series of masculinity contests, and even today most of the rules are stacked against gay boys. But academics is one competition they can master."[13]

As a way to understand why we perpetuate stories of ourselves and each other that hurt us, literary critic Lionel Trilling writes: "Ideology is not the product of thought; it is the habit or the ritual of showing respect for certain formulas to which, for various reasons having to do with emotional safety, we have very strong ties and of whose meaning and consequences in actuality we have no clear understanding."[14] He suggests that our thin stories, those that reinforce our ideological belief systems, provide a sense of safety in their familiarity and the promise that if we believe in them, we will get to or stay on top, even though most of us know that that's not really the way it works. When we passively follow the ideologies of our culture, however, we end up treating the symptoms (e.g., loneliness and mental illness) of living in "boy" culture as the problem itself. Thus our solutions are not as effective as they could be if we focused on changing the culture rather than simply changing the individual. Even the scholars who write about the limitations of our cultural belief systems don't pull the microscope out far enough. While individualism, neoliberalism, or social evaluative threats, for example, are the uneven cement on the sidewalk that makes us trip and fall, they don't answer the question of why the cement is uneven in the first place.

In *Democracy in America,* a prescient book written in the mid-nineteenth century, Alexis de Tocqueville warns of excessive individualism, what he refers to as the Achilles' heel of the American experiment: "Each one of them [the citizens], withdrawn into himself, is almost unaware of the fate of the rest. Mankind, for him, consists in his children and his personal friends. As for the rest of his fellow citizens, they are nothing."[15] Tocqueville unintentionally suggests, however, that the problem is also a culture in which women are left out, as suggested by the pronouns he chooses and the absence of the mothers of "his children" from his description of *man*kind. As sociologist Robert Bellah and his coauthors point out in their book *Habits of the Heart,* Tocqueville alludes to one of the strongest values in "boy" culture in his critique of the American compulsion of "always relying on one's own judgments, rather than on received authority, in forming one's own opinions and that one should always stand by one's own opinions" and values at all times without compromise.[16] As Tocqueville suggests in his language but doesn't explicitly state, the problem is not just individualism but a privileging of so-called masculine characteristics (i.e., standing on one's own) over so-called feminine ones (i.e., compromise). Such patterns of privileging are why we value individualism in the first place.

Habits of the Heart also blames individualism:

> Both the cowboy and the hard-boiled detective tell us something important about American individualism. The cowboy, like the detective, can be valuable to society only because he is a completely autonomous individual who stands outside it . . . To seek justice in a corrupt society, the American detective must be tough, and above all, he must be a loner . . . To serve society one must be able to stand alone, not needing others, not depending on their judgment, and not submitting to their wishes . . . And this obligation to aloneness is an important key to the American moral imagination.[17]

Not only does *Habits of the Heart* refer to stereotypic male qualities in its definition of "American," but it links them to a moral imagination bereft of the qualities associated with cowgirls and soft-boiled detectives. Pushing the male imagery even further, it says: "The profound ambiguity of the mythology of American individualism is that its moral heroism is always just a step away from despair. For an Ahab, and occasionally for a cowboy or a detective, there is no return to society, no moral redemption."[18] While one could argue that it isn't necessary to expose the masculine bias in these critiques of American society, the rebels in this book implicitly disagree. They suggest that we need to name the culture explicitly for what it is—one that values only the "hard" sides of our humanity—and thus take individual and collective responsibility for changing it so that they and we have a better chance of surviving.

Economist Noreena Hertz also blames the individualism of neoliberalism for our modern crisis of connection:

> The soaring rates of loneliness and isolation around the world go back to the 1980s when a particularly harsh form of capitalism took hold: neoliberalism, an ideology with an overriding emphasis on freedom—free choice, free markets, freedom from government or trade union interference. One that prized an idealized form of self-reliance, small government, and a brutal competitive mindset that placed self-interest [and material wealth] above community and the collective good.[19]

Solidarity, kindness, and caring are not only undervalued in capitalist culture, she argues, but "deemed . . . irrelevant human traits,"[20] with the consequence that they have "made us see ourselves as competitors not collaborators, consumers not citizens, hoarders not sharers, takers not givers, hustlers not helpers, people who are not only too busy to be there for our neighbors but don't even know their names. And we collectively let this happen."[21] While she is spot-on in her critique of our culture, by not naming the masculine bias that undergirds neoliberalism, she does not address why we undervalue our human potential to be collaborators, citizens, sharers, givers, helpers, and people "there for our neighbors." If we don't understand why and we don't know the science (and don't trust our own intuition) revealing to us that we are naturally collaborators, sharers, givers, and helpers, we feel hopeless that we can change our culture.

Unlike Tocqueville, Bellah, or Hertz, epidemiologists Richard Wilkinson and Kate Pickett do recognize the hierarchy embedded in society, which in their case is one about social status, and the negative consequence of such a hierarchy on health and well-being. They argue in their book, *The Spirit Level*, that "social evaluative threats," in which we are all trying to climb up the social ladder and get or stay on top, lead to income inequality, which then leads to social disconnection, including a lower quality of friendships for both the rich and the poor. Yet even these authors naturalize the hierarchy, as if we are born with feelings of inferiority or superiority. They quote psychiatrist Alfred Adler, who said, "To be human means to feel inferior," which they rephrase as, "To be human means being highly sensitive about being regarded as inferior."[22] The hierarchy is treated in their book as a natural phenomenon, and the problem is our sensitivity to it. In contrast, I would argue that our sensitivity is our asset rather than our problem, as it makes us aware that a hierarchy of humanness exists in the first place. While income inequality likely exacerbates our social disconnection, our natural sensitivity to such inequity is not the root of why we are so disconnected from one another but is what we need to nourish more of in each other so that we are better able to disrupt a hierarchy in which the rich are seen as more human than the poor and thus more deserving of the necessities of life.[23]

WHEN I LIVED IN Nanjing, China, in the 1980s, the young men who populated the campus on which my father worked held hands or hung on each other when they walked together, with one arm over the other's shoulders. In the summertime, they wore short shorts, plastic sandals, and nylon socks, as the nylon prevented their feet from getting hot and sticky. My American eyes coded such behavior as girlie, and I wondered whether the men who were holding hands were gay. Homosexuality, however, was outlawed at the time, so it is unlikely that the behavior I saw daily and in public spaces was reflective of a sexual identity. When I returned to live in Shanghai in 2007, China had become much more Americanized in its behaviors. I no longer saw the physical intimacy between men that I had seen in the 1980s, nor the seemingly feminized fashion that had been so popular among men at the time. In the summer of 2007, young men wore long shorts, tennis shoes, and thick white socks that went midway up their calves. Every playground in my neighborhood was filled with boys playing basketball and wearing basketball jerseys, reflecting, in part, the adoration of Yao Ming, the seven-six Chinese NBA basketball player. Chinese men looked and behaved just like men I knew at home. What became obvious to me then was that the American version of "boy" culture was spreading globally.

My ten-year-old niece told me recently that the boys in her school in Berlin, Germany, get picked on and tagged as gay if they show any physical or emotional affection toward each other. Her father, who grew up in Berlin in the 1970s, said that that kind of homophobic teasing didn't exist in his generation. It's not that it was considered okay to be gay in Berlin in the 1970s, although it was likely more okay than in the United States at that time; the desire for connection between boys was simply not linked to a sexual identity. When the Oscar-nominated Belgian film *Close,* a story of the friendship between two thirteen-year-old boys, was released, the American press turned it into a "gay drama." It was only after the director's repeated statements that the film is not about sexuality but about the human desire for deep connection that reviewers began to see and hear the story in the way he intended. The presence of American masculinity that genders and sexualizes "soft" human behavior is also evident in the Middle East, where I teach in Abu Dhabi every year and have been doing so for over a decade. When I started teaching there in 2012, men from the United Arab Emirates would often greet each other by touching their noses together. Now I rarely see such acts of intimacy between men. They appear to have gotten the message that showing your "soft" side or even touching another man makes you less of a man.

LISTENING TO MY SON and his teammates after a game, I hear them adhering to "boy" culture in their mean jokes and their stoic posing, even when I know from their mothers that they are hurting. One of the more disturbing examples of such banter includes one of my son's teammates using the word "rape" to refer to something positive ("you guys really raped that team"). I called my son downstairs and asked him to please remember that his aunt was raped and that this is not a word that should be equated with playing well in soccer. He looked deeply ashamed and made sure I understood that he had not said the offending words, nor had any of his friends on the team. But the problem lies not with specific boys or men but with a culture in which boys think that "rape" could refer to success in beating a team.[24]

Sociologists, psychologists, social activists, and journalists have long written about American norms of masculinity and the negative impact of adhering or accommodating to such norms on the well-being of boys and men.[25] Sociologist Michael Kimmel lays out what it means to be a man in the United States. This includes the dictum that boys shouldn't cry and other such expressions: "it's better to be mad than sad," "don't get mad—get even," "take it like a man," "nice guys finish last," and "it's all good."[26] Vulnerable emotions are considered weak, strength is idealized, and nuance is "soft." Boys and men are supposed to be in control and feel shame, sadness, and self-loathing if they are not.[27] In his book *Real Boys,* psychologist William Pollack defines the "boy code" required of all boys as being phobic of anything that smells of femininity.[28] It demands that they put on a "mask of masculinity," as expressed by a fourteen-year-old boy who approached him after a workshop who said: "I get a little down . . . but I'm very good at hiding it. It's like I wear a mask. Even when the kids call me names or taunt me, I never show them how much it crushes me inside. I keep it all in."[29]

Jennifer Siebel Newsom's film *The Mask You Live In* powerfully reveals the devastating impact of norms of American masculinity on boys and men, while Tony Porter's TED talk is effective in driving the point home regarding the harm of a culture that asks boys and men to fit into a literal and metaphoric "man box." Michael Reichert's and Joseph Nelson's work in schools underscores the extent to which boys and young men suffer from gender and racial stereotypes that assume that boys don't need caring relationships in school, and particularly not Black boys. They offer concrete ways to disrupt such harmful socialization in classrooms and schools.[30] Gary Barker and his colleagues at Equimundo do research around the world providing ample evidence for the devastating impact of a culture that makes men into half humans by valuing only their "hard" sides and mocking their "soft" sides that make them good fathers to their children.[31] Social activists such as Mark Greene, Mark Grayson, Kim Evensen, and Ryan Ubuntu Olson, as well as the actor Justin Baldoni, have also written or given talks about the ways that "boy" culture makes it virtually impossible for boys and men to thrive.[32] A few of these activists and educators, including Kimmi Berlin and Ashanti Branch, have also offered concrete solutions to disrupt the damage that has been done to boys and men as a result of a culture we as adults continue to perpetuate.[33]

bell hooks, a well-known Black feminist writer who wrote a book on men and masculinity, reflected on the ways her brother was pressured to adhere to patriarchal norms or norms of masculinity:

> Like so many boys, [he] just longed to express himself. He did not want to conform to a rigid script of appropriate maleness. As a consequence, he was scorned and ridiculed by our patriarchal dad. In his younger years our brother was a loving presence in our household, capable of expressing emotions of wonder and delight. As patriarchal thinking and action claimed him in adolescence, he learned to mask his loving feelings. He entered that space of alienation and antisocial behavior deemed "natural" for adolescent boys. His six sisters witnessed the change in him and mourned the loss of our connection. The damage done to his self-esteem in boyhood has lingered throughout his life, for he continues to grapple with the issue of whether he will define himself or allow himself to be defined by patriarchal standards.[34]

Even though we think that adherence to such masculine expectations will protect our sons, brothers, partners, and fathers, the research consistently suggests otherwise. Adherence to norms of masculinity has been consistently found to be linked to higher levels of depressive symptoms and anxiety, decreased self-esteem,[35] and lower levels of friendship quality, social support,[36] and academic achievement.[37] Recent meta-analyses carried out by Y. Joel Wong and his colleagues showed that higher levels of adherence to norms of masculinity that privileged autonomy over relationships and stoicism over vulnerability were associated with lower levels of reported self-esteem and social support among men and women.[38] Wilkinson and Pickett find in their study of thirty industrialized countries that those countries that promote independence at the expense of relationship (stereotypic masculinity over stereotypic femininity) are more likely than countries that don't to have higher levels of income inequality and to report more mental health problems and drug addiction.[39]

RAISED BY HIS GRANDPARENTS, Chris, one of the boys in my studies, knew all about "boy" culture:

> I'm pretty happy, yes . . . I mean, I got a few things that I'm real pissed off at in life, you know. I wasn't raised with my parents and stuff like that. But if you let that get to you, you are gonna be a messed-up person. You have to get past that, like you know what I'm saying? So if you want to sit there and cry over that, you are not gonna progress as a person. I need to progress. I need to be a man. I need to do what I gotta do.[40]

The dilemma for Chris was how to stay connected to what he knew and felt as he grew up but still become what he considered a man. When asked in his senior year of high school about arguments with his best friend, Michael replied: "Hmm, [we don't have disagreements about] nothing, really, we don't argue, and so I can't say no, can't say that, so I don't know, not much, I don't feel anything." Sounding confused, he shifted between not knowing and then not feeling. He told his research interviewer that he and his best friend no longer shared much personal information with each other because he didn't trust his friend anymore. Taking "boy" culture literally, he added: "If I wanted a best friend, I'd get a girlfriend, you know."

Omar said he wouldn't tell his best friend about his hurt feelings because "that's gay." When asked if the teasing among his male friends results in hurt feelings, Justin said, "I really wouldn't know, 'cause they never really say, 'Oh, you hurt my feelings,' 'cause guys don't share things like that . . . to my knowledge, I guess, I don't know . . . I don't share my feelings with them because then they would think you were a wuss or something like that." Recognizing his own feelings and the demands of a culture claiming he doesn't have any, Marco said in his sophomore year that while he could cry in front of his best friend, he never has. However, when asked if his best friend has cried in front of him, he replied: "Um, yes. When he found out his mom was using drugs. That's the only time. I know it's healthy or whatever." Marco understood the cultural contradiction as he stood outside ("I know it's healthy or whatever") and inside of "boy" culture (he has never cried in front of his friend).

But boys' adherence to macho norms is not always obvious. As Emilio put it:

> Um, well, with [my best friend], I, I, I, I really like talk to him on a serious level. Like we can have a serious conversation without having to always joke around, because sometimes some things

> are . . . too serious to go around joking around about—like some things like family . . . [My other friends] they're usually, um, make a joke . . . Even when, when I feel that it shouldn't really be a joke or a joking matter.

His stuttering ("I, I, I, I really") seemed to suggest the risk of taking things seriously, which is the same thing as caring, and boys learn early in life that caring is for gay-identified boys.

The fear of being laughed at during a moment of vulnerability greatly influences boys' decisions about with whom they spend time. Carmelo described his best friend as someone who wouldn't laugh at him when he is feeling vulnerable. Marcus said, "If I was with these guys and these guys didn't get along with the other guys, I'll have his back, and he'll have my back, you know . . . But that's not being trustful . . . 'cause maybe the next day, he might be the one that's joking and making fun of you." Not wanting to be the butt of the joke is what keeps boys in line, as "not being able to take a joke" means that you are "soft" and thus not a man.[41]

Carl moved in and out of adhering to norms of masculinity, often in the same response: "Sometimes . . . my friends are kind of harsh sometimes. Like sometimes I'll tell them my teachers recommended me for this award, and they were like, 'So what?' . . . That, you know, that hurts me, you know, I'll be like, 'Oh, all right, so . . .' I'll be like, 'Shut up,' you know, you just start playing and stuff." When discussing a time when he was teased, Milo said to his interviewer: "I know he's playing, so it doesn't really, it doesn't feel bad, but if I didn't know he was playing, he probably would be able to hurt somebody. He would get somebody mad enough to do something, you know." His switch from the first person ("I") to the use of "somebody" right when his vulnerability was made explicit underscores the anxiety boys feel when expressing their feelings.

Asked how his friendships have changed from his freshman year to his senior year, Justin said:

> [My friend and I] we mostly joke around. It's not like really anything serious or whatever. Nothing like serious talking whatever, 'cause I don't talk to nobody about serious stuff . . . I don't talk to nobody. I don't share my feelings, really. Not that kind of a person or whatever. I don't even share with [my girlfriend], so I'm not really like open to that . . . Like I said, I don't tell nobody my business, so it's not a . . . like it's not a trust thing. It's just something that I don't do. So with money, of course, if [my friend] needs it, I give it to him, he'll give it back or whatever, so it's not really a big thing. So with feelings, though, I don't tell nobody. So it's not basically a trust thing, it's my personal reason not to tell nobody nothing . . . So what goes on in my life I don't really wanna share, 'cause if something hurts me, I don't wanna keep bringing it up so. I just try to forget about it.

The dilemma that boys face appears to be that if they reveal their feelings to other boys, they will be left alone. But if they don't reveal them, they will feel isolated. Lyn Mikel Brown and Carol Gilligan also identified this same crisis of connection among girls in their developmental studies. For girls, the dilemma is if they say what they think or know they will be left alone.[42] Milo and other boys in my studies revealed that they, too, experience this crisis, but it's about their feelings rather than their thoughts, which is predictable in a culture that thinks feelings are feminine and thoughts are masculine.

Carlos was explicit about his fears of being perceived as gay if he showed his "soft" side. In response to the interviewer's question about what he does with his friends, he said, "That question sounded homo, that sounded homo." When the interviewer expressed confusion, Carlos laughed nervously and said that "we just do whatever, man, we like, we do whatever we can do. If we don't have money, we stay in his house, watch TV." No longer were Carlos and his friends "expressing feelings," as he had put it his freshman year; they now did "whatever we can do." When asked about his "best friend" during his senior-year interview, a friend whom he rarely saw but still considered a best friend, he said: "The relationship, I mean it's a good relationship. It's, um, it's a tight bond, whatever. Um, I can trust him. I don't know how to explain it. Somebody you feel chemistry. No homo." His qualification of "no homo" right on the heels of expressing their closeness, as well as his response of "it's a tight bond, whatever," suggests a discomfort with his feelings. Ronan said that he talks with his best friend because he "is not a homo, he's not gay . . . If I did have a gay friend and he's just a friend, you know, he pulls no move on me, then it's cool. [But if] he pulls a move, I dump him. I don't care."

Sociologist C. J. Pascoe finds that girls, too, buy into macho norms by pretending not to care[43] and seeking to be "one of the boys," or people who desire sex over emotional intimacy and who don't need anyone.[44] The kick-ass girl in this context serves as a role model for girls and women, as she is ferocious in her ability to kick your ass literally if you mess with her and doesn't need relationships, including friendships. But she is also often struggling with feelings of depression and isolation and can maintain her image only if she denies her "soft" side, which is the side that helps her feel connected to herself and to others.

In survey studies, girls report adhering to norms of masculinity almost to the same degree as boys, and in our recent analysis of a high school population in China, girls report even higher levels of adherence to norms of masculinity than boys.[45] That is not surprising at all if we understand that the real problem is not boys and men but our privileging of characteristics and qualities that we associate with masculinity. In such a culture, girls will want to be like stereotypic boys and may even want to be like such boys more than the boys themselves, given the association with such behavior and being on top of the hierarchy. Pascoe calls for a dislodging of masculinity from its biological location so that we understand that the nature of our problem is our definition of what it means to be a boy and a human, rather than what it actually means to be a boy or a human.

In a humanities class that I sat in on in a New York City high school, students produced short films, essays, and poems for their final projects on masculinity in literature. Ellie Schnayer, a senior, wrote this poem about the conflict she feels between wanting her boyfriend to "be a man," yet wanting him to be sensitive to her feelings.[46]

Women want him, men want to be him.
Sometimes I wish you would just relax, and sit down and gaze at
the world around you.
Sometimes I feel like you are trapped in a silicone bubble,
Only seeing what is fake.
What is pushed on you?
Your strength is admirable. But you don't interest me at all.
You're a tool.

You remind me of the boys I met this summer.
You remind me of the boy who said goodbye.
Sensitive one minute and then destructive the next.
I like it when you smile and I love it when you cry with me.
But this is just too much.
You cry too much and you are a pussy.
You don't stand up for me.
You let me push you around. I messed up and you told me it was okay.
But it wasn't.
Man up already. I don't want to be dating a girl.
Be the stereotype.
Be my ideology, the buff guy, the gentleman, the tough guy, the provoker, the superhuman, push the limits, the provider, the frat boy, the villain.
Each of these personas clash with the notion of homosexuality.
But you're not gay, you're not a gentleman, either. I don't want to be dating a girl.
I like when you smile and I love when you cry with me.
But this is just too much.
I told you to man up, but you couldn't.
And then it changed.
You briefly became a man.
Dinners and hangouts. You toughened up. And I melted.
But you got too tough.
I flip-flop. Masculine traits you'd drop and pick up.
It was like you had to be everything at one point.
You are trapped in the silicone bubble now, with your alcoholic vomit and oil paint thinner

I told you to man up, and you did.
If only I hadn't.
If only I didn't make you feel bad for being sensitive.
if only I didn't take advantage of you, and if only I hadn't pushed you around
Then I wouldn't remind myself of the boys from this summer
Because I was like them, the way they acted, to you.
Controlling, dominant, bitchy.
And you were sensitive, sweet, and caring.
Stereotypes of the typical male infiltrated my ideal as to what you should have been.
But weren't.
It should have been balanced. But you shouldn't have stopped being nice.
You stopped being NICE.
You'd hit the bottle till you puked and I'd smoke until my lungs shriveled.
You ruined it, dude. You changed, dude. Was it 'cause of me?
I like when you smile and I love it when you cry with me
But this is just too much.
My fault for pushing. My fault for the pressure. You snapped and I collapsed.
You don't stand up for me. I messed up and you told me it was okay
But it wasn't.

The bell rings and the students gather around Ellie and tell her that her poem was "amazing." It is truly an amazing poem in its honesty and in its window into the painful conflict that is experienced living in "boy" culture.[47]

5.

Resistance[1]

WHILE THE OVERWHELMING FOCUS of research on masculinity is on patterns of adherence to its norms, there is a small but growing body of research that suggests that boys and men not only adhere to these norms but also resist them. Such resistance appears to be more common than we think. Andrew Smiler reports that the majority of his sample of tenth-grade boys provided relational reasons for dating and having sex that included the enhancement of connection (e.g., "I wanted to get to know the person better") and the depth of feelings (e.g., "I liked the person more than I ever liked anyone").[2] Psychologist Amy Schalet uncovers similar patterns in her research with boys, finding that resistance to various norms of stereotypical masculinity is pervasive.[3] Judy Chu concludes from her qualitative study that boys during early childhood often express their feelings of vulnerability and openly acknowledge their desire for friendships.[4] In her observational research study of four- and five-year-old boys, she finds that young boys start off reading the emotional and relational world in astute ways that mirror the resistance among girls during late childhood.[5] At four, boys display a "healthy resistance" to debilitating norms of masculinity by seeking out friends, supporting other boys in the classroom, and standing up for themselves when others try to bully them, such as when Jake said, "You may think that, but I don't." Developmental psychologist Gary Barker finds that men around the world have "voices of resistance," with one young man in his studies describing his revised understanding of gender norms when his grandmother spoke of wanting to date men again after many years of being a widow. If his grandmother had a right to "sexual agency and desire," the young man realized, so should all women.

In my own studies, I, too, find evidence of resistance to norms of masculinity in which boys and young men challenge, implicitly and explicitly, the "boy code," which demands that they value only the "hard" sides of themselves.[6] In his sixth-grade interview, John presented himself as a caring boy who is eager to make friends. He mentioned that one of the things that he "hates" about his friendships is when "everyone argues and when it's more serious, like fighting, I hate that the most." The reason he and his best friend are so close is that "when I needed help, he was always there . . . I think it is important [to have friends] . . . like it would be really silent without friends, and I would probably be arguing a lot." Underscoring the importance of receiving help and talking with friends for his mental health ("I would probably be arguing a lot"), John implicitly rejected the idea that boys are interested only in autonomy.

So, too, does Ramón:

> It's weird because like [my friend] can be there for me but . . . he's not reliable . . . so I had a fight with my girlfriend and since he was like my only friend, I called him up like twice, and both times, he rejected, and he was like, "Nah, you can't come [over], man." For whatever reason, I mean I understand if I just can't come there because of his parents, or because of a bad parent . . . but if ever my friends were in that situation where they needed to leave, I would definitely be there for them. I would be, "Yeah, sure, come over . . ." I was just like, he's my best friend, but like, I was just like, I just don't understand. I'm his best friend or whatever. But you know, he's not gonna be there all the time, so I need to go to somebody else for something. I should find somebody else.

His resistance is evident in his confident assertion of the obligation to be there for each other, and that not being there is cause to "find somebody else."

When in the seventh grade Mark was asked what a good thing about being a girl might be, he answered: "Maybe hanging out with your mom more." About his mom, Mark said: "I can talk to [her] whenever I want. I have a person that I can trust. She understands my situation, so I feel good about talking with her." Mark remained close to his mother in the eighth grade, saying: "I think we have a good relationship because we don't fight a lot. We like to talk to each other. Sometimes I don't get to see her right after school 'cause she works a lot, so it would be better if I could see her more." Mark resisted the mama's boy myth that suggests that closeness between mothers and sons is problematic. He also names the "boy" culture problem explicitly, which is that his ability to be close to his mother would be easier if he were a girl.

The evidence of resistance in my research was mostly in the way they described their friendships, especially during early and middle adolescence. Lorenzo said: "Everybody needs somebody. Somebody, in other words, when you need a shoulder to cry on, . . . you need an arm to punch when you are mad, and things like that." After admitting that he doesn't have a best friend, Ryan said that he would indeed like a best friend "as long as [I could] talk to them about anything, and . . . if I tell them to keep a secret, they will keep it." Jorge added:

> [Friends are important,] as you always need somebody there for you. That's the way I see it. I always need somebody there. Someone that I could count on to talk to whenever I need anything. So I . . . I think they are really important, friendships. I don't, I mean if you're going to grow up being lonely like always, there's going to be something wrong. If you're going to be mean to people, you're going to feel lonely all the time.

When asked what type of friendship he would like to have, he said: "I would like it to get even tighter. I would like it—you know . . . like—deeper, deeper than it is now would be cool . . . there's times that you want to be even tighter with a person, so that's what I am." Eddie admitted that while friendships can cause problems, "you need somebody to be there for you, and you need somebody to let your feelings out, so it's both good and bad, positive and negative, but in the end I think we benefit from friendships." What is most remarkable in these responses is the extent to which boys expressed wanting the very thing that we assume they don't want or need naturally.

RESISTANCE TO NORMS OF masculinity among boys and young men was both implicit and explicit. In the eighth grade, Louis said: "It's kind of an image, like there's a picture of how boys are supposed to be strong and muscular and protect the women maybe, like that's the image. But it's not always like that, and you don't always have to live up to that." In the sixth grade, Kevin said: "I cried the last two weeks. My grandmother died, so I cried. Sometimes boys have feelings, too. They gotta let it out once in a while." His classmate Diego said: "A man should show his emotions like how a girl shows emotions, because it's feelings and everybody has feelings and stuff."

In response to a question of what it means to be a man, Kyle said:

> You're not supposed to be scared or you're not supposed to be worried about something. That I believe is kind of dumb because emotions are normal. But yeah, one of the things they would say about being a man is to always pretend as if nothing bothers you, which is completely wrong in my opinion . . . Emotions are normal, everybody has them . . . It doesn't make you less of a man if you feel any of those emotions . . . if you're scared about something or worried about something, then you shouldn't be told that you're being a woman because you feel—because you're feeling those emotions.

Marcus, a boy in the research of developmental psychologist Onnie Rogers, reflected on the pressures to man up:

> Well, it's not things that I think I'm supposed to do, it's things that people think I'm supposed to do. Like guys aren't supposed to be feminine or guys aren't supposed to be sensitive or show their feelings, or cry. That's a big one, like guys aren't supposed to cry . . . It's like but what if you get hit or you get a bone broken or your mama or someone close to you dies like, you know. Of course you gonna cry, 'cause that's like human nature, you're supposed to cry, that's why you have tear ducts in your body . . . I guess society thinks that if men or boys are feminine that they're gay or they just assume that they're gay. And I think that's a bad stereotype because guys need to express their feelings, too. I'm not going to say that guys are supposed to be tough all the time and they're supposed to be like man up and like cover that up with hardness or whatever. It's okay to let yourself cry and be heartbroken. I don't think that's a good stereotype because that's like telling kids not to care about anything that happens.[7]

Marcus understands what leads boys not to "care about anything that happens."

Michael, one of the boys in my studies, says in response to a question of what it means to be a boy:

> All guys somewhat have a soft spot . . . like everybody has a good heart deep down inside, and that's how I feel, I guess . . . In terms of being a boy . . . not every boy has the same feeling inside him or emotions . . . I don't know, but I think guys try to hide it more . . . Guys tend to be a little stronger when they're

> around other people and they don't really show their feelings by crying or anything like that . . . They try to act happy around their friends and like that, and I feel a guy should just act the way they need to.

Trey, who was then in the eleventh grade, said:

> T: [People] just [think] that boys as teenagers don't care about feelings. Like there are certain ones, they don't care about a girl's feelings. I think they should be considerate of a female's feelings . . . and considerate of their own feelings.
> I: So how do you know that a boy should act the way that you think that they should?
> T: Mmm, because I act like that, I act that way.

Trey's responses reveal not only resistance to "boy" culture but also a confidence in following his own path. Connor expresses a similar confidence: "As a man—a male—there's an expectation for you, you know, not to show emotion or, you know, [to] be emotional and not [to] indulge in, you know, 'sissy' things. Like, you know, cooking, for example. And like it's considered odd that I'm interested in cooking."

THE BOYS AND YOUNG men in my studies suggested both adherence and resistance to norms of masculinity in their interviews, with resistance being more common during early and middle adolescence and adherence being more common in late adolescence. In his senior year, Nick says:

> I don't give—I don't give my heart out to too many people, you know, especially when it could get broken or hurt easily. I've been through too many times of that. So it's like I don't have any room . . . to recuperate from my heart [being] broken. There's been death in my family, girlfriends, you know, guy friends. I don't have any more for my heart to get stepped on. So I've picked myself up for a while. I'm walking. But you know, you never know when you fall down again. So I'm trying to just keep my eye out.

Nick's tenderness and vulnerability is his resistance, while his shutting down and claiming not to have any room in his heart is his adherence.

When asked what he doesn't like about being a boy, Jamal replies: "Because we don't like showing our feelings to certain people—'cause it makes us feel sensitive. We don't like being sensitive around other people." When asked what life would be like if he were a girl, he says: "I'd probably be more emotional—I'd probably express my feelings more, 'cause like females—it's okay for them to express their feelings, but for boys, like you see on TV and stuff, you can't really express your feelings. You gotta be a tough guy." He critiques the expectations for boys but ultimately adheres to them.

When asked to describe his closest friends, Malcolm says:

> I might talk with people, but it won't get real deep . . . there is nobody there to talk to . . . Right now, no [I don't have a best friend]. I had a couple like once when I was real young, around ten, and then when I [was a freshman]—and then me and this dude got real close, we was cool. But right now, nobody, really,

> 'cause it seems that as I've grown, you know, everybody just talk behind your back and stuff. You know. So I just let it go because it seems like no people that can hold—well, not no people, but the people that I've been meeting can hold up to their actions. Like you know . . . something might've happened like between me and a person where other people felt that we couldn't even be friends no more. So they sit there and talk about me to that person while I'm not around or something. Then, then that person will just talk about me, too, you know, whatever, 'cause you know, all throughout my neighborhood, I always hear, "He talks about you, he says this or he says that" . . . So I just don't really bother with it, you know, trying to make best friends.

While his claim of not bothering with it is his adherence, his expression of frustration is explicitly resistant to "boy codes" of conduct.

When asked about masculine stereotypes in Megan Ryan's classroom full of seventh-grade boys[8] in an all-boys school in New York City, they reiterated many of the qualities and expectations from Kimmel's "guy code" lists: boys shouldn't cry; shouldn't be vulnerable, weak, or sad; and should be strong and love sports. And then the boys critiqued these very traits. One boy said: "Sometimes you feel sad, and you want to cry." Another said: "When my father went away, I cried because I felt sad." Then the boys were asked if crying feels good sometimes, and one boy said immediately that it does. His classmate added: "Yes, sometimes you want to really cry and then you feel better." The other boys nodded solemnly in agreement. Megan then asked them to list feminine stereotypes and to say which they most identified with—the man box or the woman box. Most of them agreed that they "kinda fit into both but not everything in either box." The boys wanted to know why we had boxes in the first place if the stereotypes didn't reflect them or their peers. Megan explained that we think our gender stereotypes represent who we really are naturally rather than something we made up. In response, one boy piped up from the back of the room: "If we make culture into nature, then we think we can't change anything." Boys at twelve already know the thick story.

The high school seniors[9] whom Sam Permutt taught, in the same all-boys school as Megan's class, resisted and accommodated to norms of masculinity in a required class on modern masculinity. When the students were asked to relate a story about when they had been "gender policed," James shared a story of telling his cousin, who was about to enter the military, that he loved him, and his cousin's response was "Don't be getting gay on me." James expressed frustration that he didn't know how to get his cousin to take him seriously. His desire for seriousness is his resistance, while his cousin's dismissal and turning James's expression into a "gay" thing is an example of adherence. Accommodation often gets provoked in response to resistance to cultural norms. Lucas responded to the question of gender policing by sharing a story of losing a tennis match to a girl. In the car on the way home, his coach said, "I can't believe you lost to a girl!" leading Lucas to feel both ashamed and irritated at his coach for perpetuating gender stereotypes. Jamie didn't have a story of being gender policed, he simply shared a story of going to a summer camp and being asked to put on a tutu as a joke. He not only put it on but then decided to wear it the entire day. The boys in the classroom looked at him incredulously and asked if he has a photo of him wearing the tutu. He pulled out his phone and showed them a picture of him in a tutu, while the other boys in the picture had on summer shorts and

T-shirts. Jamie not only didn't find it embarrassing but also didn't find it particularly funny. He said he liked wearing it and thought he would wear it throughout the day.

But resistance turned out to be more complicated in Sam's sophomore class.[10] Adrian, one of the boys in the classroom, told Sam that he wasn't willing to be vulnerable in class and that we couldn't make him because he knew from past experiences with his peers how devastating the consequences would be. The entire sophomore class tried to convince Sam and me that their sensitively written reflections they had shared with us in private were "bullshit," and that their real selves were the tough versions of themselves that they presented in class. But their cover stories had cracks in them. When Sam and I asked them what other word we could use besides "vulnerable" to describe the concept of vulnerability, one of the more stereotypically male boys in the class said "courageous," revealing that he knows what's going on. One of the boys who seemed the most irritated with the entire concept of a class on modern masculinity was the one who ended up asking me in an interview in front of the class the most tender and probing questions about my own relationships, and at the end of the school year had written a novel about friendships.

RESISTANCE TO NORMS OF masculinity is not only pervasive among boys and young men; it has been found in research to be associated with positive psychological, social, and even academic well-being.[11] In an analysis of a survey of four hundred boys from sixth through eighth grade, developmental psychologist Carlos Santos found that resistance to masculine norms is significantly associated with lower levels of depression and higher levels of math achievement as measured by standardized test scores.[12] In a cross-cultural analysis of middle school boys in the United States and China, developmental psychologist Taveeshi Gupta and her colleagues found that resistance to masculine norms is associated with lower levels of depression, higher self-esteem, and higher friendship quality among boys in both cultural contexts.[13] Boys who reported being emotionally expressive with their friends and who valued connectedness as well as autonomy reported feeling better about themselves, less likely to experience depressive symptoms, and more likely to have mutually satisfying friendships than boys who did not. Survey research with girls in the United States and China suggests a similar pattern, namely that resistance to masculine norms was associated with higher levels of self-esteem, fewer depressive symptoms, and more social support from family and friends.[14] According to the data with young people around the world, valuing the "hard" and "soft" sides of ourselves is good for our health and well-being, just as the boys and young men in my studies told us.

6.

The Story of Danny[1]

WITH PALE SKIN AND sharply defined cheekbones, wearing low-hanging jeans and a bright white T-shirt, Danny explained to his interviewer in my longitudinal research project that he immigrated from China with his mother, father, and older brother when he was six years old. Currently he lives in the same neighborhood as his school and walks to school each morning. His mother works at a local factory and manages apartment buildings in the neighborhood; his father, who immigrated to the United States a year earlier than the family, works at a restaurant as a cook. While his freshman-year interview suggested that he had resisted accommodating to the norms of "boy" culture, by his senior year Danny had begun to accommodate more in the name of "growing up" and "becoming a man."

Freshman Year: Having a Best Friend

Danny described his relationship with his mother as "very close," involving "a lot of talk about schoolwork" and about how "it was back home in China." He reported that he didn't have to hide things from her and that she always made him feel better once he shared his problems with her. He described his father as a "hard worker who provides for the family and he gives me money to buy things." Danny admitted that he rarely saw his father, since he works long hours starting in the early morning. Unlike many of the parents of the boys in my studies (according to their sons), Danny's parents strongly valued friendships and actively encouraged him to find friends who were good to him and to whom he was good in return. Danny in turn believed that friendships are among the three most important aspects of his life, next to but not beneath family and school:

> I think having friendships is good because it doesn't make you feel lonely. When you're by yourself, you feel lonely, and you feel alone, as if nobody cares about you . . . I like that my friends and I can always talk about things, and everybody doesn't say, you know, "I'm better than you" or "You're better than me." When people say, "I'm better than you," that means they think you're lower and you don't belong in the same group as them. It makes you feel down.

Acutely aware of the hierarchy among his peers, Danny wanted no part of it and sought friends he could trust and with whom he could talk openly. When asked why he felt closer to certain boys than to others, he told his interviewer: "I know how they think and feel . . . I really don't know how the other guys feel." Knowing his friends was being aware of how they thought and felt, implicitly rejecting the forced choice of "boy" culture.

What Danny liked most about his friends was that he could "talk about things" with them and they wouldn't share his secrets with other people. Much of his freshman-year interview focused on explaining to his interviewer the nuances of trust and secret sharing—who could be trusted among his peers to keep his secrets and who could not. His best friend was Anthony, who is also Chinese and whom Danny has known since he arrived in the United States. The most important component of their friendship was the trust they had between them: "I could trust him more with the important stuff than I trust the other friends . . . Having someone to trust, you don't have to worry about anything by yourself or care for yourself. There's another person who cares about you, too." Danny relied on Anthony to help him through times of distress and turned to him when the two of them simply wanted to have fun.

Danny described his ideal friendship as: "It would be like I could trust him or he could trust me, and we could play together, and he wouldn't get mad at everything. And then he could trust me when I get mad." Being able to say what you feel, even if you are angry, was critical to a real friendship for Danny:

> It's like having a second, second voice from yourself. Friends, you can talk to them about a lot of things that you would normally talk about only to yourself. So having a friend is like, um, when you're in trouble you can talk to them about things. They could help you so you don't have to worry about yourself . . . [Having a friend] means that I could have someone who's like always there, and [will] always help. And then he doesn't tell people everything about what we do and things . . . It's like another way for you to think that you have somebody else to care for you.

Danny resisted the "boy code" in that he realized the importance of having close male friends, understood the need for talking and sharing secrets with them, and used his feelings and thoughts to guide his beliefs and actions. When the choice was isolation or talking to his friend, he chose the latter.

Sophomore Year: Becoming "Autonomous"

Danny continued in his sophomore year to describe his relationship with his mother as very close, although he admitted to sharing less with her now that he had grown older. Repeating the "boy" culture mantra, Danny attributed this change to increased maturity: "Maybe like now that I'm older . . . I like to keep things to myself." His relationship with his dad continued to be close as well, but Danny rarely saw his dad and said he mostly talked to him about school and his grades. His father encouraged his independence because "he likes for me to do things on my own and not rely on them every single time." He appreciated the fact that his parents were pushing him to be autonomous because "in the future, usually I'm going to rely on myself to get like good jobs." In contrast to his earlier interview, when he described himself as "friendly and patient . . . [this year] I would describe myself as a quiet kind of person."

Danny still had a large group of friends with whom he played basketball or handball or chatted online. He continued to underscore the importance of emotional support: "'Cause if nobody helps you out, the problem's going to get more serious. If somebody helps you and they could like help you out with the problem by telling you that you're not alone or something like that 'cause you don't want to feel alone when you're having a problem. That's why having friends to help you is better." While Danny did not want to feel alone, this response suggested that he may have been starting to have such feelings at this point.

Danny made sharp distinctions between his close and his best friends, resisting masculine norms that don't differentiate these. With a best friend he could "get like close . . . and be more intimate" and "I would know him much better and be able to spend more time with him and know how he's like as a person." Knowing someone is being aware of what he is like as a person, which suggests a depth unexpected among boys.

Describing the changes in his friendships since he was younger, he said:

> I'm more to myself now, 'cause when you were little, you just hang out with everybody—like boys and girls, everybody. You're more open 'cause you don't have many problems . . . Like now you don't want people to know what's going on . . . like if you tell them what's going on in school and maybe they'll like say something like "You're slow" or something like that. You may not feel as good anymore . . . and if you like fall back from the group [of friends] in school, you will feel more lonely, even though they're your friends.

The situation had changed for Danny this year not only in his perception of himself as quiet but also in his willingness to trust others. He now keeps his "most personal" secrets to himself, including those about his family, "'cause it's a family relation and I wouldn't want anybody like saying that 'Oh, I should change my family,' or something like that . . . 'cause I know my family is good." While Anthony remained his "best friend" and Danny liked that "we could openly express ourselves," the situation was not the same as it had been the previous year: he was beginning to doubt whether Anthony could truly be trusted with his secrets. Defining trust, Danny said, "It means that he would not go around and tell everybody what you have told him," suggesting that is exactly what Anthony did.

Junior Year: "A Closed Guy"

The most obvious change for Danny in his junior year was in his description of himself: "I'm kind of like a closed guy, I don't really like to express a lot of things." This was a big shift from his earlier interviews, in which Danny saw the sharing of secrets as a core part of friendships and spoke of himself as being friendly and patient. Danny had now retreated into being a stereotypical boy who does not "express a lot of things." He continued, however, to feel close to his mother, although he often had to translate for her and that irritated him. His relationship with his father was good:

> It's not totally closed in. I mean, you can be open with him and he could be open with you, and I don't have to get like, having to pull back on some of the issues that are bothering me about somebody. It gives me the chance to tell him how I feel. I won't have to keep it inside. I mean, for some people it's hard because they don't have a real good relationship with their fathers. But I guess that's the thing I'm lucky for, 'cause I have that kind of relationship. I could tell him how I feel.

That his parents encouraged emotional expression was likely the reason for his own emotional acuity and sensitivity.

Although he had some new friends this year, Danny was no longer best friends with Anthony, as Anthony wouldn't be "serious" with him and wasn't reliable enough to trust with his problems:

> I don't know. I mean, last year, I'd say Anthony was my best friend, but things have changed now . . . I'm the kind of person who doesn't really like to consider anybody a close friend or a best friend . . . I mean, I guess it depends on different time periods. When I'm in school, I see them all the time. But when I'm outside school, it's like a whole different world. I don't see them that much.

With these new friends, he did not feel close enough to share his life, and they mostly talked about topics that did not entail confidences: "I won't tell anybody my secrets . . . If I told them something that I know, secrets or something about how I feel about them, they may be shocked about it 'cause they never heard me say these things before."

Danny knew that his public persona didn't match what he was feeling inside:

> To me, I don't really like to express my personal feelings, 'cause I'm your friend, but I'm not your close friend. If you ask me for advice, I will give it to you. But in some cases, some topics may be too serious, so you want to keep it to yourself. I mean, you wanna kill yourself, I mean—if you say you wanna kill yourself to me, I would have to tell somebody, but . . . that's a choice for you to tell me that you want to do this or do that, it's your choice . . . I mean it's up to you, to them, whether they are gonna tell me.

Underscoring the importance of keeping secrets rather than sharing them, Danny resisted *and* accommodated to norms of masculinity. His not liking to express feelings aligned with the "boy code," while his willingness to raise serious topics in his interview and to go into detail about his moral obligation if someone confessed wanting to kill himself revealed his resistance. He expressed his real feelings, at least with his interviewer, even though it sounded like he wasn't able to with his friends.

When asked why he didn't speak openly with his friends, he said: "I guess it's just what I have to deal with by myself. I mean, everybody has to deal with their own personal situations. Life is complicated as I see it, 'cause if I don't deal with it myself and I rely on people my whole life, I won't be able to learn the lessons that I need for me to grow." Transforming isolation into a "life lesson" necessary for growing up is one of the most insidious and harmful thin stories in "boy" culture. Asked what he doesn't like about his friendships, he said with a sigh: "Not much. I mean, we don't talk to each other a lot, so I don't really know the bad or good sides to them . . . So there's not much, really, that I don't like." While Danny said that his ten male friends were all his "best friends," he picked himself when asked with whom he was closest. When pushed to choose someone, he stubbornly said, "My shadow." Danny was clearly feeling alone.

Yet he tried to convince himself throughout the interview that the norms of masculinity to which he was adhering and resisting actually make sense:

> [Friendship is] unconditional. I guess that means for sure that we will be friends even if we don't see each other, 'cause I've

> known him for such a long time. And we know how each other feels. And we don't have to tell each other every single day how we feel—how he feels. We know how each other feels already without telling each other. We don't have to worry about each other. I mean, I don't have to worry about him when he has a problem. He knows he could come to me when he has a problem or something . . . And he knows I could go to him . . . if I tell him how I really am and then he goes to other people and tells them that same thing that I told him.

Trying hard to believe in the thin story of boys' friendships, Danny finally broke down and told his interviewer about his friendship becoming "one big mess." Danny attributed the meltdown to Anthony's being a "jokester, he didn't know when to become serious," a common problem in "boy" culture. Thus, Danny no longer shared anything with Anthony.

Rather than trying to work it out with Anthony, Danny chose the less risky stance of not saying anything and giving up on that friendship and friendships entirely: "I keep my secrets to myself . . . Um, people say . . . if you have a friend, you could trust them with anything, and you could, like, tell people—tell them what—how things are. I mean, I don't believe that, 'cause if it's your secret, you should keep it to yourself, 'cause why should you tell other people how you feel if it's personal to you?" And then repeating one of the thinnest stories we tell in "boy" culture, Danny said: "You know, friends could help you, but you actually wanna do it—figure it out for yourselves before anybody could help you . . . It's just that you kind of feel in a sense that you're in a weaker state 'cause you can't figure out the problems yourself and the problems are happening to you because of that."

The interviewer asked him if his friends really knew him:

> D: They know the outside perimeters of my personal feelings, 'cause it's like—
> I: Could you, like, clarify that?
> D: My personal feelings are like how I feel about everyone. But I—but they only know what my personal ideas are of how I feel about someone.
> I: You are gonna have to give me an example, 'cause I just—I'm not getting it.
> D: All right. My personal feelings about like some people in this school, like all trying to be all gangsters and stuff, and I don't, I don't think that's the way they really are. That's my personal feelings. But my personal idea is that let them be what they wanna be, and I'll just leave my—I'll leave them alone and they'll leave me alone.

In a telling moment at the end of his junior-year interview, Danny redirected his wariness toward his male peers at the interviewer herself. After responding to numerous questions about his male friendships, Danny said in a loud and exasperated voice to her: "I do not like boys." Fearing that her persistent questions about male friendships were framing him as gay, he felt compelled to clarify the record and thus revealed the cultural norms that led to his problems in the first place.

Asked about the type of friendship he would like, he answered sarcastically:

> D: Ideal friendship? The perfect friendship? *The Brady Bunch* style. I don't know, I guess it's just everything goes well. You don't have any problems to worry about. Every day you wake up and you walk to school. You meet the friends. And then you just have your perfect little day with the butterflies flying around outside, and that little music that you do. Stuff like that.
>
> I: Music? Butterflies? What is that?
>
> D: That's cartoon style. You said ideal.
>
> I: Well, tell me real-life wise what a perfect friendship means to you?
>
> D: [I] don't really believe in a real-life wise kind of perfect friendship. I don't believe there's anything as a perfect friendship for anyone. [If there were] it would be having no problems whatsoever. You don't have any problems with that person and you don't have any problems with yourself and that person doesn't have any problem with you.

And then in his desire, perhaps, to be seen by his interviewer as he sees himself, Danny followed up with:

> Talking is—it's a better way of expressing how you feel. I mean, having someone to talk to basically means you have someone that like wants to hear what you say and wants to know like how you're doing. So it gives you a sense that there's somebody out there who I can say is a close friend to me and they could listen to me when I have a problem. And there there's someone I could turn to when I have a problem or I'm someone they could turn to for someone who has a problem . . . Friendships are important. It gives you a sense of purpose in life. I mean, it's

> part of . . . how you think in life. I mean, [let's say if] everybody is gone in the entire world and I was the only one left, [then] I would be happy, 'cause I'll get anything I want without anybody to compete with me. However, . . . even though I have all these special things, I'm not able to share it with somebody. I'm not able to share it with a family member or a friend. I'll be all alone. And that friend acts like a secondary family member to you, 'cause you could turn to your friend for help.

Senior Year: Being Alone

Danny's senior-year interview was short. He told his interviewer that he was ready to go to college and assume the responsibilities of manhood. Danny was still close to his mother, understood the way she thought and felt, and believed that she was sympathetic about most things. He was less close to his father than in the previous year but still believed that his father was supportive and would encourage him to try new things and meet new people so that he had friends and new experiences. He reiterated that both of his parents wanted him to have friends and that they had friends themselves. The biggest change over the last year had been:

> The way I view myself has changed, 'cause I mean I try to change in my own way, too, like I am doing things differently, and like being more of my own character and not the character that like other people might try to be, somebody else they are not. Like I guess in truth, I was trying to be somebody else I wasn't before. But right now, you discover new things, like once you're like grown up, like once you get older, you discover new

> things, and you don't have to be that type of person or have that type of style to fit in.

Danny's desire to be his own person appeared to be in response to his alienation from his friends. When asked why he didn't share his private thoughts and feelings with anyone anymore, he said:

> Maybe like your personal status, like what you're going through now, like if anybody's hurting you or stuff like that. I mean, if it goes to a certain extent, of course, you would tell somebody, but I mean if you think that you can fix it yourself, like solve the problem on your own, you will. You might get advice, but I guess you wouldn't share it . . . It's just that, like I guess some people like to keep their own personal issues, like they like to solve it themselves before they kind of ask people for help and stuff. So I mean, sometimes you want to solve it like yourself and not [involve] someone else.

Experiences of betrayal had led to what appears to be feelings of isolation under the rubric of growing up and solving problems by himself.

Danny described playing basketball and walking around with his friends that year, as well as being online playing games or on the phone chatting and sharing things—but nothing "really personal." He still retained, however, his awareness of the importance of talking with others, even though he didn't do it: "You get a sense that you have somebody your own age to talk to about things, [and] you know, if you talk, if you think about it, you tell him and then he's not gonna maybe like, he probably won't laugh at you. But I mean, he'll—you'll be able to talk to somebody about that." While his close friendships had disappeared, his sensitivity had not.

Danny claimed that Anthony remained a friend but not a best friend: "It's like any friend, it's great, 'cause I mean, I've known him for that long. I know how he's like and I can basically talk to him about almost anything that comes to mind. I guess." His stoic cover ("it's great") was exposed as false when he confessed to his interviewer that in fact he never talked seriously to Anthony because Anthony was never serious. Asked what he disliked about Anthony, he said there was nothing he didn't like "'cause I don't know, I've known him for a long time, and . . . most of his dislikes I've gotten used to. I mean, I don't really care . . . Like he's always making jokes and stuff like that." Even though Danny didn't seem to like it, he understood that joking even when things are serious was all part and parcel of "boy" culture.

Danny admitted in a soft tone of voice that Anthony and he did not know each other: "I don't know, maybe I don't know just how he feels inside. 'Cause he usually keeps his thoughts like most, I guess most important thoughts or [what] he's thinking about like—what's going on for him. Maybe that's, maybe it's too personal to share, stuff like that." He recognized that his lack of knowledge about Anthony and "just how he feels inside" was mutual, but he justified it as being "too personal to share." He wavered between telling a thick story he knew to be true and telling a thin one that was widely shared.

During the last part of his final interview, Danny reflected:

> I guess for me . . . keeping in touch is like an important thing for a friendship, 'cause you gotta like talk to the person you are

> friends with and see what's going on so that they know that you care. [They have to] know that, um, you're the type of person that wants to help you when you have a problem and wants to do something about it. I guess, you know for me, in order for a friendship to work, you can't like just say hi and "How are you doing?" and that's it. I mean, sometimes you have to talk to people in order to find out how they are feeling so that they have somebody else to express themselves to and they don't have to feel alone and like they're the only person in the world that has this problem.

Even amid what appeared to be stark feelings of loneliness, Danny remained connected to what he knew and felt. He knew that such mutual sharing was necessary for the friendship itself but also for making someone feel less alone in the world.

While Danny started off in his freshman year resisting a culture that makes male friendships "girlie and gay," he finished high school accommodating to it. His fear of appearing gay names explicitly the underlying ideology that led to his change in perspective. His transformation appears to be the product of a clash between what Danny wants, which is close male friendships, and the culture in which he lives, which doesn't value them and even mocks them and thus makes them feel almost impossible to find. This clash between what boys and young men want and what "boy" culture tells them that they should want is at the heart of more than just Danny's suffering. It's also why suicide and homicide are so much higher among boys and young men than others, and why many of us who grow up in "boy" culture are so depressed, anxious, and lonely.

Part Three

THE NATURE/ CULTURE CLASH

Every instance of severe traumatic psychological injury is a standing challenge to the rightness of the social order.

—JUDITH LEWIS HERMAN[1]

7.

Suicide

When my uncle was sixteen years old, he died by suicide. The story of my mother's brother was that he killed himself with a shotgun to his head in my grandfather's den because a girl had recently broken up with him. After years of reading suicide notes posted online and sent to me privately from mothers and sons who wrote them, I realized there is often more to it than a single breakup. In my uncle's case, his "friends" apparently taunted him to do it when he told them he felt like killing himself, which likely exacerbated his depression and suggests that his suicide may have also been a consequence of uncaring peers.

Rates of depression, anxiety, loneliness, and suicide are soaring around the world, especially among young people. Self-reports of clinical levels of depressive symptoms are 14 percent higher among teenagers in the last decade than those in the previous decade. The Youth Risk Behavior Survey[1] shows that more than one in three teenagers reported persistent feelings of sadness and hopelessness in

2019, a 40 percent increase since 2009.[2] In a meta-analysis comparing over 269 studies of 52,000 people, Jean Twenge found that anxiety has risen dramatically since 1952.[3] A national health council recently recommended that *all people* under the age of sixty-five get screened for anxiety symptoms.[4] Loneliness[5] is also reaching epidemic levels, with 60 percent of people born between 1995 and 2010 in the United States reporting feeling "left out or isolated from others," and 61 percent of young adults in 2021 reporting "serious loneliness," compared to 54 percent in 2018.[6] U.S. Surgeon General Vivek Murthy recently claimed that loneliness is the public health crisis of our times.[7]

Suicide rates are also increasing dramatically, with a 30 percent increase in the United States during the last two decades. Males are three to five times more likely to kill themselves than females, while females are significantly more likely to attempt suicide, a pattern likely explained by the methods employed, with boys more likely to use guns and girls more likely to use pills. A recent ABC News report indicated that the number of suicides in the United States in 2022 reached record levels, matching the levels during World War II, and the numbers are likely to be even higher once pending death certificates are ruled as deaths by suicide. Between 2007 and 2018, suicide rates in the United States for those aged ten to twenty-four increased by 57 percent, with rates tripling among children ten to fourteen years of age and increasing by 76 percent for older teenagers.[8] Boys and young men between the ages of fifteen and twenty-four are having the most dramatic increases in suicide rates, with the rate of suicide among Black boys between ten and twenty-four *rising* by 36.6 percent and rates of suicide being highest among Native American and Alaska Native people, at 26.7 deaths per 100,000.

Death by suicide is now more likely to occur than by being hit by a car.[9] The problem is not just in the United States. The term *hikikomori* (meaning "socially isolated") is used in Japan to describe the newest generation of young people, and a few years ago the UK appointed a minister of loneliness to tackle the problem. The suicide rate in South Korea was 9 per 100,000 in 1985. In 2015, it was 30 per 100,000, with similar rates in England and France. In countries that are deemed less "modern," however, the suicide rates are significantly lower, at about 1 in 100,000, suggesting that our modern problem is rooted in our uncaring culture rather than in our people.[10]

At the edge of manhood, right around the time that my uncle died by suicide and that the suicide rate among boys in the United States rises dramatically, the boys in my research suggested in their interviews feeling pressured to "man up" and hopeless about finding the friendships that they want and need so that they won't "want to kill" themselves. The two experiences are likely linked. The "boy code" makes male friendships unmanly, and thus boys and young men will likely struggle to find the very relationships that they want and need for their mental health.

This loss of or struggle to find close male friendships among boys and young men has been documented not only in my own research but in coming-of-age movies such as *Stand by Me,* in which Richard Dreyfuss, who serves as the adult narrator, describes the process of such loss among boys during adolescence. Another coming-of-age movie is *The Breakfast Club,* in which a character says, "When you grow up, your heart dies," suggesting that this loss has consequences. The Grand Prix–winning and Oscar-nominated Belgian film *Close* reveals the homophobic teasing that can lead to the loss of male friendships and the suicide that can result from such loss in "guy" culture. Lukas Dhont, the director of and screenwriter of *Close,* told me in a Zoom call that he realized while he was reading my book *Deep Secrets* that his yearning for close male friendships when he was a teenager was not just about his sexuality but also about his human desire for such friendships. He didn't realize that his story was the story of many boys and young men until he read my book. The fact that his film was nominated for or won some 110 awards around the world underscores that the story told in my previous book and his story resonate with a lot of people.

But suicide among boys and young men isn't always about the betrayal by a loss of friends or about friends at all. It also appears to be for some a consequence of the clash between a culture that doesn't care and a human who does. The mother of a young man who died by suicide described her son to me as deeply upset by the social injustices in the world and his sense of helplessness in trying to effectively address them. Similarly, Senator Jamie Raskin of Maryland writes about his sensitive son, who died by suicide when he was twenty-five:

> From a very young age, he was an enormously sensitive person. He felt the pain of other people and of animals in a way that certainly I had never seen before, and [which] people describe as unique. He would read an article in the newspaper about the civil war in Yemen and the hunger of children there, or about children who were displaced in Iraq, and it would stay with him the entire day and he would think about it, and then he would get in touch with groups that were working on it. He felt these things like these people were members of our family. So he was

> an extraordinary empath and had this overwhelming sense of responsibility for the world. And so these episodes of war and civil war and famine and hunger and violence, it struck him really hard. That was just in his nature . . . Tommy never stopped looking at that level of the Maslow hierarchy of needs. He understood there are people who could focus on nothing other than where their next meal is coming from. Or how are they going to be safe from violence? Or how do they get out of a war zone? And so before we think about, OK, how are we going to get people on trips to Mars and stuff like that, we've got to be thinking about [helping] people who are just struggling to survive, even at a subsistence level.[11]

The suicide note of Raskin's son urged everyone to "look after each other and the animals. Don't forget the animals and the global poor."[12]

Maya, the daughter of a close friend of my parents and now a close friend of mine, describes her brother who died of a drug overdose at age twenty-six in a manner similar to the way Raskin described his son:

> When I think about Josh these days, a lot of what I think about is how incredible he would have been with my kids. My son Hestu is 3.5 years old and very interested in how things work. It's the incessant "why" of toddlerhood coupled with an urgency to really grasp the fundamentals of the environment around him . . . Josh was similar. He loved books. He surrounded himself with them and used them, as many of us do, to make

> sense of what he was feeling, why he was experiencing the world as he did . . . Josh would have really loved talking to Hestu. He had a profound respect for curiosity and would have, I imagine, fully engaged with Hestu in honest and respectful conversation without pandering or oversimplifying because he was speaking to a three-year-old . . . Josh was always a little boy in my mind. He was gentle and kind and curious and loving and really just felt too fragile for the world he was entering, moving in step with his peers through high school, experimenting with drugs and going to parties. It all just seems like these things were forced onto him and he was anxious to keep up out of social pressure more than active engagement and exploration. I don't know, maybe that's just what school and growing up is. When I think about Josh at his happiest, I always think about us playing outside . . . We invented great games that involved prolonged narratives which we would return to for days and weeks running . . . Josh was usually the driver of the story. He was fascinating to listen to and would talk for hours developing characters and building plots. I think Josh was happiest when he felt in control and unchallenged—at home surrounded by his books, nature, animals, and his younger sister.[13]

In a suicide note written by a middle-aged man and posted on the internet, we hear a similar theme of being "too fragile for the world."[14] Nicolas (not his real name) explains in his post that at the root of his impending suicide was that he never felt that he fit into a society in which few people listen to one another: "I rarely felt that I was successful explaining my ideas, perceptions, understandings to others." His struggles began in the second grade, when he discovered that "there were all these [confusing] unwritten rules governing my classmates' behavior, as well as a slew of them that governed my teacher's interactions with us." He wondered why his classmates weren't interested in talking about the topics he was curious about and preferred to talk about things he found boring. Attributing some of his struggles to his shy nature and self-diagnosed autism, he makes it clear, however, that those characteristics were not why he died by suicide. It was, according to his own account, a result of living in a world where lying is considered a form of politeness: "The best way for me to articulate why I valued honesty is that it hurt to lie. White lies (told to spare another's feelings) hurt. As Holden Caulfield [in *The Catcher in the Rye*] puts it, being 'phony' hurt."

Nicolas also indicates in his note that there are three periods of life that everyone goes through: "As a child you are taught to conform; as a teen you struggle to conform; and as an adult you struggle to make sense of a world that doesn't make any sense." In the final part of his note, he writes: "And so the simple way to say it is this: I was done. I was tired of fighting to try to share my experiences, ideas, and views . . . Perhaps that is true for most people. Perhaps it is part of the human condition. But I had enough and just wasn't up for the continued effort . . . Live well, and to steal a line from one of my fraternity brothers, 'Go hug somebody!'"

At the turn of the twentieth century, French sociologist Émile Durkheim wrote about the anomie and suicide that result from a society that does not address the needs of its people.[15] But this clash between the values of the society and the needs of humans who live in it fosters more than just mental health problems, loneliness, and suicide. It also produces violence. What we haven't realized in our rush to blame one another for such violence is that our impulse to see it as another person's problem rather than an outcome of the culture that we help to perpetuate is precisely what leads to more violence. According to the rebels, the solution is to listen *to* them to learn *from* them and about ourselves, and care—even when they have committed a violent crime like those I discuss in the next chapter. While these young men you are about to hear from are not the rebels that I am celebrating in this book, as their cause is not for a common humanity but simply for revenge, they do teach us something important about them, us, our "boy" culture, and how to prevent further violence.

8.

Mass Violence[1]

SITTING IN HIS MERCEDES-BENZ in 2014, twenty-two-year-old Troy says into his cell phone: "Tomorrow is the day of retribution. The day in which I will have my revenge against humanity, against all of you [because] for the last eight years of my life . . . I have been forced to endure an existence of loneliness . . . I've had to rot in loneliness."[2] The following day, near a local college campus, he mortally stabs three roommates, one of them ninety-four times, and shoots and kills two women standing outside a sorority and a man shopping inside a deli. He also shoots himself in the head.

Mass violence, in which at least four people are targeted, has increased dramatically over the past twenty years in the United States, with those under the age of eighteen now being called "children of the mass-shooting generation."[3] Having lockdowns to prepare for such events is part of the regular school day for most children in the third decade of the twenty-first century.

Two days after another mass shooter killed himself, his mother, twenty children, and six staff members at his former elementary school, I ask a classroom filled with twelve-year-old boys what they thought were his reasons for suicide and homicide. They respond by telling me that he was "crazy." I then ask them what made him crazy, as there is no evidence that he was born that way. Two boys say, "Loneliness," in unison, and then one adds, "Sometimes feeling lonely makes you feel angry because you think that no one cares and then you act crazy." Boys around the room nod in agreement and slowly begin to share moments in their own lives in which they felt lonely and then acted out aggressively. With tears in his eyes, one of the boys discusses a time when he broke off the head of his little sister's favorite Barbie doll because she and her friends had excluded him from their games, and so "I had no one to play with." Boys and young men who do not commit violence often provide insight into the reasons for the boys who do. They also reveal, as do the mass shooters themselves, that mental health problems, loneliness, and violence are tightly linked together.[4]

In a study of 7,000 adults in England, people who were depressed were over ten times more likely to be lonely than those who were not depressed.[5] Even short periods of isolation had a long-term impact on mental health and can also lead to violence. Primatologist Harry Harlow in the 1950s isolated infant and juvenile macaques for different periods of time to chart the social and emotional consequences. He and his research team found that monkeys placed in isolation exhibited different levels of social deficits when introduced or reintroduced into a peer group, depending on the length of isolation.[6] For those monkeys who were partially isolated—they were allowed to see, smell, and hear other monkeys but had no physical contact with them—the consequences included blank staring and self-mutilation. Monkeys who were repeatedly separated from their peers and isolated were severely psychologically disturbed.[7] Those monkeys raised in total isolation with no contact with other monkeys[8] usually "went into a state of emotional shock, characterized by . . . autistic self-clutching and rocking," with the effects being more severe the longer they were isolated: "12 months of isolation almost obliterated the animals socially."[9] Conducting similar experiments with mice, Graziano Pinna and his colleagues discovered that when you put male mice in a cage for a period of enforced solitude over four weeks and then put another mouse in the cage with the first mouse, the mouse who was in solitude will initially explore the other mouse and then "stand up on his back legs, rattle his tail and aggressively bite the intruder wrestling him to the ground."[10] The longer the mouse is isolated, the more aggressive it will become when another mouse is put into the cage to join it.

Lonely men are more likely to administer hostile shocks to confederates in a laboratory experiment than those who do not report feeling lonely.[11] People who are socially isolated or reported feeling lonely are more likely to commit violence against intimate partners, children, or elders, and are more likely to commit homicide or kill themselves. A study of incarcerated youth concluded that those who were most aggressive also had higher levels of loneliness, and those who were more socially isolated were more likely to be in the violent crime group.[12] Social neuroscientist John Cacioppo notes: "No matter what social species you're talking about, all the way down to the fruit flies, if you isolate them, they die earlier. It lowers your impulse control and essentially triggers a self-preservation mind-set. A lonely person's brain is always on the lookout for social threats," and thus a lonely person is more likely to commit violence than one who is not lonely.[13]

Social psychologist C. Nathan DeWall and his colleagues state that "even seemingly minor or vague manipulations of social exclusion produce significant and sometimes substantial increases in aggressive behavior, even toward people other than the rejectors."[14] They explain such behavior by proving through a series of well-designed experiments that social exclusion leads people to perceive neutral information such as ambiguous words and actions as hostile, and act aggressive not only toward people they saw as unfriendly but also toward those with whom they had no previous contact. Cognitive distortion often leads socially excluded people to perceive a threat when there isn't one and thus to respond with a fight-or-flight reaction, which in turn causes others to exclude them even more.[15]

Every few weeks in the United States, we are hit with a story of a man, almost always between the ages of eighteen and thirty years old and typically white, who has committed an act of violence with a gun and/or other weapons in a public space in which multiple people are wounded and/or killed. The numbers of such incidents vary depending on how you define "mass violence" and where it happens. Such incidents are more common in private homes than in public spaces, but mass violence committed in public spaces is more likely to be in the news. Mass shootings have tripled since 2011.[16] By the end of 2019, there were 417 mass shootings; in 2020, there were 611; and in 2021, 693.[17] The year 2021 ended with 690 mass shootings; from January to November 2022, there were more than 13 mass shootings per week on average.[18] Following the news of such violence, there is typically a discussion regarding why the man did what he did. There is also a wave of support for gun control of some sort.

Our response also includes figuring out who is to blame. Was it the perpetrator's school, family, mother, or peers? Or was it just the perpetrator himself, who was perhaps a loner or an inherently evil person? But those questions never address why girls and women—not to mention most people who are lonely, including those with mental health problems—*don't* commit such violence. Nor does it address the fact that the perpetrators are almost always men who are young, white, and/or middle and upper class, suggesting another story about the hierarchy of humans and not wanting to be demoted to the bottom.[19]

BRIAN WHITNEY, EDITOR OF *Exit Plan: The Writings of Mass Shooters,* attempts to explain the violence by drawing from the social media postings of mass shooters:

> Mass shooters usually want to get even. The motivation for a mass killing is almost always revenge . . . Almost every mass shooter has two very distinct characteristics. They are miserable and depressed enough to be willing to die, and either paranoid or angry enough that they blame others for their suffering, which for them has become unbearable . . . Some are motivated by fame, the desire to impress, or for attention. Others do it simply for the thrill.[20]

Mental illness and access to guns are indeed the problems, as Whitney states, and the solutions are thus to employ more mental health counselors, to identify the problems sooner, and to prevent the shooters from getting weapons. These solutions, however, don't address why boys and men are killing in the first place.[21] Undoubtedly weapons, especially automatic guns, should not be accessible to anyone. In fact guns should be hard for all of us to get, including those who are minors and/or have mental health problems. Mass shooters are indeed depressed and anxious, often do want revenge, and are resentful of and target those who they perceive get more attention than they do (girls, women, people of color, gay people, immigrants, jocks, popular kids). They are also often paranoid and delusional, and they do want to kill people and sometimes themselves. Parents and school systems often do miss what seem like obvious signs of distress, and they, too, should be held accountable. But none of the perpetrators were born killers. Thus the question we should be asking is, What happened to them to turn them into mass shooters?

The reports of the early life of Yahya, a twenty-two-year-old who killed ten people in a grocery store in 2021, suggest that he got along with others and was a "happy boy," but then during his late adolescence, everything fell apart. A middle school teacher said: "[Yahya] was the sweetest kid ever. Really quiet and respectful. He got along with everyone. And he talked to everybody. He would play with everyone." She added: "He was a good kid. I just don't know what happened." A classmate who ate lunch with Yahya in high school said: "He was a pretty chill kid from what I can remember. He wasn't like a popular kid or anything. And he wasn't like the high school loser, either. He was just kind of in between. He was like me, I guess." A classmate in a tenth-grade English class, however, remembered Yahya as not really "having a lot of friends, and that's why [the other student] and I tried to reach out and make him welcome. He was alone and he was just kind of shy." His brother told CNN that he was often the recipient of bullying for his religion and for his feminine-sounding name. He added that those factors may have contributed to his becoming antisocial and mentally ill. One of his peers said that he had indeed become increasingly isolated during high school.

Yahya was convicted of a misdemeanor assault against another student in a classroom in his senior year and told the police at the time that the victim had made "fun of him and called him racial names." Three years later, he became a perpetrator of mass violence. His action was likely, given what we know from the research, the result of a combination of bullying, harassment, isolation, mental health problems, and rage. His cousin responded: "Are they seriously saying he killed ten people? This doesn't make sense. How can this be true? [Yahya]'s whole family are good people. They never had problems." Sharing a PBS link about the impact of immigration on the U.S. economy, Yahya wrote a post titled "Why Refugees and Immigrants Are Good for America," suggesting that he was hearing otherwise and that he was offended, given the immigrant status of his own family. When Yahya was twenty, he posted #NeedAGirlfriend. One of his brothers said to a reporter: "The entire thing surprised me. I never ever would have thought he would do such a thing. I never thought he would kill. I still can't believe it. I am really sad for the lives that he wasted, and I feel sorry for all those families . . . We lost a brother even if he is the killer." Yahya was a killer, but his violence was not inevitable.

Mass shooters often report feelings of loneliness and isolation and anger at some form of harassment, rejection, and discrimination by their peers. One of the mass murderers in 2013 openly discussed on social media that he longed for a close friend.[22] Even though his peers considered him popular, his postings suggested that he wanted a friend who understood him, saw him for who he was, and listened to him. He may have also been angry at the racism that was likely directed at him, his brother, and his family, given where they came from. This mixture of loneliness, anger, and the mental health problems that can result is toxic when, like mice trapped in a maze, these young men see no way out. Mark, who was arrested with his brother for building bombs in their apartment, was reportedly lonely and looking for a close friend to understand him and see him as he saw himself. Another mass shooter writes just before he is caught and after he has committed his crime: "I am writing this more for my own comfort than for anything. I do not want to feel the loneliness that I do. Though it is ironic that I feel this loneliness when surrounded by people." In 2019, police arrested two young men who had an arsenal of weapons they were planning to use for a mass murder. The father of one of them said that his son had been wanting to escape the pain of loneliness for a very long time and described him as "angry, hateful, and needing unconditional love."

Loneliness does more than just make you sad and sometimes angry, especially for boys and men, as the only acceptable emotion for them in "boy" culture is anger. It can also cause you to look for love in all the wrong places. Mass shooters, particularly those who are white and who feel discriminated against for various reasons, link up with groups that promote hate ideologies. In her book *The Origins of Totalitarianism,* Hannah Arendt writes: "For those who feel they have no place in society, it is through surrendering their individual selves to ideology, that the lonely rediscover their purpose and self-respect . . . the experience of not belonging to the world at all . . . [is] the essence of totalitarian government."[23] Those who commit mass violence likely find the ideology of hate attractive because they are searching for connection and think they will find it among others who hate like they do.

Perpetrators of mass violence have also typically been diagnosed with one or more of the following problems, which may be both a cause and a consequence of their distress: sensory integration disorder, oppositional defiant disorder, intermittent explosive disorder, ADHD, anxiety, depression, autistic spectrum disorder, juvenile bipolar disorder, post-traumatic stress disorder, dysgraphia, or just social awkwardness.[24] Their self and medical diagnoses are often reported as if these are explanations for why they were bullied or harassed, or even for why they became violent. Questions are rarely asked about why these young men were so explosive, defiant, depressed, or anxious; what has triggered their bipolar disorder or PTSD; or why being socially awkward or being on the spectrum can translate into being isolated.[25]

Answers to this question may lie with the ways we treat boys and young men with such diagnoses, often blaming them implicitly or explicitly rather than considering the impact on them of living in a culture that doesn't nourish their nature. Evidence of our tendency to blame them is that we often move them out of the damaging context when troubles arise rather than seek to change the context. Thus, perpetrators of mass violence have typically experienced a lot of school transitions. Troy, a mass shooter whom I quoted in the beginning of this chapter, changed schools six times in the span of fourteen years because his parents wanted him to be in a safer context. He needed, however, a safer culture to grow up in as well. Mateo, another mass shooter, had had behavioral issues since middle school,[26] had transferred schools six times in three years in an effort to deal with these problems, and was eventually transferred to a school for children with emotional or learning disabilities,[27] which simply banned him from wearing a backpack on campus.[28] While some perpetrators have had mental health problems from early on in their lives, most began to experience problems at early adolescence, right at the age that school transitions begin to occur. Developing close friendships is hard enough for boys without diagnoses or who are not socially awkward or on the spectrum. For those who are and who experience numerous school transitions, it can feel impossible.

While we often hold the perpetrator solely responsible for his crime, the perpetrator almost always blames us and thus doesn't see the culture that makes it impossible for us to see our own humanity, let alone theirs. Troy says he is going to get revenge "on all humanity" who has let him rot in loneliness.[29] Sixteen-year-old James, who killed two and wounded two, says in a note: "I am not really depressed just the fact that I want people, the world . . . to know how fucked up and cruel the world is and can be. This school has to get its shit together. 'Cause there are too many deaths this past 2–3 years . . . But anyway, I'm dead. You guys are living, you should be happy."[30] William, a seventeen-year-old who shot six students, had written a post before he committed his crime:

> In a time long since, a time of repent, The Renaissance. In a quaint lonely town, sits a man with a frown. No job. No family. No crown. His luck had run out. Lost and alone. The streets were his home . . . His only company to confide in was the vermin in the street. He longed for only one thing, the world to bow at his feet. They too should feel his secret fear. The dismal drear. His pain had made him sincere. He was better than the

> rest, all those ones he detests, within their castles, so vain. Selfish and conceited. They couldn't care less about the peasants they mistreated. They were in their own world.[31]

Noah, a sixteen-year-old who shot and killed two people and injured seven others, writes:

> I am not insane! I am angry. This world has shit on me for the final time . . . I killed because people like me are mistreated every day. I did this to show society "push us and we will push back!" I suffered all of my life. No one ever truly loved me. No one ever truly cared about me . . . And all throughout my life I was ridiculed. Always beaten, always hated. Can you, society, truly blame me for what I do? . . . But I shall tell you one thing, I am malicious because I am miserable. The world has beaten me . . . It was not a cry for attention. It was not a cry for help. It was a scream in sheer agony saying that if I can't pry our eyes open, if I can't do it through pacifism, if I can't show you through displaying intelligence, then I will do it with a bullet.[32]

George, who killed four people, asks, "Why do people put up with all the injustice around them, why don't they fight it?"[33] He expresses his rage toward humanity:

> You aren't human you are a robot. You don't take advantage of your capabilities given to you at birth, you just drop them and hop into the boat and head down the stream of life with all the other fuckers of your type. Well goddammit, I won't be part of it . . . The human race sucks, human nature is smothered out by

> society, jobs, work, and school . . . People don't take any advantage of the gift of human life. They waste their minds on memorizing the stats of every college basketball player or how many words should be in a report when they should be using their brain on more important things.[34]

Thomas, an eighteen-year-old who shot and wounded five people and killed himself, said:

> People told me that I have to go to school, to be able to lead a beautiful life later. But what's the point of the fattest [most expensive] car, the biggest house, the most beautiful wife, if in the end it doesn't matter anyway. When your wife begins to hate you, when your car uses up gas that you can't pay for, and when you don't have anybody that will come visit you in your fucking house! The only thing that was taught to me at school was that I am a loser . . . [and] you can only be happy, when you conform to the masses. But I couldn't and didn't want to do that . . . My actions are a result of your world, a world that won't let me be the way I am. You made fun of me, I did the same to you now . . . On a final note, I want to thank those who mean something to me or were good to me, and I want to apologize for all of this! I am gone.[35]

IN HIS BOOK *Achilles in Vietnam,* Jonathan Shay draws from the stories of veterans who sought his help as a psychiatrist to describe "moral injury," which he defines as a traumatic reaction to an experience of a "betrayal of what's right" by someone in authority.[36] He provides a thick story that explains how "boy" culture, although he does not name it as such, gets under the skin and can lead to violence. Shay, whose work is widely referenced in the world of trauma treatment, explains that when those in authority—a commander in chief, a parent, a teacher, a boss, or one's peers—put pressure on a person repeatedly to engage in activities that go against what that person knows to be morally responsible or right, this can lead to "psychological injury" that can have "disabling psychiatric symptoms" and "ruin good character."[37] The effects will be particularly dramatic if that person has no one with whom to discuss the moral trauma.

The symptoms of moral injury that can "devastate life and incapacitate its victims from participation [in it]"[38] include

- Loss of authority over mental function—particularly memory and trustworthy perception
- Persistent mobilization of the body and the mind for lethal danger, with the potential for explosive violence
- Chronic health problems stemming from chronic mobilization of the body for danger
- Persistent expectation of betrayal and exploitation; destruction of the capacity for social trust
- Persistent preoccupation with the enemy
- Alcohol and drug abuse
- Suicidality, despair, isolation, and meaninglessness[39]

Moral injury and the PTSD that often results from such injury, according to Shay, consist of a five-stage process that at first entails the betrayal itself of what's right,[40] which could be anything that involves behaving in a way that harms one's internal sense of right and wrong or witnessing such behavior. For veterans, it includes being required to harm or kill innocent people or witnessing the harm or killing of innocent people without being able to intervene. For all others, it may include experiences of physical, sexual, or emotional abuse or even being asked by someone in authority or a peer higher in the hierarchy to lie, participate in, or remain quiet when others are being bullied. It may also involve being the victim of such bullying, as victims often feel as if it were their fault and thus that they somehow participated in their own violence. When I ask my students to tell me moments when they have experienced a feeling of being injured morally, they immediately tear up and tell me times when they have been asked to do or say something that they know isn't right or not to do or say something that they know they should. Their reaction suggests that moral injuries, at least the physically nonviolent forms, are not only common but also painful.

After experiencing repeated and long-term betrayals of what's right, in combination with a lack of support, victims of moral injury can then in the second stage exhibit what Shay calls "indignant rage."[41] Such rage can lead them to the third stage, which is to isolate and create a self-fulfilling prophecy in which few want to spend time with them, thus exacerbating their isolation. Shay notes that he prefers the term "indignant rage" to "rage" because he can hear the word "dignity" in the word "indignant": "It is the kind of rage arising from social betrayal that impairs a person's dignity through violation of 'what's right' . . . and that rupture[s] social attachments . . . and chok[es] off the social and moral world."[42] It creates an "us versus them" mentality and "severs all other attachments or commitments."[43] In the words of a mass shooter who spent most of his childhood being bullied by his peers, the indignant rage mixed with isolation and the corresponding mental illness that such rage often triggers sounds like this: "Humanity has rejected me. Humanity has never accepted me among them . . . Humanity is a disgusting, depraved, and evil species. It is my purpose to punish them all."[44] The "us versus them" mentality explicit in this statement is not a natural component of human nature, as most social psychology articles would have us believe, but a response to a culture that can lead to moral injury and, in the case of those who are most isolated and unsupported, to a desire to bond with an "us," which in the case of the mass shooter is a "me," through creating divisions from a "them."

For those who have experienced the more extreme forms of moral injury—witnessing or being the victim of violence—the fourth stage of moral injury is often grief and suicidal longing, in which the victims of moral injury feel like they are already dead, tortured by shame and humiliation and guilt, especially if they participated in or witnessed the moral offense repeatedly. In Shay's words: "Severe, prolonged traumatization [based on betrayal of what's right] can bring wholesale destruction of desire, of the will to exist and to have a future."[45] Depression, hopelessness, feelings of complete isolation, and a longing for death are all symptoms of moral injury and of PTSD when the trauma is left untreated.

And finally, the veterans in Shay's clinical practice who experience the fourth stage of moral injury can enter a fifth stage when they don't get help at the fourth, a stage in which they go berserk and "commit atrocities against the living."[46] Shay describes this stage in reference to a soldier who feels "trapped, surrounded, or overrun and facing certain death." Shay argues that "the berserk state has apparent survival value, because [the soldier] apparently has nothing to lose and everything to gain from reckless frenzy."[47] In the words of a soldier: "It was a mission that we didn't have to be on."[48] In the words of a mass shooter: "What I am about to do didn't have to happen." The soldier's and the shooter's recognition of the unnecessary nature of their "reckless frenzy" suggests it could have been prevented had we recognized the nature of their injury and cared. While the vast majority of people who have experienced moral injury do not end up committing homicide, it is important to recognize that the roots of violence likely lie in our immoral culture.

In his book, Shay also describes how moral injury is transmitted through the values of an organization, which helps illuminate how values in a culture get transmitted:

> [The expectations and values] are embodied in formal regulations, defined authority, written orders, ranks, incentives, punishments, and formal task and occupational definitions. Others circulate as traditions, archetypal stories of things to be emulated or shunned, and accepted truth about what is praiseworthy and what is culpable. All together these form a moral world that most of the participants most of the time regard as legitimate, "natural" and personally binding. The moral power . . . is so great that it can motivate men to get up out of a trench and step into enemy machine-gun fire.[49]

What he describes in this passage is, in essence, how thin stories become naturalized and thus perceived to be immutable.

Shay notes that while our individually focused responses to the consequences of moral injury (e.g., medication or therapy) may alleviate some of the individual suffering, they are not going to stop it from spreading. To properly heal, he says, victims of moral injury should be listened to and given opportunities to tell their story to those "who can be trusted to retell it truthfully to others in the community . . . So before analyzing, before classifying [or labeling], before thinking, before trying to do anything—we should *listen.*"[50]

9.

The Story of Troy[1]

THE MOST SURPRISING ELEMENT of Troy's 141-page, single-spaced manifesto[2] is not the rage and misogyny that dominate the pages. It is instead the love he felt for and from his mother, his grandmother, and his nannies, and his desire to find close male friendships, especially during his first decade of life. Evidence of such love starts on his third birthday and appears to last, although it diminishes over time, until the day he mortally stabs or shoots six people and then turns the gun on himself at the age of twenty-two. Troy divides his manifesto into four segments: his childhood, early adolescence, middle adolescence, and late adolescence. He begins by stating: "[My story] is a dark story of sadness, anger, and hatred . . . a war against cruel injustice . . . This tragedy did not have to happen. I didn't want things to turn out this way, but humanity forced my hand, and this story will explain why" (p. 1).

The Elementary School Years: "A Blissful Beginning"

In the first thirty pages, Troy describes moving to the United States from England at the age of five, traveling around the world on vacation with his parents and sister, and receiving a lot of attention from his parents, nannies, and grandmother. His mother and grandmother are given the credit for trying to give him a happy life in which he could enjoy the privileges of being rich and living in a wealthy neighborhood. He believes himself to be lucky that his mother dated a famous movie director for a brief time and thus he got opening-night tickets to the director's very well-known movies. His stories during this early part of his manifesto include detailed descriptions of each of his early birthday parties, in which he names who was there, what activities they did, and his enjoyment or lack thereof during the party:

> I started out as a happy and blissful child, living my life to the fullest in a world that I thought was good and pure. On the morning of July 24th in a London hospital, I was born . . . My father . . . was only 26 and [my mother] was 30 . . . My father was a professional photographer at the time . . . My mother gave up her nursing career to stay at home and look after me. My grandma on my mother's side . . . moved in with us to help out my mother. I would spend a lot of time with [her] during these years.
>
> This was a time of discovery, excitement, and fun . . . I enjoyed life with innocent bliss. I can remember playing in the fields and going on long walks with [my grandmother] to pick berries. She would always warn me not to touch the stinging nettles that sometimes grew in our fields, but my curiosity got the better of me, and I got stung a few times. There was a swing in the back of our yard, which I had many good times on.

For preschool, I was enrolled at . . . an upscale all-boys private school in the countryside . . . I was very nervous and I cried on my first day there. I can remember two friends I made by name . . . I would always play in the sandpit with them.

I didn't like school . . . very much. I found the rules to be too strict. My least favorite part of it was the football sessions. I never understood the game and I could never keep up with the other boys in the field, so I always stood by the goalkeeper and pretended to be the "second goalkeeper." My favorite part was playing in the woods after lunch . . .

There was one very special place that my father would often take me to . . . The hills were full of tall straw-like grass, and the weather was always windy—perfect for kite flying.

It was a time of utmost happiness and joy for me. My father taught me to fly a kite by myself. The wind was so strong that I feared it would lift up my frail little body and carry me into the clouds. Once I got the hang of it, it was exhilarating. We would fly our kites together and run with the wind. I will never forget that place.

My favorite childhood film was *The Land Before Time.* I used to watch that movie all the time with [my grandmother] . . . I remember the feeling of utter sadness I felt during the scene when [the baby dinosaur's] mother died, and the triumphant and happy emotions that swept over me when he finally discovered the Great Valley, after going through all the hardship to get there. I watched this movie so many times that just thinking about it brings the emotions back. It was a big part of my childhood. (pp. 1–3)

Unlike most of the boys who have written social media postings or manifestos and who have perpetrated mass violence, Troy insists on sharing his feelings not only of sadness and anger but also of joy, suggesting that he didn't start off life being psychologically damaged.

Troy's seeming empathy for others is evident throughout his description of his early years. Reacting to his father, who had just received news of the death of his own father, he writes that it was "the first time I saw my father cry. My four-year-old self could not imagine my father ever crying, and so when I saw him cry that day, I knew how shaken he was. It was a very sad day for all of us." Troy's memories of his dad in these early years are very positive:

> [When I was eight years old, my] father decided that I was old enough to climb Big Rock . . . I had already conquered every other rock in the area . . . there was only Big Rock left. And so I set out with father and a few of father's friends to finally climb to the top . . . The second half of the journey was quite a challenge, but it was so exhilarating! I was very nervous the higher we climbed. The best part, of course, was reaching the top, and the sense of accomplishment I felt. I finally did it! Looking down, I could see the vastness of the canyon region, and father's house looked tiny down there. I was too scared to venture close to the edge, and I felt a sense of dread at the prospect of falling from such a height. The way down was even more challenging, but I felt so proud of myself for climbing that rock that it wasn't as scary as I thought it would be. (p. 12)

Following this proud moment, he shares the first of many difficult experiences in his life:

> I was very small and short statured for my age. I never gave this much concern during my early childhood, but this fact fully dawned on me the day my family took a trip to Universal Studios. At the time, I loved dinosaurs. I was fascinated by them. I had just recently watched the movie *Jurassic Park,* and when I found out that there was a *Jurassic Park* themed ride at Universal Studios, I couldn't wait to go on it. We queued up in the line and waited for an hour. When I reached the front, the park staff presented me with a measuring stick, and I didn't fit the requirements. I saw other boys my age admitted onto the ride, but I was denied because I was too short! The ride that I was so excited to enjoy at the theme park was forbidden to me. I immediately fell into a crying tantrum, and my mother had to comfort me.
>
> Being denied entry on a simple amusement park ride due to my height may seem like only a small injustice, but it was big for me at the time. Little did I know, this injustice was very small indeed compared to all the things I'll be denied in the future because of my height. (p. 6)

His sadness and sense of powerlessness over the injustice in which tall people, in this case, are valued over short ones particularly when they are male are the themes of his manifesto. Switching between tender feelings and outrage, Troy wants the reader to know the reasons for his suffering. Jonathan Shay writes extensively about this phase of moral injury.[3] Traumatized people want others to know what happened to them.

Troy's first friend is a girl. While he will eventually seek revenge against girls and women, these early entries suggest that it didn't start off that way:

> Monica and I started playing together at Farm School, and eventually my parents became very good friends with her parents . . . I was a five-year-old boy playing with a girl my own age like any normal boy would do. I was enjoying life in a world that I loved . . . I was playing innocently with this girl, in the manner that all children play. We even took baths together . . . When I think about the experiences I had during my friendship with her, it makes me think ominously of the fact that all children, boys and girls, start out the same. We all start out innocent, and we all start out together. Only through the experiences and circumstances of growing up do we drift apart, form allegiances, and face each other as enemies. That is when wars happen. (pp. 5–6)

His problems, in his mind, began at the edge of adolescence, the point in development in which the demands of "boy" culture intensify.

Troy meets his first and only male best friend in first grade:

> During recess at school, I started noticing this boy with slightly long blonde hair who also enjoyed kicking dust. Before I met him, I always mentally nicknamed him the "King Arthur Kid," due to the regal look his hairstyle gave him. It was only a matter of time before our dust kicking antics would collide with each other. We then teamed up and started playing the game together, and this was the start of a long and interesting friendship . . . [He] would become my best friend for the next 14 years of my life . . . Soon enough, I would start having frequent playdates with [him]. (p. 8)

Bryan becomes the only friend with whom he shares his secrets throughout his life, including his confusion about his parents' divorce and the difficulty of living in two households.

Troy describes his relationships with his mother in these early years as supportive, disputing the stereotype that troubled boys are troubled because of their mothers. His "mother's kind and loving nature" made the divorce easier for him, as "she turned her household into a fun environment which I enjoyed living in." In fact, Troy preferred staying at his mother's house because of her "gentle and fun attitude" and the "energy of her household." He adds: "My mother indulged me more than my father and [his wife] ever did. She knew what I liked and what I didn't like, and she would go out of her way to make my life pleasant and enjoyable. She always arranged playdates for me, because she knew I was too shy to initiate them myself. She always made everything fun."

Following the announcement of his parents' divorce shortly after his seventh birthday, Troy discovers his father's "acquisition of a new girlfriend," a woman who would become his stepmother and would try to help him make friends with other children. His father having a girlfriend so soon after his parents divorce "impresses" Troy, as it suggests to him that women find his father attractive: "I subconsciously held him in higher regard because of this. It is very interesting how this phenomenon works . . . that males who can easily find female mates garner more respect from their fellow men, even children. How ironic is it that my father, one of those men who could easily find a girlfriend, has a son who would struggle all his life to find a girlfriend" (p. 11). Rather than critiquing the culture that privileges "getting a girl" over anything else, he turns it on himself and makes the failure his own:

The first frustration of [my ninth] year, which would remain for the rest of my life, was the fact that I was very short for my age. As fourth grade started, it fully dawned on me that I was the shortest kid in my class—even the girls were taller than me. In the past, I rarely gave a thought to it, but at this stage I became extremely annoyed at how everyone was taller than me, and how the tallest boys were automatically respected more. It instilled the first feelings of inferiority in me, and such feelings would only grow more volatile with time.

I desperately wanted to get taller, and I read that playing basketball increases height. This sparked my brief interest in basketball, and I would play it all the time during recess and lunch . . . During my time at father's, I would spend hours playing basketball at father's basketball court, shooting hoop after hoop long into the evening, and I also remember lying on the ground in the basketball court trying to stretch my body as much as I could in between basketball sessions. (pp. 15–16)

As my fourth-grade year approached its end, my little nine-year-old self had another revelation about how the world works. I realized that there were *hierarchies* [italics mine], that some people were [considered] better than others. Of course I was subconsciously aware of this in the past, but it was at this time of my life—at nine years old—that I started to give it a lot of thought and importance . . .

The peaceful and innocent environment of childhood where everyone had an equal footing was all over. The time of fair play was at its end. Life is a competition and a struggle, and I was slowly starting to realize it . . . (p. 17)

> Again, I repeat, that as children we all play together as equals in a fair environment. Only after the advent of puberty does the true brutality of human nature show its face. Life will become a bitter and unfair struggle for self-worth, all because girls will choose some boys over others. The boys who girls find attractive will live pleasure-filled lives while they dominate the boys who girls deem unworthy. And I will go on to be rejected and humiliated by girls . . . Life is such a cruel joke. (p. 25)

His description of what happens during early adolescence is startling in its consistency with my research with boys who do not have mental illness and who do not commit crimes. He explicitly calls out the hierarchy that most young people find so unjust and that privileged boys who expected to be at the top find particularly unjust. Yet like many men, Troy blames girls and women for his problems, unable to see that by doing so he is only flipping the hierarchy in which he perceives himself to be at the bottom:

> When I became aware of this common social structure at my school, I also started to examine myself and compare myself to these "cool kids." I realized, with some horror, that I wasn't "cool" at all. I had a dorky hairstyle, I wore plain and uncool clothing, and I was shy and unpopular.
>
> This revelation about the world, and about myself, really decreased my self-esteem. On top of this was the feeling that I was different because I am of mixed race. I am half white, half Asian, and this made me different from the normal fully white kids that I was trying to fit in with. (p. 17)

Troy understands the nature of his problem but idealizes the "fully white" boys at the top and yet continues to believe in a thin story that it is only a matter of his wearing uncool clothing, having a dorky hairstyle, and being "different" that make him unpopular.

Sharing another traumatic memory, Troy reveals what will be a theme for the remainder of his manifesto:

> This man [my dad and I] were talking to at a party . . . he patted me on the back and told me that I have a great life ahead of me. With a grin on his face, he told me that "in the next ten years, you'll have a great time . . . a great time." I had no idea what he meant by that. I wasn't even thinking about my future at that point; I was living in the moment.
>
> Now I know what he meant. Childhood is fun, but when a boy reaches puberty a whole new world opens up to him . . . a whole new world with new pleasures, such as sex and love. Other boys will experience this, but not me, it pains me to say. That is the basis of my tragic life. I will not have a great time in the next ten years. The pleasures of sex and love will be denied to me . . . Instead, I will only experience misery, rejection, loneliness, and pain.
>
> At that moment in time, I didn't think much about this man's comment. I don't even remember who he was. But after those ten years have passed and I've experienced what I've experienced, I can't help but think about that moment. If only I knew what was in store for me, right then and there. (p. 20)

The cruelty of the exchange with the man at the party was not, in Troy's view, his low status, but that the man promised him a promotion that never arrived.

The Middle School Years: The Last Period of Contentment

> On the first day [of middle school], I was shaking with anxiety and fear. I didn't know what to expect. Transitioning to middle school was a big deal for me, even more so than starting elementary school. I was much older and I cared more about what people thought of me. I was no longer an innocent little child who didn't have to worry. I had to worry about a lot of things, and oh, did I worry! It was a whole new school full of people I didn't know. They all previously went to elementary school together, so most of them already knew each other. That made me even more nervous . . .
>
> I also felt an intense fear of what middle school life would be like. I didn't know how to act around girls, I didn't know what was cool anymore, I had no friends there. I simply didn't know what to do. I felt like I was walking into a snowstorm without a coat. (p. 27)

His evocative metaphor suggests an emotional depth to Troy that is unexpected in the narrative of a mentally ill boy who eventually causes so much heartbreak.

> I observed the popular kids of seventh grade . . . In a way they visually mimicked the popular kids of my own grade. They

were all the same, though the seventh graders seemed a lot meaner. (p. 38)

[I] didn't really talk to anyone. I did observe, however. I observed how everyone acted, who the "cool kids" were, what they were like . . . and it was all so intimidating. The social challenges that I faced in fifth grade were intensified tenfold.

I noticed that there were two groups of cool, popular kids. There were the skateboarder kids . . . and then there were the boys who were popular with girls . . . They all seemed so confident and aggressive. I felt so intimidated by them, and I hated them for it. I hated them so much, but I had to increase my standing with them. I *wanted* to be friends with them.

I also observed the girls. I was still very short for my age, and most of the girls were taller than me. I hadn't reached puberty yet, but I was starting to admire female prettiness . . . I didn't yet desire girls sexually, but I still felt envy towards [others] for being able to attract the attention of all the popular girls.

I thought all of the cool kids were obnoxious jerks . . . and yet somehow it was these boys who all of the girls flocked to. This showed me that the world was a brutal place, and human beings were nothing more than savage animals. Everything my father taught me was proven wrong. He raised me to be a polite, kind gentleman. In a decent world, that would be ideal. But the polite, kind gentleman doesn't win in the real world. The girls don't flock to the gentlemen. They flock to the alpha male. They flock to the boys who appear to have the most power and status. And it was a ruthless struggle to reach such a height.

It was too much for me to handle . . . I tried not to think about this new revelation and enjoy life in the moment . . .

> The "cool" thing to do now was to be popular with girls. I didn't know how to go about doing that . . . I didn't even understand what was so special about it either, but everyone seemed to place so much importance on it. This made me even more shy, and I became known as the "shy new kid." (pp. 27–28)

While Troy seems most angry at the alpha males who get all the attention, he ultimately blames girls for his problems, as they don't give him the attention that he needs to draw the attention of the alpha males. Most the boys in my research studies indicated that what they really wanted is close male friendships. Troy is no exception.

After a failed attempt at friendship with a boy in middle school, Troy began to fill the social void by playing video games:

> [Middle school was] the beginning of a very lonely period of my life, in which my only social interactions would be online through video games, with the sole exception being my friendship with [Bryan]. The ability to play video games with people online temporarily filled in the social void. I got caught up in it, and I was too young and naive to realize the severity of how far I had fallen. I was too scared to accept it. This loss of a social life, coupled with the advent of puberty, caused me to die a little inside. It was too much for me to handle, and I stopped caring about my life and my future. I even stopped caring about what people thought of me. I hid myself away in the online World of Warcraft, a place where I felt comfortable and secure . . . (p. 40)
>
> [Bryan] would be my only friend throughout the next depressing and lonely period of my life. My friendship with

> [Bryan] helped me cope with the loneliness. The very few fun times we would have were like a light in the darkness for me . . .
>
> I was so immersed in the game that I no longer cared about what people thought of me. I only saw school as something that took time away from WoW. I became very bored at school, mainly due to the fact that I was still the invisible quiet kid. To alleviate this boredom, I started to act weird and annoying to people just to gain attention.
>
> I became known as the "weird kid" at school, and people started to make fun of me, but I didn't care. I had my online games to distract me from the harsh realities of life that I was too scared to face. The only time I did care was when a group of popular seventh grade girls started teasing me, which hurt a lot. (p. 41)

As his middle school years progress, Troy's isolation appears to get worse:

> As middle school approached its ultimate end, I was having a miserable time there. I was extremely unpopular, widely disliked, and viewed as the weirdest kid in the school. I had to act weird in order to gain attention. I was tired of being the invisible shy kid. Infamy is better than total obscurity.
>
> The teasing I received was bittersweet. It felt horrible to be teased and bullied . . . It caused me a lot of pain and anger . . . but at the same time I got a kick out of getting so much attention. It felt good to be confident enough to pick fights with the popular skateboarder kids. It was either that or continue to be

> ignored by everyone like I was in sixth and seventh grade. I never knew how to gain positive attention, only negative. (p. 42)

Troy's ability to be self-reflective is evident in his comment that the teasing by his peers makes him feel both terrible and visible. He also remains remarkably empathic even as he sounds increasingly disconnected:

> One day at school, I was sitting in my class when I was suddenly called to the office. My mother was there, waiting to pick me up. I got into her car . . . She told us the dire news. [Bryan]'s mother . . . had just passed away from breast cancer. I cried for a bit. [She] was a very kind-hearted person, and the mother of my best friend. She had been suffering from breast cancer for several years, but I never thought she would die from it. I immediately thought of how [Bryan] must be feeling. He just lost his own mother! It made me think of how horrible I would feel if the same thing happened to my own mother, just the thought alone filled me with pain.
>
> There was to be a get-together of family friends at [Bryan]'s house that night. On the way, I thought about how I would approach [Bryan] on the subject. The amount of grief he must be feeling . . . I couldn't even imagine it. The last similar experience was the death of my grandfather, and I was only four years old then. When we arrived, I looked for [Bryan], and found him sitting in his room. I gently offered my deepest condolences for his loss. He remained very strong, obviously hiding his emotions. He looked very sad, in an extremely stoic sort of way. He told me he fully accepted what had happened, that his mother was dead

> and that was the end of it. That was all we spoke on the matter. We tried not to think about it for the rest of the night, and later on I played tag in his backyard with him and some of his friends. (pp. 29–30)

Suggesting a similar softness with his grandmother, Troy wrote: "She is just like my mother, she always knew what I liked and went out of her way to get it for me, just to put a smile on my face. She brought with her some of my favorite English chocolates, along with her famous peanut cookies that I loved so much." When his stepmother told him she was pregnant, he writes:

> I was going to have a baby brother. I felt elated. I remember when I was a bit younger, I always asked my father and his wife if they were going to have a baby, and they said they would like to. I still felt surprised when it was actually confirmed. It was that warm feeling that would envelop me when a good change happened in my life. I had no idea what it would be like, but I welcomed it. (p. 36)

His transition from middle to high school, however, marks the end of his empathy for anyone but himself and more overt signs of "boy" culture in its misogyny and homophobia.

The High School Years: Stuck in the Void

> The dreaded day arrived all too soon. I had to start high school . . . My father drove me there on the first day. When we got there, I was intimidated by all the huge high school boys,

and I cried in the car for a few minutes, telling my father that I was too scared to get out.

I had to go, and eventually I did . . . As I expected, I failed to make any new friends. I was so overwhelmed by the brutality of the world that I just didn't care anymore. In this very first week, I had my first experience of true bullying, not just the teasing I had at middle school. Some horrible twelfth graders saw me as a target because I looked like a ten-year-old and I was physically weak. They threw food at me during lunchtime and after school. It enraged me, but I was too scared to do anything about it. *What kind of horrible, depraved people would poke fun at a boy younger than them who has just entered high school?* I thought to myself.

After the first few weeks of high school, I concluded that my time at [my new school] would not be pleasant at all. I withdrew further into the World of Warcraft, neglecting my homework and spending all of my free time playing it. (p. 45)

[As the year progressed] my life [at school] got even worse . . . They teased me because I was scared of girls, calling me names like "faggot." People also liked to steal my belongings and run away in an attempt to get me to chase after them. And I did chase after them in a furious rage, but I was so little and weak that they thought it was comical. I hated everyone at that school so much.

It got to a point where I had to wait in a quiet corner for the hallways to clear before I could walk to class. I also took long routes around the school to avoid bullies . . .

I felt very small, weak, and above all, worthless. I cried by myself at school every day. (p. 46)

His parents move him to another high school soon after he starts in an apparent attempt to find a school in which he is not being bullied, which Troy says was even more "terrifying as it was a bigger school and had girls in it." It would be the fifth time he had switched schools since he was in kindergarten. Of his new school, he writes: "I had never been so scared in my entire life . . . [the school] would eat me alive and spit me out."

> *Toxic* is the word that describes my first day of tenth grade . . . It was a toxic nightmare. Every single second of it was agony. I continued to beg my parents to not make me go, but it was to no avail. My father drove me there, and I didn't want to get out of his car. He almost had to drag me out. I somehow found the will to put one foot in front of the other and walk towards that awful, ugly front building.
>
> The first week of [the new school] was living hell. I was bullied several times, even though I didn't know anyone there. After being so used to wearing a polo shirt with khaki pants as a school uniform at private schools, I continued to dress like that even after leaving [that school]. I didn't give any thought to how nerdy I looked. I was too withdrawn, like a turtle tucked into his shell. I was still in the process of going through puberty at the time, so I still looked and sounded like a ten-year-old. Such a persona attracted zero attention from girls, of course, but it did attract bullies like moths to a flame.
>
> I was completely and utterly alone. No one knew me or extended a hand to help me. I was an innocent, scared little boy trapped in a jungle full of malicious predators, and I was shown no mercy. Some boys randomly pushed me against the lockers

> as they walked past me in the hall. One boy who was tall and had blonde hair called me a "loser," right in front of his girlfriends. Yes, he had girls with him. Pretty girls. And they didn't seem to mind that he was such an evil bastard. In fact, I bet they liked him for it . . . This was what truly opened my eyes to how brutal the world is. The most meanest and depraved of men come out on top, and women flock to these men. Their evil acts are rewarded by women; while the good, decent men are laughed at. It is sick, twisted, and wrong in every way. I hated the girls even more than the bullies because of this. The sheer cruelty of the world around me was so intense that I will never recover from the mental scars. Any experience I ever had before never traumatized me as much as this.
>
> I couldn't do it anymore. On the morning before the second week of [school] started, I broke down and cried in front of my mother, begging her not to make me go to that horrible place. I was so scared that I felt physically sick. I continued crying in the car on the way there, and my mother gave in. Instead of taking me to school, we went to the café . . . where we had a big talk. I tried to explain how much I was suffering there. She just could not take me to school after that. When we were finished . . . she drove me to my father's house and told him about what happened. They agreed to take me out of [the school]. (p. 48)

Wavering between self-denigration, anger, and sadness, Troy suggests that he wants to be included in the very culture in which he has been demoted to the bottom. The problem is no doubt Troy's, as he is likely provoking other kids at this point, but it also lies with a culture that has a hierarchy of humans and human needs in the first place. Troy gets this. Like all boys and young men in my studies and in my classrooms, he already knows the thick story.

His parents transfer him for the sixth time in the eleventh grade to a school where students spend three hours a day at school and do the rest of their work at home: "All I wanted to do was hide away from the cruel world by playing my online games, and [this] high school gave me the perfect opportunity to do just that." Troy stays in this school until he graduates from it two and half years later. Troy decides in his senior year to stop playing World of Warcraft, as it is no longer enjoyable: "On my last day on the game, I had a long, emotional conversation with Bryan where I opened up about all of my troubles. I told him about all my newfound views of the world, and my belief that sex must be abolished. He seemed to be supportive of my stance, and I was glad that he understood me. It was a very memorable day" (p. 56).

One of the last times Troy connects with Bryan is when he has a sleepover and tells him about his hatred of people who have sex: "[Bryan] quickly deduced the reason for why I was so fervent about abolishing sex . . . that in truth I really want to have sex but I feel like I can never have it, so I wish to take it away from everyone else. He read me very well. I had to admit that he was right. That *is* the exact reason for it" (p. 57). While appearing to be supportive, Bryan must have been tortured by his desire both to help Troy and to escape him.

Post High School: "The Endgame"

> Once summer started [at the end of eleventh grade], I sank into a major depression . . . It was at this time that I was just begin-

ning to realize, with a lot of clarity, how truly unfair my life is. I compared myself to other teenagers and became very angry that they were able to experience all of the things I've desired, while I was left out of it. I never had the experience of going to a party with other teenagers, I never had my first kiss, I never held hands with a girl, I never lost my virginity. In the past, I felt so inferior and weak from all of the bullying that I just accepted my lonely life and dealt with it by playing WoW, but at this point I started to question why I was condemned to suffer such misery . . .

There was nothing I could really do about my unfair life situation. I felt completely powerless. The only way I could deal with it was to continue to drown all of my troubles with my online games. I played WoW really hard, leveling two new characters to 70. At my mother's house, I sometimes played it for fourteen hours a day. (p. 54)

The more lonely I felt, the more angry I became. The anger slowly built up inside me throughout all of the dark years. Even after the release of the new WoW expansion, I noticed that the game's ability to alleviate my sense of loneliness was starting to fade. I began to feel lonely even while playing it, and I often broke down into tears in the middle of my WoW sessions. I began to ask myself what the point was in playing this game anymore. I spent less and less time playing it. (p. 56)

Repeating what the seventh graders in his classroom told him after hearing about a mass shooting, Troy makes explicit the links among isolation, anger, and violence. After giving up on video games and having no friends, Troy plots his revenge "against humanity."

I began to have fantasies of becoming very powerful and stopping everyone from having sex. I wanted to take their sex away from them, just like they took it away from me. I saw sex as an evil and barbaric act, all because I was unable to have it. This was the major turning point. My anger made me stronger inside. This was when I formed my ideas that sex should be outlawed. It is the only way to make the world a fair and just place. If I can't have it, I will destroy it. That's the conclusion I came to, right then and there. I spent more time studying the world, seeing the world for the horrible, unfair place it is. I then had the revelation that just because I was condemned to suffer a life of loneliness and rejection, doesn't mean I am insignificant. I have an exceptionally high level of intelligence. I see the world differently than anyone else. Because of all of the injustices I went through and the worldview I developed because of them, I must be destined for greatness. I must be destined to change the world, to shape it into an image that suits me.

In what is one of his final events, he describes a Halloween night:

Young thugs drove by me in a pickup truck and proceeded to throw eggs at me, laughing while they did it. They seemed intoxicated, and they missed me. I picked up one of the shells and threw it right back into their car. I was no longer a weak little kid who would take a hit without fighting back. I was stronger now. They got out of their car and tried to attack me, and they would have beaten me bloody if I didn't pull out my trusty pocketknife, which I usually carried when I walked alone by myself. Thankfully, the thugs backed away and drove off. Perhaps it was

> the knife, or the look of extreme hatred in my eyes. I quickly ran home, terrified. It was an unsuccessful and misfortunate night. For a few days after Halloween, I kept thinking about that incident with the horrible thugs who almost attacked me. They must have seen me as a weakling who they could bully for their amusement. I didn't want the world to view me as weak.

But it is the loss of Bryan that ultimately pushes Troy to his "end goal."

> I went over to [Bryan]'s house during my visit home [from college]. The two of us chatted online a lot, and when I told him that I was in town, he seemed eager to see me. I was eager to see him too, as he was my closest friend and I had a lot to talk to him about. I drove up . . . to his house, not knowing that it will be the last time I ever visit him.
>
> The two of us did what we usually did. We walked out to [the Bluff] where we discussed our hopes and dreams. We then went to the town center to have dinner . . . While we were eating, some high school kids walked in. [Bryan] saw them first, and right when he saw them, he said the words "We're fucked." [Bryan] knew I would have trouble with them. They were popular boys who had a flock of pretty girls with them. One of them sat down with two of the girls, putting his leg up on another chair with a cocky smirk on his face. I was livid with rage, and I wanted to pour my drink all over his head. [Bryan] knew exactly what I was planning to do; we had been through similar incidents before. He made a lot of effort to try to dissuade me from acting on my anger, pointing out that there was a security

guard nearby. I did the only other thing I could do; I packed up my dinner and left the restaurant, fleeing in defeat and shame. [Bryan] soon followed, and we decided to finish our meal at his house . . .

When the two of us got back to [Bryan]'s house, I was still seething with rage. I didn't understand why [Bryan] wasn't angry like me. The sight that we just witnessed was horrible to watch. To see another male be successful with females is torture for males like us who have no success with females. I was so angry that I told [Bryan] of all of the acts of revenge I wanted to exact on those popular boys. I told him my desire to flay them alive, to strip the skins off their flesh and make them scream in agony as punishment for living a better life than me. [Bryan] became deeply disturbed by my anger. I wished that he wasn't disturbed. I wished he could be a friend that felt the same way about the world that I did. But he wasn't that kind of person. He was a weakling.

Once I had calmed down, the two of us had a long conversation in his room, and I ended up crying in front of him as I explained how hopeless I felt about life. Soon after that, I left his house, never to return there again. He will never invite me over after that incident, and our friendship will slowly fade to dust . . . (p. 91)

[Bryan] blatantly said he didn't want to be friends anymore. He didn't even deign to tell me why. After he said the fateful words, he refused to talk to me ever again. That was the last time I ever spoke to him.

It was the ultimate betrayal. I thought he was the one friend I had in the whole world who truly understood me, who truly

> understood my views and the reasons why I thought the way I did about the world. I confided everything to him, because I thought we were on the same page. To be betrayed in such a manner wounded me deeply, though I never admitted it to anyone . . .
>
> I didn't have any friends left anymore. No friends in the entire world . . . I was completely and utterly alone, in the darkest pit of despair. And in that pit I withered in agony. (p. 105)

His feeling of being "completely and utterly alone" leads Troy to not just plan but also pursue his revenge:

> For the next month, I barely left my room. I was completely and utterly at the end of all hope. *My life is over,* I thought . . . what was there to live for in the future? I still couldn't believe I didn't win. I kept thinking about the heavenly life I would be living if I had won. I was certain of my victory, right at the moment of the drawing. Instead, it turned to a crushing defeat, just like everything else in my life. Everything I had tried to do in the past, ever since childhood, had been a failure. It was very hard to feel good about myself anymore. I spent all of my time drifting aimlessly, doing nothing with my time except brooding over my fate. I didn't want to think about anything. I could barely breathe from the stifling loneliness. All of my energy had been sapped out of me. (p. 105)

The breaking point for Troy is at a party in which he provokes the violence, expressing, most likely, a death wish, in what Jonathan Shay described as the final stages of moral injury:

They were all obnoxious, rowdy boys whom I've always despised. A couple of pretty girls came up and talked to them, but not to me. They all started socializing right next to me, and none of the girls paid any attention to me. I rose from my chair and tried to act arrogant and cocky toward them, throwing insults at everyone. They only laughed at me and started insulting me back. That was the last straw, I had taken enough insults that night. A dark, hate-fueled rage overcame my entire being, and I tried to push as many of them as I could from the 10-foot ledge. My main target was the girls. I wanted to punish them for talking to the obnoxious boys instead of me. It was one of the most foolish and rash things I ever did, and I almost risked everything in doing it, but I was so drunk with rage that I didn't care. I failed to push any of them from the ledge, and the boys started to push me, which resulted in me being the one to fall onto the street. When I landed, I felt a snap in my ankle, followed by a stinging pain. I slowly got up and found that I couldn't even walk . . . I tried to get away from there as fast as I could . . .

I realized that someone had stolen my Gucci sunglasses that my mother had given me. I loved those sunglasses and had to get them back. I vehemently turned around and staggered back towards the party. At that point, I was so drunk that I forgot where the party was and ended up walking onto the front yard of the house next to it, demanding to know who took my sunglasses. The people in this house must have been friends with the ones I previously fought with, for they greeted me with vicious hostility. They called me names like "faggot" and "pussy," typical things those types of scumbags would say. A whole

> group of the obnoxious brutes came up and dragged me onto their driveway, pushing and hitting me. I wanted to fight and kill them all. I managed to throw one punch toward the main attacker, but that only caused them to beat me even more. I fell to the ground where they started kicking me and punching me in the face. Eventually, some other people from the street broke up the fight. I managed to have the strength to stand up and stagger away.
>
> It was the first time in my life that I had been truly beaten up physically to the point where my face was bruised up. I had suffered a lot of bullying in my life, but most of it wasn't physical . . .
>
> The worst part of this whole ordeal was not getting beaten up, oh no . . . No one cared about me. I was all alone . . . (p. 122)
>
> It was time for Retribution . . . On the Day of Retribution, I will finally be able to punish them *ALL* . . . I want to feel worthy. There is no pride in living as a lonely, unwanted outcast . . . I wasn't the one who struck first. But I will finish it by striking back. I will punish everyone. And it will be beautiful. Finally, at long last, I can show the world my true worth. (pp. 135–36)

Troy puts "boy" culture in plain view with his aggressive targeting of girls, his Gucci sunglasses, the homophobic violence, and the desire for homicidal and suicidal retribution. Believing that his "true worth" will be proved only by striking back and punishing everyone, Troy commits his crime against humanity and leaves in his wake the crushing despair of the friends and families of his victims, as well as his own family.

FOR BOYS SUCH AS Troy, their violence seems to reveal a truth as they see it. Another mass shooter writes in his journal: "When mankind can't find truth, untruth is converted to truth via violence." But then he adds a few lines later: "Violence is a false response to truth while giving the illusion of truth." Boys and young men know the deal, even those who commit monstrous acts. Picking up on this theme, Barbara Deming, a feminist activist, says, "I think the reason that men are so very violent is that they know, deep in themselves, that they're acting out a lie, and so they're furious at being caught up in the lie. But they don't know how to break it . . . which means that in some deep part of themselves they want to be delivered from it, [and] are homesick for the truth."[4] But when rebellion against a culture that doesn't care turns into murder, the perpetrators don't seem to recognize that the very culture they are attacking through their violence reifies its hierarchy by suggesting that certain lives are more valuable than other lives. Thus while boys such as Troy appear to be critiquing the hierarchy through their violence, they are in fact reinforcing it and thus making sure that boys like them who feel like others don't care will continue to be at the bottom and have no one to care.

Part Four

SOLUTIONS

Hatred is increased through the return of hatred but may be destroyed by love.

—BENEDICTUS DE SPINOZA[1]

10.

Joining Their Cause

IN THE SPRING OF 2022, I am sitting by a tree-lined path on the campus of NYU Abu Dhabi reading *Social* by Matthew Lieberman—in which he says that about 70 percent of our conversations are spent inquiring about the thoughts and feelings of others and by the age of ten we have spent approximately 10,000 hours asking questions of them—when an eight-year-old girl with long black hair pulled back in a ponytail and riding a scooter abruptly stops and asks me what I am reading. I respond in a condescending and vague way: "Oh, it's just a book I like." The girl looks at me as if I am a bit dense and repeats her question. I respond, amused that I just tried to short-circuit her curiosity while reading a book about that very topic, and tell her about the book and why I like it. She then asks, "What are you writing in that other book next to you?" I show her my notes in my journal and explain what I have written down. She listens intently and then rides off on her scooter. *Bam.* I have just been reminded of what the rebels in this book have taught me regarding what it means to be human, how our culture gets in the way and leads to a crisis of connection, and how we already have it within us to solve our own problems.

While humans are social animals, want to connect, and do so by listening with curiosity to one another, especially when we are around five years old, we live in a society that doesn't value these desires and capacities and thus don't nourish them. Interpersonal curiosity, our natural interest in another person's thoughts and feelings and our capacity to learn from them, is not a topic of research in the field of child development outside of a few exceptions.[1] We even have a slur word for it, "gossip," but sharing negative information about other people is not the same as wondering about how others think and feel and what we can learn from them about them and about ourselves. This human capacity, as the young girl suggested to me, is critical for forming meaningful connections with others and allowing us to see others as they see themselves rather than as we stereotype them to be.[2] I had assumed the girl wouldn't understand what I was reading. Once she insisted on getting the answer to her question by repeating her question, a strategy children often use, I told her what I was reading and why. In doing so, I not only recognized her intelligence but saw myself in her and remembered the intense feeling I had when I was a child of wanting to know the answers to my questions.

Underscoring our incurious culture, a recent article in *The New York Times* provided "nine ways to improve your relationships" and didn't include curiosity in the list except for offering the tip to ask someone who is suffering if they want to be "helped, heard, or hugged."[3] But a teenager would likely respond to this tip by saying, "If you want to help me, hear me, and if you truly listen to me, I will want to hug you." When we listen with the intent to learn about the answers to our own questions from another person and thus learn about them and about ourselves, we cut off the circulation of a culture that relies on outdated stereotypes and makes up stories that aren't true. Once we act on our affective knowledge and engage with our natural social, emotional, and cognitive intelligence, we join the cause of boys and young men in this book and begin the process of solving their and our own problems.

In *The Dawn of Everything,* anthropologist David Graeber and archaeologist David Wengrow tell thick stories about human evolution, nature, and society that contradict many of our well-established "facts." They arrive at conclusions different from those of others because they start from different questions and draw from different data sets than their predecessors did. Rather than asking about the roots of inequality, as many historians and philosophers have done before them, the authors start by asking why it is that Europeans became so obsessed with questions of inequality during the eighteenth century. To answer this question, the authors examine the texts produced during that period that reflected the ongoing debates between North American Indigenous leaders and European leaders. What they discovered in exploring the "hard" data that most people in the twenty-first century don't even know exists is that the questions posed by the Europeans about inequality were in response to an Indigenous critique of inequality among the Europeans. Indigenous leaders were challenging the Europeans in the eighteenth century as to why they would choose to live such brutal lives in which they didn't care for each other and acted "like slaves" to their king and their god. Kandiaronk, a leader of the Huron-Wendat community, challenged Europeans as to their reasons for being so willing to "bend to the will" of an individual perceived to be more powerful than themselves and of not insisting on their own autonomy. In response to this critique, the Europeans held essay contests on the origins of inequality, one of which Jean-Jacques Rousseau won in 1750. Rousseau argued in his essay that inequality is rooted in the natural development of a civilized society, suggesting that Europe was a more civilized society than the Indigenous communities who were critiquing such inequality. The Europeans also had revolutions, according to the authors of this paradigm-shifting book, to prove to the Indigenous leaders that they could in fact be independent from the British (although not from their god). By drawing from texts that include the voices of those who hadn't been listened to, Graeber and Wengrow were able to tell a story that is thicker, or uses the historical data more thoroughly, than the one we know not only about the Europeans but also about us and our propensity—especially for those of us at the top of the hierarchy—to tell one-sided stories that subsequently become established and naturalized facts.

Similarly, when we listen with curiosity to the boys and young men in this book and place them in a cultural context, we learn not only about them but also about us and the culture in which we live. Their stories suggest that we humans have extraordinary social and emotional capacities and very similar needs across our social and political identities. From a young age, we read one another's thoughts and feelings and notice contradictions and patterns. We wonder why we fake our feelings, and we already know at five years old that violence can be transmitted across generations. We ask questions and won't stop asking them, especially when we are young, until we get answers that make sense to us. Not only do we want close relationships—including, and perhaps most important, friendships—and know how to create and maintain these through our curiosity but we need them for our mental *and* physical health. We are also born with a moral compass and become upset when it hasn't been followed; we resist the push to follow a path that doesn't feel right or true to us. Yet we grow up in a culture that diminishes our curiosity—both interpersonal and intellectual—our sense of wonder, and our capacity to resist, listen, care, and take responsibility.

The boys and young men in this book also reveal how this culture of ours leads them and us to feel lonely, depressed, anxious, suicidal, and, in some cases, homicidal, with the last being especially likely for those who are the most isolated and feel as if they have been demoted to the bottom of the hierarchy of humans. While sociologist Émile Durkheim blamed our "anomie" on people not fitting into their prescribed roles in society, the data suggest that our alienation results from a society that doesn't align with our nature or our needs.[4] Yet we are not passive recipients of our own socialization, as boys and young men so brilliantly reveal throughout this book. We have a natural capacity to resist or rebel against that which harms us, and this is precisely what they are asking us to engage.

IN 1899, EIGHT-TO-TEN-YEAR-OLD BOYS who sold newspapers on the streets in New York City went on strike across all five boroughs. These "newsies" were street children who purchased a set of papers in the morning but got paid only if they sold their newspapers. Since the news was outdated by the late afternoon, it became impossible to sell their papers by then, and so they were forced to purchase papers that they weren't able to sell. Thus they rebelled. For several days, these boys successfully shut down access to printed news for the entire city of New York. They eventually settled with the publishing tycoons Joseph Pulitzer and William Randolph Hearst to get reimbursed for their unsold papers. Their efforts were the beginning of the child labor movement in the twentieth century.[5]

Undocumented college students started the Dreamers movement in 2010 by occupying the Arizona office of Senator John McCain. Frustrated by the inaction of Congress on the DREAM Act, they wanted the legal right to stay in the United States. Other young people quickly followed their actions by holding similar types of rebellions, including hunger strikes, demonstrations, and marches. Their movement led to the Deferred Action for Childhood Arrivals (DACA), an executive order issued by President Obama that allowed those who entered the country who were younger than sixteen years old and not older than thirty when they applied for DACA to gain renewable two-year permits to work and study, obtain driver's licenses, and qualify for educational grants and loans, as well as state-subsidized health insurance. Since 2012, U.S. Citizenship and Immigration Services has approved over 830,000 applications.[6]

After the shooting in 2018 by a lonely, angry, and mentally ill young man that left seventeen people dead at Marjory Stoneman Douglas High School in Parkland, Florida, teenagers from the high school protested, wrote letters, lobbied local politicians to pass stricter gun laws, and urged Congress to enact tougher background checks for gun buyers and impose a ban on assault rifles. They organized the March for Our Lives student-led demonstration in 2018 that catalyzed over 880 similar events throughout the United States. In a newspaper article, these rebels were called "warriors of a new youth crusade for stricter American gun laws—an impromptu movement born out of frustration and outrage over last week's mass shooting at their Florida high school . . . They are leading the charge with a simple message—'Never again'—and they say they will continue to speak out until their demands are met, unlike protests that broke out and then quickly faded away after other mass shootings in recent years."[7] A sixteen-year-old student at Marjory Stoneman Douglas said: "What we need is action, and we need it now more than ever because people are losing their lives and it is still not being taken seriously."[8] Another student said: "I think that this current fight for gun control is a fight that students and teenagers and children are having to fight . . . We're the ones who need to stand up and call attention to it and change it."[9] A fifteen-year-old organizer of one of the protests said in an online petition: "We are the students. We are the victims. We are change. Fight gun violence now!"[10] Since their protests began, states—including fourteen with Republican governors—have enacted at least fifty new laws restricting access to guns, ranging from banning bump stocks to allowing authorities to temporarily disarm potentially violent people.[11]

Inspired by the anti-gun movement of her peers from Marjory Stoneman Douglas High School, fifteen-year-old Greta Thunberg sparked a youth-led climate change movement, Fridays for Future, that inspired hundreds of thousands of students to hold strikes of their own in at least 270 cities.[12] It eventually grew to become a global movement that brought more than 10 million people onto streets worldwide to demand action on climate change, and public concern about climate change has reached record highs.[13] These youth-led efforts also led Fridays for Future to partner with UNICEF to support youth climate activists around the world. The UN secretary general has stated: "My generation has failed to respond properly to the dramatic challenge of climate change. This is deeply felt by young people. No wonder they are angry."[14] He added that we are "not winning the battle against climate change"[15] and that it was up to the youth to "rescue the planet."[16]

These examples represent only a small set of hundreds of rebellions by teenagers and young adults with a righteous cause. They each underscore not only our human capacity to resist or rebel against harm but also the problem with a culture that implicitly asks children and teenagers to solve our problems in response to the lack of action by adults. We ask them to "rescue the planet" while blaming others for our problems, rather than taking individual or collective responsibility for the damage we have done to ourselves and to our children. We blame everyone, including men, women, immigrants, poor people, Biden supporters, and Trump supporters. The culpability for "boy" culture is certainly not equal across groups, given that the folks at the top perpetuate "boy" culture significantly more than those at the bottom; in fact one could argue that they created the hierarchy in the first place. But we all need to take some responsibility, even if it's just recognizing the way in which we value the "hard" over the "soft" and have helped to create our billionaire "boys," who became so because most of us buy their products or use their services. Once we take responsibility for our part in this "boy" culture of ours, we can begin creating a different one that doesn't flip the hierarchy of humans and of human qualities but disrupts it entirely so no one is at the bottom and neither part of our humanity is left out of our definitions of being human, manhood, maturity, modernity, science, and success.

But how do we do that? The first step is to identify and name the problem as a crisis of connection[17] rather than a crisis of loneliness or of mental health, as the latter two problems either ignore our disconnection to ourselves or treat what is a symptom of a crisis of connection as the fundamental problem. If we identify *the* problem as one of mental health rather than a crisis of connection, we respond with ineffective long-term solutions and thus don't solve the public health crisis of our times. Short-term solutions such as therapy and medication may feel good now, but they won't lead us to change the culture doing the damage in the first place. They won't allow us, as Bishop Desmond Tutu reminds us, to stop people from falling in the river. Once we recognize that we are facing a crisis of connection caused by a culture that is out of sync with our nature and our needs, we can begin the work of changing that culture so that it better aligns with our nature and our needs. Boys and young men not only teach us about the culture/nature clash and its consequences, they also teach us about the solutions to the crisis in our schools, workplaces, and homes.

11.

Schools

EVIDENCE OF A CRISIS of connection in schools and universities is seen in the high rates of depression, anxiety, loneliness, and suicidal ideation among young people, as well as in its behavioral correlates, such as bullying, discrimination, stereotyping, suicide, and school-based violence. My students at New York University, like others around the world, are at times too depressed to come to class; can't give presentations because they are too anxious; feel lonely, stereotyped by, and discriminated against by others; and are exhausted from the constant onslaught of messages about what they are doing wrong and how they could be doing better if they only tried harder. Eating disorders, cutting, drug and alcohol abuse, and other self-harming activities remain at high levels among middle and high school students, with many students on some form of medication and/or in therapy. All I have to do is mention these problems and some of my students tear up. They feel powerless to do anything about it, and they think it is their fault. They also often think they are the only ones who are suffering.

Responding to this crisis of connection, I created two types of school-based solutions: one is a course on the science of human connection and the other, created in collaboration with activists and educators, is a school-based curriculum called the Listening Project, which has been implemented in middle and high schools across New York City and has been taught in modified forms on the campuses of NYU Abu Dhabi and NYU New York.

"The Science of Human Connection" Course

After many decades of my own research and reading across the sciences—including social neuroscience, primatology, evolutionary anthropology, medicine, and social psychology—I discovered that the sciences were telling the same five-part story about the crisis of connection and its roots, consequences, and solutions as the boys and young men in my studies. The sciences are segregated to such an extent that, like the blind men registering parts of the elephant but not grasping the elephant as a whole, they don't see that there is a larger story being told by their research, and it is the story in my research as well.[1]

The first part of the five-part story in both sources of data (theirs and mine) underscores our social and emotional capacities and needs. The second part exposes the ways in which our cultural beliefs and practices, including our "macho origin myths,"[2] get in the way of our nature and needs and often lead to a crisis of connection. The crisis is the third part of the story, evident in my own research as well as in the health-based research. The fourth part of the story focuses on the violent consequences of the crisis, which are evident not only in the sociological research but also in the manifestos of mass shooters and in the responses by boys and young men in my classrooms when you ask them about the reasons for the violence. The fifth part of the story is the solutions suggested by the first and second parts of the story that reveal the clash between our nature and our culture and the solution, which is to create a culture that better nourishes our nature rather than gets in the way.

To share this five-part story with my NYU students, I created a course called "The Science of Human Connection," which is part of a list of core offerings that NYU students can take to fulfill their social science requirements. Students in the course first explore the science, including my own, that emphasizes our social and emotional nature and needs (see chapters 1 through 3 in this book). Then students read the sociological research (see chapters 4 through 6 in this book), which underscores the impact of our cultural belief systems—including our stereotypes about gender, race, social class, sexuality, and religion—on our understanding of ourselves and each other. To learn about the third and fourth parts of this five-part story, students read the research from the health sciences, social neuroscience, and developmental psychology that provides empirical data on the crisis of connection and its physical, mental, and behavioral consequences (e.g., rising rates of depression, anxiety, loneliness, suicide, and violence). To learn about the solutions, the fifth part of the story, students explore the work of practitioners, educators, social activists, and interfaith leaders who bring us back to the first part of the story and remind us of who we are as humans and of what we need to thrive.[3]

Required reading in this fifth part of the story includes chapters from my co-edited book *The Crisis of Connection: Its Roots, Consequences, and Solutions.* These chapters describe the work of educators and social activists such as Lisa Arrastia, who writes about the love pedagogy that she practices in college classrooms; Mary Gordon, whose empirically tested program Roots of Empathy fosters empathy in young children around the world; Dana Edell, an educator and social activist who helps to create radical theater with teenage girls and young women that fosters resistance to harmful stereotypes; Michael Reichert and Joseph Nelson, who train teachers in strategies of relational teaching in all-boys schools across the nation; and social activist Khary Lazarre-White, whose Brotherhood Sister Sol offers a wide range of opportunities for youth of color to resist and engage in just and humane practices within and outside of their own communities. The students in my class are also required to read a chapter about love written by leaders across the three Abrahamic religions—an imam, a minister, and a rabbi—that underscores our common humanity. Each of the solutions reveals the ways in which we can create a culture that better aligns with our nature by actively fostering resistance to "boy" culture.

To teach the course, I use John Dewey's technique of learning by doing by promoting listening with curiosity to one another in each session of class and thus enhancing connection among the students—and not just reading about the need to do so. At the beginning of class, students often take turns conducting a six-to-eight-minute interview in pairs, with each partner having the same amount of time to ask questions and then answer questions focused on a topic that they read about or that they are simply curious about that relates to the class. Their interviews are aimed at sharing their own experiences of a particular topic with each other rather than what the reading said about it (e.g., friendships, empathy, stereotypes). Students ask questions of each other such as "What type of friendships would you most like?" "What does 'belongingness' mean to you?" "Tell me about a time in which you felt listened to." In the five years that I have taught the class, I have never had a student who didn't want to answer the questions that were posed by their partner, even though they are given the choice not to answer them.

The goal of these short interviews done in pairs at the beginning of each class is to remind them of their natural curiosity about each other, what I call their "relational intelligence," and their ability to gain answers to their questions from the experiences of another person and thus to learn about others while also learning about themselves. Students in the class are often stunned at how effective this approach is in helping them connect to another person, even during such a brief period. Some report to me finding new best friends and even romantic partners in the class—relationships that last long past the class itself. They also begin seeing themselves in the course material even when it appears that they have nothing in common with the participants in the research that they are reading about (e.g., research about boys of color or about mostly white girls). Students also keep curiosity journals throughout the class, in which each week they are asking questions about the content of the class and trying to answer them by drawing on readings from the class, their personal experiences, and class discussions. Keeping such a journal reminds them that they can answer their own questions by drawing not only from the readings and lectures from class but also from listening to each other and reflecting on their own personal experiences.

For the final assignment in the course, students work in groups of two or three to propose a solution to a societal problem that is inevitably a symptom of a culture that clashes with our nature and needs and leads to a crisis of connection (e.g., loneliness, depression, anxiety, suicide, violence, drug and alcohol abuse, income inequality, discrimination of all types, homelessness, the climate crisis, social media addiction, and police violence).

In the fall class of 2021, four young men in the class picked male suicide on campus as the focus of their final paper. They chose to create a theater-based solution to disrupt the hierarchy of human qualities that lies at the root of this crisis. Their goal was to help the men on campus value their "soft" *and* "hard" sides, thus not flipping the hierarchy but simply getting rid of it. In an email to me, they write:

> *Boys Will Be Boys* will be a theater-based approach to curbing the male suicide epidemic, hinging on restoring the emotional vocabulary deemed impermissible by traditional notions of "masculinity." It has two main goals. The first is to give men opportunities to freely express emotion, and to connect this experience to their own lives. The next is to foster strong and emotionally deep male friendships among participants. As such, on the first day of the program they will be paired with a static scene-partner; unchanging throughout the duration of the process. While everyone will grow in this course, these men will grow *together,* fostering a relationship not built on macho self-reliance.[4]

They chose theater, as they felt that "the theatrical stage offers a non-judgmental environment for boys to embrace vulnerability and learn to manifest the complexities of their long-suppressed feelings through the eyes of imaginary characters . . . it is a rejection of the 'I don't care' mindset forced on boys in adolescence and politely requests that this toxic credo go jump off a bridge." For these young men, theater is a "potentially life-saving apparatus for a demographic not properly catered to by mental health resources." They underscore that they "do not need to be taught to be emotional; rather, they need to be reminded. They are not strangers to the grammar of emotion, feeling, and connection . . . Therefore, our theater work to combat male suicide will not be an uphill battle."

When I asked Wyatt, the leader of the group, why he chose theater, he responded via email:

> Why theater at all? I should start by mentioning that in my young childhood I loved acting, especially in plays. I can't remember how many I was in, but vividly remember multiple rehearsals and a legendary performance as the Scarecrow in a rendition of *The Wizard of Oz.* Sometime early in elementary school I came under the impression that theater was a "girlie" activity and felt the need to shed it entirely. This was, of course, an oversimplified way of saying that the qualities theater necessitates you access have been traditionally labeled as feminine. These include things such as expressing emotion and being generally vulnerable. In other words, I came to believe that theater was only for girls because it engages ideas that are uniquely intrinsic to our humanity. It is for this same reason that I now see it as a prime means of combatting male suicide.
>
> I am realizing now that most of my major hobbies and activities post-theater revolved around performative expression; but a watered-down version endorsed by stoic and combative masculine stereotypes. When my elementary school mandated that my sixth-grade class put on a play (it was a mock-trial take on the *Wizard of Oz*, where Dorothy was put on trial for

> manslaughter), I insisted on being a prosecutor. In eighth grade, I did another mock trial (this one involved less magical slippers and more homicide) and I again made sure to be a prosecutor. This role is a blatant endorsement of male stereotypes. The intrinsic purpose of a prosecutor is to ensure that a punishment is inflicted. Regardless of the offense, a prosecutor is, by nature, combative.
>
> Throughout middle school and high school I was on the debate teams. That activity was, again, performative but incredibly impersonal. It endorsed only argumentation and celebrated traditionally male stereotypes via the guise of "perceptual dominance." Finally, towards the end of high school, I started doing stand-up comedy. Stand-up is the most liberal of the bunch, but it still comes short of true emotional expression. Describing an emotion to a crowd is far less vulnerable than actually displaying it. Moreover, using humor as a defense mechanism is a cliché I embody in my day-to-day life; it's the grammar I adopted. As a child, I rejected theater for being feminine, but substituted it with a series of activities which drew increasingly closer to it. In other words, I was aching to express myself and didn't realize it or know how. Truly all it takes to save lives is an environment encouraging emotional expression and a close friend. It may sound overly simplistic but that's a testament to how intuitive it is. The hierarchy of humanness has gotten in the way. A theater-based intervention would address it directly.[5]

Wyatt's recognition of the importance of his so-called feminine side and of his friendships to his health and well-being is common among all my students by the end of the course. The irony, of course, is that it is their peers, albeit a few years younger, who taught me this kernel of knowledge in the first place, so the course constitutes my reminding them of what they and their peers already know.

The Listening Project

While "The Science of Human Connection" course offers students insight into our crisis of connection and its roots, consequences, and solutions, it doesn't teach any specific method to effectively address the crisis of connection. The Listening Project,[6] with its school-based method of "transformative interviewing," does. It is a method that not only builds human-to-human connection but also breaks down stereotypes and helps each person discover their own humanity and the humanity of others. It grew out of my training as a graduate student back in the 1980s,[7] from conducting research interviews with adolescents over the past almost four decades, and from teaching interviewing research methods to doctoral students at NYU over the past two decades, particularly co-teaching the course over the past decade with my former student and now colleague at Swarthmore College, Joseph Nelson. When I was an assistant professor, I thought my method of semi-structured research interviews was simply a way to gather data. But after many years of teaching my research methods class and having students report that the method helped improve their relationships, and having readers of my research ask, "How did you get the boys to talk like that?" I realized it was more than just a research method. It was a way to build human connection and to get a thicker story.

The method of transformative interviewing is best summed up as a way of interviewing that nourishes our natural capacity to listen with curiosity to learn the answers to our questions from the experiences, thoughts, and feelings of another person. Because the method focuses on asking real questions—questions that we are genuinely curious about—and following up those questions with further ones that allow for real answers, not just the answers that are culturally expected, it leads to the discovery by the interviewer and even by the interviewee of their "hard" and "soft" sides and thus is transformative in nature. Our evaluation of this research suggests that the method effectively challenges the stereotypes or single stories we hold of ourselves and one another and allows each person to see themselves in the other and thus to recognize both our common humanity and our differences.

Transformative interviewing is not just a way of learning from another person about the answers to your questions, though; it is also a method of unlearning cultural norms that often exacerbate feelings of alienation and loneliness. One of the most damaging norms is we think listening is simply not talking when another person is talking. This form of listening, in which the listener doesn't ask any type of follow-up questions, is not only unsatisfying for the respondent, as it can often feel as if the other person is not listening, but also unsatisfying for the listener, as they often don't know what the other person is talking about and thus become bored and stop listening. Another damaging cultural norm is that we think we can predict other people's responses based on our stereotypes of them. While this is mostly a problem when we don't know the other person, it can also be a problem when we do. We also often think that asking real questions, or questions you really want to know the answers to, is rude, when the data suggest that people want others to ask them meaningful questions, even on the subway.[8]

Furthermore, we often believe that talking about oneself in a vulnerable way will make the other person feel connected to us. But meaningful connection happens only when we ask real questions of each other and follow up with even more questions and get the details of the other person's experiences in response to our questions so that they feel listened to, heard, and seen (and then they might even want to hug you). Connection is not based on how much we share. It's based on the quality of our questions and the extent to which we followed the logic of their responses and asked good follow-up questions so that they can articulate the nuances of their responses and they in return offer us the same gift of listening with curiosity. The parallel play that we call listening in "boy" culture—in which both people speak (or only one person speaks) and neither asks questions of the other—enhances our feelings of alienation and loneliness and is definitely depressing, as people in this dyadic act rarely feel listened to, seen, or heard.[9]

The method of transformative interviewing also helps us unlearn the cultural norm of giving clichéd or stereotyped answers to genuine questions, as we often don't trust that the other person really wants to know the details, so we skim the surface.[10] In my interviews with adolescent mothers in a study I did many decades ago with developmental psychology professor and thick storyteller Bonnie Leadbeater, we would ask these young women questions about the quality of their close friendships, and they would often respond by saying, "I tell them everything." When I would follow up with a question about a time in which they didn't tell their close friends something, they would have much to share with me and thus communicate a thicker story about their friendships than simply that they trust their friend with "everything."[11] Asking follow-up questions, in other words, is necessary to get a thick story.

When Joseph Nelson and I first developed the Listening Project to teach transformative interviewing methods to seventh-grade boys in an English class taught by Ethan Podell at an all-boys school in New York City, we immediately discovered that seventh-grade boys are far better at the method of transformative interviewing than our NYU doctoral students. They don't ask us if their questions are good, they just ask their questions, as they know their questions are good because they are genuine. It typically takes us at least a month to get our doctoral students to ask questions that they really want to know the answers to and don't already know the answers to. They have been trained in their research-oriented education to believe that they should only ask questions that they know the answers to in the form of a hypothesis. Seventh graders, in contrast, take only a few minutes to come up with what they believe are their "thick" questions, including of their peers, family members, and teachers.

WHEN YOU ASK SEVENTH-GRADE boys what listening looks like, they purse their lips tightly. They have been taught that listening means not talking or, in the language of a grouchy teacher, "shutting up." They tell me that they often don't feel listened to when someone doesn't ask questions to get the details while they are talking. They want the other person to want to know more, to probe about the whys, whats, whens, and hows of their experiences. When the other person does, they report that they feel listened to, heard, and seen by the other person. As one boy in Ethan's class said, "It makes me feel that the person really cares about me." According to Kate Murphy, the author of one of the few books that make a similar point, listening with curiosity heightens our awareness of the other person:

"It makes you feel. As you become more attuned to the thoughts and emotions of others, you become more alive to the world and it becomes more alive to you."[12] Developmental psychologist and thick storyteller Deborah Tolman describes the process:

> As a listener I bring myself knowingly into the process of listening, learning from my own thoughts and feelings in response to what a girl is saying in her story, and using clinical methods of empathy and associative logic to follow and make sense of her story. This attention to myself increases my ability to stay clear about what my own ideas and feelings are and how they do or do not line up with a girl's words, thus avoiding "bias" or imposing my own story over the girl's.[13]

Following our work at the all-boys school in which we first taught transformative interviewing to middle school students, we received funding to develop and evaluate a Listening Project curriculum in middle and high schools across New York City. Our training with students and teachers, but also with over a hundred professors and administrators at NYU during the COVID period, includes imparting not only our method of transformative interviewing but also our framework for understanding the crisis of connection's roots, consequences, and solutions, as our method of interviewing is a part of the solution. My team at NYU[14] have spent the last six years creating and evaluating a twenty-six-lesson Listening Project curriculum and adapted versions of it that we have implemented in English and humanities classes as well as in advisory groups, and science classrooms, in middle and to a lesser degree in high schools.

In our quantitative and qualitative evaluation of our curriculum, we find that it effectively builds curiosity and listening skills and enhances connection, academic engagement, and a sense of a common humanity.[15] It also increases teachers' satisfaction and sense of connectedness with their students. We are now in the process of making a film about it with Dana Kalmey to make the framework and method of transformative interviewing more accessible to schools around the world.

Our method of transformative interviewing currently includes the following nine practices, although we are still adding to our list as we learn from the students and teachers whom we train:

1. Start with a real question.[16]
2. Ask open-ended follow-up questions (don't "lead the witness").
3. Ask curated follow-up questions.
4. Ask for examples or stories.
5. Get "gold nuggets."
6. Ask clarifying questions.
7. Ask contrasting questions.
8. Ask how, what, why, when, and where questions.
9. Listen for the unexpected and expected and probe both.

Asking real questions, the first practice, is difficult, as it requires the person to unlearn the cultural norm that such questions are rude, as they are "too personal." Yet real questions are by definition coming from a place of genuine curiosity, humility, and openness to learn something new from another person from the answer to the question. Such questions are never rude, although interviewees may choose not to answer the question, which when you are following our method is always their choice. In the over two decades of applying various versions of our method in my research studies and in my classrooms, however, I have never had anyone tell me or my team members that they didn't want to answer the question. But to create a safe space to allow trainees to answer what they may perceive to be sensitive questions, those training them in the method must model the openness that is necessary for hearing thick stories.

It is a fall day in 2016 and I am in a classroom with Joseph training a group of twenty twelve-year-old boys in the Listening Project. As part of their training in transformative interviewing, they are asked to interview either me or Joseph as a class. They decide they want to interview me first. I tell them that they can ask any questions they want and that I can decline to answer their questions if I don't want to answer them. One boy begins by asking me if I am married. I tell him no, offering a one-word response, as I am trying to encourage them to follow their curiosity and don't want to be too easy an interviewee. Then another boy asks if I have ever been married, and I say yes. They laugh, as they know that I am intentionally being difficult. Then Anthony raises his hand and asks me if I still love my ex-husband. My eyes immediately fill with tears, as I can't believe that within five or six seconds, we are getting to the heart of the matter. I respond as honestly as possible because real questions deserve real responses. Sam raises his hand the minute I finish my response and asks, "Does he know that you still love him? And if he does, how do you know that he knows?" I am now in a deep and meaningful conversation with these boys, primarily of color from poor and working-class communities to boot (in other words, those who are most negatively stereotyped as not being curious). Eric, another boy in the class, asks me if my children know that I still love my ex-husband and how do they know. The boys look pleased with themselves, as they recognize that their questions are genuine or thick and listen intently to my responses. They want to know the answers to their questions, and their silence in a situation where they would normally be fidgety underscores their curiosity. What I learn from this interview (and hundreds like it) is that children and teenagers—including twelve-year-old boys—are teeming with thick questions, and they can easily follow their curiosity if given the permission by the adults in the room.

Examples of thick questions asked by middle school students include: Who do you trust the most and why? What do you fear the most and why? What do you want most of all in life and why? When do you feel listened to? When don't you feel listened to? Where is home for you? What does love feel like to you? The questions generated by children and teenagers are almost always better than those generated by older people, who inevitably want to sound smart rather than follow their curiosity. In a training on Zoom during the pandemic, we asked seventh-grade students what their thick questions were that preoccupied them in their lives. I worried that the concept of thick stories would be too complicated for them and they wouldn't understand what I was asking. (I stereotyped them given their young age.) David, an Asian American boy who didn't show his face on Zoom and had a Transformer cartoon picture on his screen, which suggested a boyish identity, offered his question in a quiet voice with his video off. I asked him to repeat it so that we could hear it. He turned on his video so we could see him and repeated it again. I still couldn't hear him and told him to repeat it one more time. He then put his mouth close to the microphone and said loudly, "I want to know where you feel safe." According to a study of 1,800 people,[17] humans "secretly crave deeper conversations with strangers." We want to be asked "What's your life's greatest regret and why?" or "When was the last time you cried and why?" Researchers also found that conversations with strangers, particularly when they asked deeper questions, were significantly less awkward than people thought they would be and were also more enjoyable and resulted in a greater sense of connection than chitchat did.[18]

Asking open-ended follow-up questions, the second practice in our method, allows interviewees to elaborate on their experiences rather than responding to a yes-or-no question. It has long been the definition of active listening.[19] Rather than the question "Do you like your teacher?"—a form of leading the witness by providing a possible response (i.e., that liking their teacher is a way to understand how they feel about their teacher)—an open-ended question would be "How would you describe your relationship with your teacher?" or "How would you describe how you get along with your teacher?" These questions allow the interviewee to provide any type of response they want and don't prime them with a particular response. My NYU students have a difficult time making their questions open-ended, as they are used to partially, if not fully, providing the answer to the person whom they are asking. They are seeking to confirm their own views and want to know whether the other person has these same ones, rather than trying to learn something new from the answers to their questions.

When I was in my early years of graduate school, my friend Amy Grillo was willing to be my interviewee for a research project I was doing on friendships. The task I was told to do by my professor was to show the interviewee a diagram of concentric circles and ask the person to put the name of their best friend in the middle of the innermost circle, and then to put the name of their closest friends and then friends and then acquaintances in layers moving out from the middle, with each outward layer representing a less significant friendship. When I asked Amy to complete the diagram, she immediately said she didn't know what I was asking of her. I repeated the instructions, and then she repeated that she was confused. With increasing frustration, I said that I didn't know why she didn't know what I was asking her to do and would she please just do it. Finally, with a stroke of insight, I asked her to draw how she sees her friendships, as it occurred to me at that moment that perhaps she doesn't see her friendships as a series of concentric circles. She then drew her friendships in what looked to me like a random assortment of stars, with big stars representing certain types of friendships and little stars representing other types of friendships and the lines connecting them being sometimes squiggly, sometimes straight, and sometimes completely absent. What I learned from Amy is the importance of open-ended questions and not imposing my framework on other people so I could learn about their way of making meaning and not simply their reaction to my meaning-making.

The third practice is asking curated follow-up questions, which means following the logic of the response given by the interviewee while staying focused on the original question. This process is a metacognitive task that takes years to become good at, but seventh graders have an easier time doing it than doctoral students as they are simply more curious. Asking curated follow-up questions means that the interviewer must pick up when the interviewee trails off onto another topic and ask a question that brings it back to the original question while incorporating into the follow-up question what was just said. They must, in other words, follow their own curiosity but keep to the story that the person is telling and curating it so that it stays on topic.

While there are numerous question games on the market,[20] few ask the players to ask follow-up questions, and certainly not curated ones. But as students always tell us after learning our method, it is the follow-up questions that lead to the connection, as they allow one to understand the details of someone's responses. One of the most popular of these question games is the *New York Times*'s "36 Questions That Lead to Love," which is commonly played by millennials and Gen-Zers. The questions include

> "Given the choice of anyone in the world, whom would you want as a dinner guest?"
>
> "What would constitute a 'perfect' day for you?"
>
> "When did you last sing to yourself?"[21]

Students claim that it is fun to play, but it doesn't make them feel closer to the other person and certainly doesn't lead them to fall in love. My response to the dinner guest question would be Kazuo Ishiguro, the Nobel Prize–winning novelist, and Shirley Jackson, the spooky fiction writer who died just after I was born. While that may be somewhat revealing about who I am, it doesn't reveal much. Follow-up questions that explore why I would want to have them over for dinner, what questions I would want to ask them, what questions I would not have the nerve to ask them but would want to ask and why I would want to ask them those questions, and who else would be at the dinner would offer much more insight into who I am and what I care about than simply knowing their names.

The fourth, fifth, and sixth practices of transformative interviewing entail getting stories, gold nugget stories specifically, and getting clarification in response to what the storyteller just said and only to those parts that relate to one's original question. Getting stories or "a time in which" examples is critical, as they allow the interviewer to hear exactly how the interviewee experienced something. A response such as "I am close to my mother" means nothing until you hear a story or "a time in which" the interviewee felt close to their mother. A gold nugget story is one that is a meaningful moment for the interviewee. Sharing a time in which the interviewee went with their mother to the store and bought milk together might be an experience of closeness but is not necessarily a gold nugget story, although it could be if buying milk together was a new experience for them or if the interviewee just moved to a new city and went shopping with their mother for the first time. Sharing a time in which a newborn sibling came home from the hospital is more likely to be a gold nugget story, but it's not a gold nugget unless one gets the details and clarifications that allow the interviewer to see the experience through the interviewee's lens and understand why and how it was so meaningful. We almost always assume we know the meaning or significance of what someone has just shared, especially when we have had a similar experience, when in fact we rarely do.

When Alex, one of the boys in our Listening Project, interviewed his seventh-grade peer Mark about his relationship with his English teacher, Mark said that he didn't think his teacher liked him. Alex assumed that Mark's teacher did not like him because Mark didn't do well in the class. Yet when Alex asked Mark why he thought the teacher didn't like him and if he could provide an example of a time he felt that way, Mark recounted an exchange when the teacher didn't have time to help him and Mark felt rejected. At the end of his interview, Alex said that he had a totally different understanding of Mark. He had assumed that Mark didn't care about his schoolwork, which is why he didn't do well, when in fact Mark suggested that it was his feeling that his teacher didn't like him that led him not to do well.

When Felix interviewed his father, he initially wanted to ask him only questions that he already knew the answers to, as he assumed his father didn't want to share any stories Felix didn't know, and certainly not the details. After getting feedback from his peers, Felix decided to ask his father about their relationship and discovered that not only did his father want to talk about it but he was willing to share the details, even the vulnerable ones. Felix said he had made a lot of assumptions about his father that weren't true. After that interview Felix came to see his father in an entirely new light and felt much closer to him.

The seventh practice is asking contrasting questions. This practice comes from the simple observation that we often understand each other more when given the opportunity to compare two experiences. According to Asma, an NYU student in Abu Dhabi, there is a popular Arabic philosophical saying لولا وجود عكس المعنى، لما كان للمعنى معنى, which she translates as "Without the existence of antonyms and opposites, meaning would cease to exist." Asking someone about friends who are not close, for example, provides insight into their close friendships. Contrasting questions also allow the interviewer to understand the experience of absence in an interviewee's life in contrast to presence, such as when people speak about the meaning of an "absent parent," who might be literally absent but not psychologically so.

The eighth and ninth practices of our transformative method are asking the how, what, why, when, and where questions—grasping those details—and exploring both the unexpected and expected responses so the interviewer gains a full grasp of the meaning of the stories being told by the interviewee. When we asked boys to describe the details of their male friendships, they often said things that surprised us ("I can't live without him") as well as what was predictable ("It's all good"). When we ask them to describe what they mean and to provide stories illustrating what they mean, thick stories emerge. Not doing so produces thin stories, as the meaning that will be given to the interviewee's responses after the interview is completed will be the interviewer's rather than the interviewee's.

In one of our seventh-grade classrooms, Marco described how people stereotype him as not wanting friends because he is a boy: "But I do want friends, real friends, friends I can trust. Friends who won't laugh at me when I say something stupid." Following his confession, students reflected on why interviews might be a good way to disrupt stereotypes and build connections. When Joseph was interviewed by a classroom of boys about a challenging time in his life, he told the students about feeling lonely and isolated as a child because he wore thick glasses that prevented him from playing with his older brother and friends. As the students asked him questions, Joseph provided details so that they could visualize his story—how big the glasses were, how they made his eyes look to others, how they helped him see clearly but made others who looked at him see him as different. Joseph felt seen by the boys, as they got gold nugget stories, and the students saw themselves in Joseph, even though they were from a different generation and many of them didn't share his African American identity. Most of them, however, had had experiences in which they felt left out. They were able to see Joseph in his full humanity and see their own humanity in Joseph.

OUR TWENTY-SIX-LESSON CURRICULUM THAT is part of our Listening Project is divided into five parts.[22] In the first part, we engage the class in a conversation about the crisis of connection, its roots, consequences, and solutions. The purpose of starting from this thick story is for the class to understand the method is not just a method of connection but an urgent response to a devasting crisis around the world. This conversation is often lively and eye-opening, as it uncovers the extent to which students feel lonely and would like to find ways to better connect to peers and adults in their school. We also discuss how cultural belief systems and the stereotypes that reinforce them (e.g., boys don't want deep secret friendships; girls can't be trusted) get in the way of connection. Students typically have examples of the ways they have been stereotyped or have stereotyped others and understand intuitively why it's necessary to listen in ways that challenge such stereotypes.

The second part of the curriculum asks students to generate their own questions and practice interviewing with each other and with an adult, including someone in their school whom they know but who doesn't get listened to (e.g., lunch lady, security guard). These interviews allow students to learn our practices and unlearn those that I described earlier that get in the way of listening, curiosity, and connection. During this part, students discover that while the practices may look easy and are natural to five-year-old children, they are not as easy as we get older and our curiosity declines as a product of a culture that doesn't value it.[23] The third part of the curriculum asks students to pick a focal person whom they interview repeatedly (three to five times) using the practices of the method, focusing on finding gold nugget stories in response to their questions. For this part of the curriculum, students almost always pick a mom, dad, grandma, or grandpa to be their focal interview and interview them with the goal of learning something new from the answer to their question about the person they are interviewing.

We teach the curriculum exactly how we teach our doctoral students. They are asked to tape-record and transcribe their interviews, or parts of them, and play them back or read them for each other in small groups. Their peers who are listening are asked to provide feedback on where the interviewer may ask additional questions to get at the meaning of the experiences being shared. Middle school students are good at this peer feedback process and often give better feedback than the trainers. The reason, of course, is that they are more connected to their natural curiosity than the adults are. Michael, one of the students in one of our trainings, said to James, another student being trained, "You need to ask your dad about why he did that, as you really don't understand why he chose to do that." James wrote down Michael's suggestion for his follow-up question with his dad, focusing on his favorite memories as a child. Family members often tell us that the depth of the questions that their child or grandchild asked astounds them. That is, in large part, a reflection of the astute quality of the feedback they received from their classmates.

The fourth part of the curriculum involves having the students write a short biography of their focal person using their interview data. During this phase, students learn not only how to use interview data to write an essay but also how to embed quotes from their interview into their paper. Teachers have reported that this phase is an effective way to teach literacy skills. In the final part of the five-part Listening Project curriculum, students present their biography to the classroom or to the entire school, as well as to those whom they have interviewed, after receiving their agreement to have their story presented publicly. Watching young people present their findings to their school community and family members is a moving experience. The pride of the students in their family members when they speak about, for example, their mothers' immigration experiences or their fathers' best friends is readily apparent.

Not only do our surveys, completed before and after the curriculum is completed, indicate that the method of transformative interviewing effectively addresses the crisis of connection,[24] but students and teachers report that they are transformed by the training. One student said that he didn't know that he was "so good at understanding other people" and didn't realize that he didn't know much about his mother's or his friends' personal experiences. Another student said that the project made him see how he was like his older brother. One boy said that he didn't know much about his grandmother but learned that there were a lot of similarities between them, and now he wants to spend more time with her. Rather than simply knowing that his mother immigrated from the Dominican Republic, a student wrote on his evaluation form that he learned about his mother's experiences of immigrating by interviewing her and consequently reported feeling much closer to her. A seventh-grade boy wrote that the project made him more confident with others and better able to find friends, and a girl in the same class wrote: "The most interesting part was learning a lot about someone and realizing that everyone has 'gold nugget' stories, and everyone is more complex than you thought they were. They have their own thoughts and emotions, and it was just interesting to realize this through the interview process."

Another girl wrote: "It affected how my classmates interact with each other now, acting more passionate and curious because we learned something new about each other." Students also reported feeling closer to their teachers: "I see my teacher as more of just a person who teaches me, rather than just a teacher who teaches me. I learned so much about her that I can really understand better the concept of common humanity"; "I really just see my teacher as another human, one with feelings and stories just like me." One of the boys in our seventh-grade class wrote: "I now know that I can open up to people I don't know that well. I also learned how to explain what I'm feeling."

Teachers also told us or wrote to us about the transformative effects of the project:

> I loved when students interviewed me. There was a distinct moment of silence after I thought class was over and I'd announced to the kids in the section that class was over . . . I stood up and opened the door for the kids and told them, "Hey, guys, class is over!" and they all just kind of sat still. And then one by one, the kids gave me a hug as they left. They didn't need to and I wasn't expecting (nor did I even want) that, but it was that tiny moment of silence, the pause in between my words and their movement. It was another one of those "being seen" moments. It was like a thick silence where I could feel a change happening.

Another teacher wrote:

> In general, it changed how I see the seventh-grade mind. It really did. It helped me to see their process, their needs, their hesitations and worries, and it helped me to understand rules and behaviors in our SOCIETY (such as not wanting to probe into sensitive topics, or come close when someone appears upset, or misunderstanding/reading emotions/tears as defense mechanisms, or . . .) and it helped me see kids as maybe a product of our society. That's kind of big-picture stuff.

Gina Voskov, a seventh-grade teacher who helped us create the Listening Project, describes how the training infiltrates her professional and home life:

> Karen (the music teacher) wanted to know how to bring transformative interviewing into her class to help her students connect to the music they're singing. So we spent almost an hour imagining what it might look like to bring the LP method into class . . . We began to imagine how students might ask questions of each other: "Tell me about a time you felt really alive." "Tell me about a time you noticed beauty." "Tell me about a time you were moved to tears." I've never had such an experience at work. We find ourselves so caught up in standards and lesson plans and backed into the walls of our hectic days. This moment slowed me down. And it started with curiosity.
>
> I never would have had that discussion if it weren't for the LP. Nor would I have had the second one, just a few hours later, with Linda, who was wondering about the ways she can help

revise a fifth-grade unit about migration and place the LP methods at the heart of the process. I had come to her with some ideas about a different focus for the unit—having students interview each other about the objects they take with them as they travel through their own worlds—and Linda happened to mention the word "belonging." And just that word! "Belonging." "Belongings"! Aren't we all, in every possible way, seeking belonging? Aren't we united in this search for belonging and in the weight of what it is that we carry? When do we belong to each other?

Without the LP, I'm not sure I'd be able to identify the underlying causes of the problems I saw on the surface. Maybe without it, I'd have said that the problem with middle school students is that they don't know how to be responsible digital citizens. I'd have very passionately argued that what we need to do differently at school is to teach in Advisory about digital citizenship. And I probably would have been a little sad about it all, knowing that I was missing something but not being able to put my finger on it.

But I realize now how I'd have been rushing to just scratch the surface or to slap a Band-Aid on an open wound. I wouldn't have known to examine the wound itself. Now, because of the LP, I see the aching need for connection, understanding, and common humanity wherever I look. It is the single greatest tool I have at my disposal to get to the heart of a person or a problem. And to be clear, it's not just in my work world where I see and pause and notice that I am naturally armed with what I need to understand people and problems.

I constantly use my natural curiosity—that the LP has reminded me I have, actually—to talk with my daughter, my family, my friends. When I think about it, I feel like I made an active decision to step into LP methods with my family. It's so easy not to. It's so easy to just have a busy day, get dinner on the table, do a bedtime routine, and talk with my family without actually listening to them. I feel like what my relationships with them require is more than "togetherness," more than being in the same room or doing the same activities. So I turn to questions.

I now pause when I hear my daughter ask, "Mama, can I ask you a question?" Because this idea of asking questions is so central to being human, and if I can coach into and preserve her curiosity about people, "sustain" is maybe the more accurate word, then I want to make sure I hear her and help her. For years she's been asking me to tell her true stories from my history. But I need to say that it wasn't until recently that I realized how important her curiosity about me and my past was. And I admit to brushing off those questions earlier, claiming I was too tired from my day, that I would tell her later. But now? Now I realize that when my kid is asking me about me, when I answer her or engage in a winding conversation, she is fully present to me, she is nurturing her own interpersonal curiosity, she is seeing me in new ways, probably seeing herself in new ways, and learning. And honestly, that's everything.

It's not hyperbole to say that there is a before and an after. In the before, I was good at what I did. Before, I was aware, active, engaged. And it's fair to say I was hovering at or near the surface of every interaction and interpretation. In the after, I am still most of those things, but what rests in me like a precious calm is an excitement about living that I haven't experienced

> ever before. It comes from a knowing that each of us is full and layered and deeply sensitive *and* that I was born with an ability to see every single person for the human they are, and learn from them, if only I care to ask. While the world we're living in has tried its best to beat it out of me, my own revolution is within me. It's in each of us.

The principal of a middle school reported after being interviewed by a seventh-grade boy that it was "the best therapy session" she ever had. She couldn't believe that an introverted seventh grader could provide such a transformative experience.

Social neuroscientist Matthew Lieberman notes about schools: "Consider that a huge portion of [our] amazing brain helps to make us more social. Yet for a large part of our day, whether we are at work or at school, this extraordinary social machinery in our heads is viewed as a distraction, something that can only get us into trouble and take us away from focusing effectively on the 'real' task at hand."[25] Not allowing students to engage their curiosity about the thoughts and feelings of other people, however, is like "telling someone who hasn't eaten to turn off the desire to eat."[26] By strengthening their natural capacities to listen with curiosity, students and teachers replace judgment with curiosity and connect more meaningfully with each other, and each person involved feels heard, respected, and valued. Schools are a perfect place to nurture the "soft" skills that are necessary to nurture if we are going to effectively address our crisis of connection and disrupt the culture that leads to such a crisis. So, too, are workplaces and homes.

12.

Workplaces and Homes

THE CRISIS OF CONNECTION in the workplace is evident in the Great Resignation, or the Big Quit, during which large numbers of people left their jobs starting in 2021 and continuing to this day, although to a lesser degree than during COVID. Those numbers still, however, surpass pre-COVID ones, with more than 4 million workers per month now quitting their jobs,[1] and most citing mental health issues as a large part of their decision. An employee of Amazon Global contacted me a while ago to inquire whether I could help their employees with their loneliness crisis. The crisis in the workplace, as in schools, is evident not just in high rates of depression, anxiety, and loneliness but also in the sharp divides across political, racial, ethnic, gender, sexuality, and religious lines. Bridging such divides in the workplace is now a priority for a growing number of organizations and is the goal of a "new pluralism" movement that aims to help us learn how to live and work together more peaceably even if we don't share the same views.[2] These divides or symptoms of the crisis of connection lead to job instability among employees, who change jobs hoping to find more responsive employers who will provide a living wage and good benefits *and* workplaces in which they feel valued for what they add and are listened to and treated with dignity by their peers and their bosses.

To address this crisis, companies are now trying to transform the culture of work. Work climates that privilege competition over cooperation and cutthroat strategies over more humane ones have been proved to be "10 times more predictive of having a higher-than-industry-average attrition rate."[3] Leading the effort for more equitable and connected workplaces is the U.S. surgeon general, Vivek Murthy, who released a detailed framework to address these problems.[4] With more than 160 million people in the U.S. workforce and with the average full-time worker spending about half of their waking life at work, addressing this crisis in the workplace is urgent:

> A healthy workforce is the foundation for thriving organizations and healthier communities . . . As we recover from the worst of the pandemic, we have an opportunity and the power to make workplaces engines for mental health and well-being . . . It will require organizations to rethink how they protect workers from harm, foster a sense of connection among workers, show workers that they matter, make space for their lives outside work, and support their growth. It will be worth it because the benefits will accrue for workers and organizations alike.[5]

The model he proposes includes creating policies and practices that provide protection from physical and psychological harm, connection and community, and cultures of inclusion and belonging, and that cultivate trusting relationships and foster collaboration. We are already seeing the national impact of the surgeon general's model, with the new norm in corporate culture being "huddles," in which employees are asked to share something work-related but personal (e.g., what are you struggling with right now? what recent successes did you have?) at the beginning of team meetings. The idea behind such a change is that each person in the workplace is supported in their work-related stresses and their successes. The fact that huddles have over a very quick period become a norm at work, with my peers outside of academia telling me that they, too, are asked to do that in the workplace, underscores the intensity of the desire by both employers and employees to have a more caring and connected workplace. It also emphasizes how easy it is for us to create change when we understand intuitively that it might improve the culture of workplaces.

While such efforts in the workplace are essential, they are based on the implicit assumption that the change needs to take place only at the individual or workplace level rather than in the larger cultural framework in which work takes place. They don't address the privileging in the workplace of "hard" skills like number-crunching over "soft" skills like being relationally intelligent and listening intently and with curiosity to others. Such a hierarchy of the "hard" over "soft" leads to most jobs being depressing, anxiety-provoking, and lonely regardless of where you are in the hierarchy, but especially when you are perceived to be at the bottom.

Blair Miller, a business leader who writes about the future of work, argues that nurturing "soft" skills in the workplace is critical for achieving the outcomes in Murthy's model. According to Miller, as technical skills such as finance and analytics are automated and implemented via AI, the ability to listen with curiosity, to build empathy across lines of difference, to care about another person's thoughts and feelings, and to incorporate another's perspective even when we disagree is essential to workplace productivity and retention. Miller goes on to argue in her op-ed for *The Hill*[6] that the winners of this "soft" skills revolution will be those whose talents have historically been undervalued. She notes that "outsider talent" like women and people of color have had no choice but to cultivate these skills to survive and thrive in the workplace. Paradoxically, they are best positioned for the future. This shift in the skills needed for job retention, success, and productivity combined with a world of unstable employment and hiring may lead to the recognition that hiring candidates with strong "soft" skills and providing a living wage and good benefits are ways to achieve real economic value. These are the first steps toward a more stable and sustainable human-centered economy.

While most company bosses and economists still believe that workers will be more motivated and work harder if they earn more money, the evidence suggests that employees are driven more by feelings of connection with their fellow employees and with their bosses than by the pay they receive, as long as they receive a living wage. Employees were polled to see if they would prefer a raise or a better boss, and 65 percent said they would prefer a better boss. Furthermore, in a study in which thousands of employees were asked to score the effectiveness of their boss, bosses who were considered great leaders were always those who had interpersonal skills. Many dimensions of leadership were assessed, but if a leader was considered as focused on results and talented in building relationships, there was a 72 percent chance that this person would be rated by the employees as a great boss.[7]

In his chapter on workplaces, Matthew Lieberman writes:

> The best bosses understand and care about the social motivations of all the members of their team. Bosses have to foster better connections between themselves and their team, among team members, and between the team and other outside groups and individuals critical to success. Better [relationships] will reduce the mindreading burden on everyone on the team, and it will allow social issues to be nipped in the bud, rather than festering from one project to the next.[8]

The truth is that feeling connected in the workplace, rather than money, motivates employees to try harder, increase their productivity, and stay with a job.

Evidence of old ways of thinking about the workplace are readily apparent in training programs that I came across on the web, with the five qualities of effective leadership being as follows:[9]

1. Being self-aware and being emotionally intelligent.
2. Developing others by delegating, coaching, and mentoring.
3. Encouraging strategic thinking and action, and maintaining a flexible mindset.
4. Being ethical and civic-minded and taking responsibility for one's own mistakes.
5. Practicing effective cross-cultural communication.

While these are all good practices in the workplace, the definition of the softer elements on this list such as emotional intelligence is almost always interpreted as emotional regulation, or controlling negative emotion, and doesn't include emotional sensitivity, suggesting, once again, our privileging of the "hard" over the "soft."[10] Furthermore, relational intelligence—or the capacity to listen with curiosity and learn from others—is rarely if ever mentioned. This omission is especially surprising because, as we all know, engaging with what someone is saying by asking them follow-up questions affects the quality of what is shared. In a study on the impact of inattentive listening, researchers found:

> Speakers remembered less information and were less articulate in the information they conveyed. Conversely, they found that attentive listeners elicited more information, relevant detail, and elaboration from speakers, even when the listeners didn't ask any questions. So, if you're barely listening to someone because you think that person is boring or not worth your time, you will actually make it so.[11]

If the skill of listening is included in the leadership training programs, it is almost always the thin version. In Google's attempt to foster listening in their teams, they focused on "taking turns, hearing one another out, and . . . non-verbal cues to pick up on unspoken thoughts and feelings."[12] While these are certainly important skills, they don't necessary foster listening, as can be attested to by anyone who has been in a meeting in which everyone speaks but no one is addressing what the others have just said. Only when people are asked to elaborate on their experiences—what exactly happened (he said/she said version) and how they interpreted what happened—will they feel listened to and understood. Ingvar Kamprad, the founder of IKEA, provides us with an example of such listening. Kamprad would often show up at stores and anonymously stroll the floor, asking questions of customers. He showed "an eagerness to understand someone else's worldview and an expectation that you will be surprised by what you hear and will learn from the experience."[13]

The absence of listening with curiosity, or what I call relational intelligence, in leadership training programs means that they are not fully tapping into our human potential to be truly great leaders. If these programs did, they would emphasize the importance of making everyone on the team feel valued by listening with curiosity to how they understand and want to approach a task or a problem—communicating that leaders want to learn from their employees and not just tell them what to do. They would also offer opportunities in which people can share, if they want, details about who they are and what is important to them outside of the workplace, as well as offering work-related insights during work hours. This type of intimacy—sharing thoughts and feelings about the workplace and about one's own life in spaces outside the workplace, so it's optional rather than required—will likely enhance job stability, retention, and satisfaction.

Relational intelligence is also essential, of course, for conflict resolution, including those related to a diverse workforce in which the values and perspectives of employees and employers may be different from each other. Having the person who committed what seemed like a microaggression ask questions of the person who was angered by it can be an effective first step in understanding how the recipient interpreted what was said and why it led to anger. Taking this first step and then figuring out together how to prevent it from happening again will likely diminish the number of such aggressions in the workplace. When people ask questions with the intent of understanding rather than "proving a point, setting a trap, changing someone's mind, or making the other person look foolish,"[14] the conflict is more easily resolved. However, such resolution can happen successfully only when the culture of the workplace doesn't implicitly or explicitly replicate the hierarchies found in the larger culture. Social activists Saliha Bava and Mark Greene argue that listening with curiosity is critical for creating an inclusive work environment in which everyone feels that they belong. In their book *The Relational Workplace,*[15] they offer concrete ways to practice such listening. Once we listen to and see the other person as they want to be seen and not how we stereotype them to be, we are more willing to work with others even when there is conflict. Listening with and leading with curiosity creates an environment in which, as Doug Guthrie, the CEO at On Global Leadership, puts it, "we ask rather than tell, connect rather than compete, listen rather than judge, and join rather than take sides."

WHILE THE CRISIS OF connection is relatively easy to address in the structured environment of schools and workplaces, it is harder to deal with in our homes. For women, the crisis often entails remembering to take care of themselves, as they are typically the primary caretakers (including of their male partner if they have one), the therapist, the organizer, the lover, and the parent who is most likely to be blamed for the problems of any children they may have.[16] For men, the crisis is often dealing with their own emotions, especially their feelings of vulnerability, as they have been raised in a culture that tells them that the only respectable emotion is anger. That message means that they often rely entirely on their female partners for their emotional sustenance, as that feels like the only safe space that they have,[17] and are often hesitant to go into therapy because that, too, has been feminized. According to a 2021 survey, only 21 percent of men said they received emotional support from a friend within the past week, compared to 41 percent of women.[18] Men also often struggle to be good listeners in a culture that doesn't value listening and in which they may not need to listen as much as women do to get their needs met. While women may be better at looking like they are listening than men, they, too, struggle with listening while negotiating a wide range of demands, including those of their own parents, which makes it difficult to listen and seemingly impossible to listen with curiosity. Thus, the crisis of connection for women is remembering to take care of themselves while caring for others, while the crisis for men is remembering to care for others, including their partners and their parents, while trying to take care of themselves.

The crisis of connection between parents and children, however, is often similar across different types of households. Parents often feel the pressure to abide by the rules of their culture, which means, in the case of the United States and many other countries, making sure that every moment of their child's life is productive, as they fear that if it isn't, their child won't get into a good college or get a decent job. Their children, in turn, are often angry at their parents for not seeing them as they see themselves and not listening to what they have to say or taking their desires seriously, which are almost always focused on wanting to spend more time with their friends or finding friends with whom they want to spend time. Ginia Bellafante, a journalist at *The New York Times,* calls this style of not listening to one's children "anxiety parenting" and believes that mothers are particularly victims of it, which is not surprising given that they will be blamed when things go wrong:

> Just as women entered the workforce in unprecedented numbers [in the 1980s], the laissez-faire parenting style that had defined the previous three decades—a style in which the various responsibilities of child-rearing were shared with television, the frozen-food aisle, Jane Jacobs's "eyes on the street," and the random neighbor in 3F—came in for stampeding indictment. Now mothers were always to be "on," engaged in relationships with their children that were at once kinesthetic, tirelessly management oriented, and unrelenting in their emotional solicitations. Across demographics, American mothers have absorbed the cultural pressures to beat the odds, whether that involves navigating charter school admissions in West Baltimore or shepherding the diligent but ordinary son of Winnetka toward Yale.[19]

While my daughter was in high school, I spent a good deal of time asking her whether she was doing her homework. I missed out on large parts of her adolescence with my concern that she was not doing her schoolwork in a timely manner (in fact she was). I also spent most of my time with my son pressuring him to do extracurriculars that would make his college application stronger. Now that they are in or have graduated from college, I wish that I had spent more time with them asking them about their friendships and helping them find mutually supportive ones, as that is what both continue to care about the most in their lives. At the time, however, I parented according to what I thought was the best way to protect their futures. Other parents do the same thing, with a study from the Harvard Making Caring Common Project suggesting that most parents nationwide believe that academic achievement is more important than kindness.[20]

Addressing the crisis of connection in our homes takes the same relational and emotional intelligence necessary to address the crisis in our schools and workplaces. Listening with curiosity is always part of the first step to address the crisis in any context. When Jane Goodall was asked in a talk she gave on the campus of NYU Abu Dhabi who had influenced her the most in her life, she said her mother. She then told two stories that underscored the importance of not only listening but also listening with curiosity. One was about when she was a very young girl and wanted to put worms on her pillow at night so she could see what happens to them. Rather than being upset because Jane wanted to put worms on her pillow, her mother gently explained that the worms would die if she kept them overnight on her pillow, so she should put them back into the dirt where they belong. Jane explained that her mother didn't shame her for wanting to do something that would make her pillow dirty but simply made the case for removing them in a way that respected Jane's curiosity. The second story she told was about wanting to see a chicken lay an egg. Jane was six or seven years old and remembers hiding in the barn near their house to see if she could see an egg emerging from a chicken. While she was hiding, she heard her mother calling for her and demanding that she come out from wherever she was. She didn't want to lose the chance to see an egg coming out of a chicken, so she chose not to respond to her mother, who continued to call out. After a while, she saw a chicken lay an egg and then came rushing out of the barn to tell her mother. When Jane's mother saw Jane, she came running toward her with an angry look on her face, probably intending to yell at Jane for not responding to her calls. As her mother came closer and saw the expression of excitement on Jane's face, her mother simply said when she was right in front of her, "What have you discovered, Jane?" Rather than getting angry at her daughter, she chose to prioritize her daughter's curiosity.

A similar story was also told to me by Sky, an NYU New York student, who told me the following story via email:

> When I was around five or six, I visited my aunt in Minnesota. For as long as I've known her, she has had a passion for gardening, which she poured into the most sprawling, beautifully lush garden. Because we were visiting in the middle of summer, all the flowers she had planted were in bloom. I remember I asked her if I could pick some flowers, and she said that I could pick as many as I wanted. I took that literally and picked almost every flower she had, putting them in a massive plastic bucket with water from the hose to make flower soup. I don't remember the moment when my aunt discovered that I had essentially axed her entire garden; I remember her response: she asked me about my soup. I told her that I was making perfume and she nodded, listening closely, then offered me some small glass bottles from her kitchen and assisted me in bottling the soup. I don't remember feeling any anger from her, she didn't react at all. Looking back now, I am positive she was upset on some level, and it would make sense for her to have felt angry and disappointed.

> But the single element that makes this memory significant for me is that she, as the adult, put her feelings aside to recognize me as a child and treat me with gentleness and care. If she ever did say something to me about maybe picking fewer flowers next time, I don't remember it, leading me to assume she said it casually. It was no big deal.

What these stories remind us of are the possibilities of listening with curiosity and thus with care in our own homes and the significant impact of doing so on the recipients of such responses.

Critiquing the way we raise our children by "miss[ing] the profound ways in which we are immersed within relationships, even when alone,"[21] Saliha Bava and Mark Greene in *The Relational Book for Parenting* encourage us to create spaces that include asking questions of our children and partners and encouraging them to ask questions of us as well; holding uncertainty; staying playful; reframing our stories; and always considering the context when responding to them.[22] Listening with the intent of understanding, they wisely claim, helps us set aside our assumptions about what the other person meant. Telling another person including a child about what they felt rather than asking them how they felt shuts down their ability to articulate their own thoughts and feelings. Even when the other person is expressing strong emotions, Bava and Greene emphasize the importance of not "collapsing" into our own or their strong emotions. They urge parents to be open to gaining new knowledge from their child and their partner that helps nourish their understanding not only of the other but also of themselves. Such parenting and partnering, they conclude, "loosens the grip of individualism" that inhibits our relational and emotional intelligence from flourishing.

When we ask questions of other people, we reach outward and learn from them—an act of connection in and of itself—and when we also allow them to reach outward toward us, no one is left alone.[23]

Curiosity, of course, is a catalyst of empathy, as it requires us to "understand the inner emotional worlds of other people and then act in ways that benefit other people and our relationships with them."[24] But empathy without asking questions often doesn't feel empathic. My students tell me that responses like "I am so sorry that you are feeling bad" irritate them, as such a response suggests that the person doesn't really want to hear about why they are struggling, what happened, who said what, and how they are thinking and feeling about it. They just want to say something that sounds empathic and move on. A colleague recently told me that after his parents died, most people said to him, "I am so sorry for your loss." One of his friends, however, asked him about his parents and wanted to hear stories about what they were like. He said he immediately teared up. That was the response that felt the most supportive to him and was what he had wanted someone to ask him, as it allowed him to tell stories about the people whom he loved and had just lost.

We listen with curiosity not only by asking questions but also by being present when someone is talking. During a recent Zoom call in which my daughter was telling me about her essay for one of her classes, a text message popped up on my computer screen, telling me disappointing news. My eyes flashed to the top of the screen and I quickly moved back to "listening" to my daughter. After I spent ten seconds trying to focus on what she was saying, she said, "Mom, you are not listening to me." I provided an unconvincing response of "Yes, I am, I am totally listening," but I knew that I wasn't. She was not satisfied and reiterated: "No, you are not listening, I can see it in your eyes . . . they kind of glazed over." While I still protested, I was struck by the fact that listening with curiosity entails not only questions but also physical presence. When we offer neither, the other person doesn't feel listened to and thus stops talking.

Developmental psychologist Judy Chu's ethnographic study of four- and five-year-old boys and their fathers suggests that listening with curiosity is a large part of good parenting. She and her collaborator, Carol Gilligan, asked fathers what qualities they see in their sons that they hope their sons will never lose and how they nurture them. The fathers responded by saying that what they cherish and wish to preserve most is their sons' openness and willingness to "feel their feelings fully" and "'to be honest,' 'upfront,' and 'expressive' in their relationships . . . they could 'let things come right out,' and they were not hesitant about 'saying what they feel' and telling others what was on their minds."[25] They were also delighted with their sons' curiosity. Fathers spoke about their sons being able to closely "[read] people's facial expressions [and] tone of voice."[26] The fathers were also appreciative of their sons' acute abilities to ask questions that reflected a deeper level of understanding than one would expect from a four-year-old. They suggested that their sons' emotional and relational intelligence was a large part of the reason that they felt close to them.

The fathers of the young boys also spoke of how they nurtured curiosity at home. One father told a story of how he and his son would often just have these "great conversations . . . so unselfconsciously":[27]

> He was taking a bath and I'm sitting there talking to him and he's sorta playing, fooling around with bubbles and just

> hanging out . . . and he was telling me some stories about his buddies and how much he likes his buddies and then he was asking me about my buddies . . . just like "So, what's friendship about?" you know, "What's it mean to you?" kind of thing . . . He was just talking and I was talking. We were playing, you know. There was nothing to accomplish . . . It's not about anything in particular . . . There's nothing else going on.[28]

Another father said:

> These boys [in this classroom] . . . they're very sensitive, they're emotional, they seem to like each other very much. There's this soft side . . . but somehow they can't show this. I feel like they have to hide it and they've learned *so* fast how to hide it, except for these moments, you know, with my kids it's usually in the car . . . or at nighttime after reading to them. [I'm] sort of lying with them a little bit, and then [they ask] these incredible questions and it opens up.[29]

The fathers chose to counter mainstream messages about being a boy by finding ways to stay close to their sons through talking and asking questions. They wanted their sons to maintain their emotional acuity, not only for their sons' sake but also for their own, as their sons "'get at the heart of you,' they 'want the real thing' . . . it's the only thing they'll respond to . . . Adults have to face it, own up to their feelings and experiences . . . Kids unravel what's been carefully tucked away."[30]

The fathers in Chu's study also expressed the yearning to "join" their sons by "meeting [them] where they're at"[31] and creating emotionally connected relationships driven by mutual curiosity. While acknowledging that it can be exhausting and "requires patience, energy, and focus" and listening "without judging,"[32] they said it is the only way to keep their sons close and to make sure they hold on to their emotional and relational acuity. They want their sons to "develop and maintain close relationships in which they could 'confide in others,' 'talk to someone,' ask questions, and feel 'acknowledged,' 'recognized,' and 'validated.'"[33] They knew that their sons "need 'relationships where they feel safe and O.K.,' where there is 'someone to meet them half way,' 'someone willing to join them,' 'so they can read the world in a way that makes sense to them.'"[34] Among their greatest fears for their sons was that they wouldn't feel like they could turn to anyone for help and thus would feel alone. They seemed to know intuitively, however, how to prevent that from happening.

Studies show that children and adults who are securely attached to at least one parent "tend to be more curious and open to new information . . . You know you will be okay if you hear something or find out things that upset you because you have someone, somewhere, you can confide in and who will relieve your distress."[35] Psychologist Constance Flanagan finds that families who value social compassion, reciprocity, and giving the benefit of the doubt, qualities that are linked to listening with curiosity, are more likely to produce empathic children who have a sense of social responsibility and will more likely have friends.[36] Neuroscientist Lise Eliot concludes that "children who are raised in more emotionally intelligent homes—where parents talk about feelings and their causes—score higher on empathy tests than children from families who talk less about feelings, and the influence is every bit as strong for boys as for girls."[37] Talking about thoughts and feelings and asking others about their thoughts and feelings fosters intra- and interpersonal curiosity, which in turn fosters deep and meaningful connections and thus social and emotional well-being, in and out of the home.

Nurturing our relational and emotional intelligence in schools, workplaces, and at home is necessary to disrupt a culture that brings out the worst in us and makes us treat ourselves and one another poorly and sometimes even makes us kill ourselves and/or each other. Listening with curiosity and asking each other not what is wrong with you but what I can learn from you about yourself and about myself and about the world around us are the first steps toward creating a society in which our human capacities are nurtured and our human needs are prioritized and we are able to thrive without preventing someone else from surviving. Once we understand that no one will listen and learn from us if we don't listen to and learn from them, we will remember what we have known all along, and what the boys and young men in this book have shown us through their stories and their actions, which is that we have a natural capacity to solve our own problems, and now all we need to do is begin doing it.

The Story of Us

If everyone had been in love, they would treat their children differently. They would treat each other differently.

—JAMES BALDWIN[1]

IN A CLASSROOM OF seventh-grade boys, I asked the students to read a line from my book on friendships. It's a quote from a fifteen-year-old boy: "My best friend and I love each other . . . that's it . . . you have this thing that is deep, so deep, it's within you, you can't explain it. It's just a thing that you know that that person is that person . . . and that is all that should be important in our friendship."[2] The boys in the classroom start to giggle and tell me that the quote sounds gay. When I tell them that most teenage boys sound like this at some point during adolescence, they look at me with amazement. "For real?" they ask. I confirm that it is indeed. A moment of silence ensues. Then, as if they are literally taking off their masks of masculinity, boys begin to share their own feelings about wanting or having close male friendships. Two boys in the classroom speak together about a recent disagreement that led them to "break up" and how their hurt feelings had driven them to it. Boys know the thick story about friendships but are willing to share it only if the adult in the room makes it a safe place to do so.

A parable that I read in a book long ago involves a tourist and a local who meet on a street corner. The tourist asks the local for directions, and the local responds, "If I wanted to go there, I wouldn't start from here."[3] If we want to create a society that better aligns with our nature and our needs, we need to start from a new place. The rebels in this book offer us a way to do that by providing four insights in our reimagining of boys, ourselves, and our culture, with the most obvious being that if we want to address our crisis of connection, we should start by asking questions of one another and should listen and, in the workplace, should lead with curiosity, as those will allow us to see each other and ourselves outside of a set of negative stereotypes and learn something about the other person as well as about ourselves. And not just listen with curiosity to those we know but to everyone else, including those in kindergarten classes (perhaps especially them because they appear to be the wisest among us) and those who teach them and the elderly people in assisted living and those who care for them. We should ask thick questions of our neighbors, of those who sit next to us on the bus and the subway or who ring up our groceries or take care of our children. The research repeatedly suggests that most people are hungry to be asked questions that allow them to reveal what they value, who they are, what they care about most, and what they want in their lives in addition to money. We should also ask questions of our own children and of the other people with whom we live, using the same curiosity we had when we were five years old to understand who they are and what they want, regardless of how young they are. And we should persist in our questions until we get an answer that makes sense to us and to them.

We should also remember to give the persons whom we are asking the choice of whether to answer our questions. Sometimes people aren't in the mood. I have found, however, that people generally love to answer real questions, even on the subway. We should also ask questions of people who don't agree with us and those who do, as they can teach us a lot about us and them and why their values and ways of living may be different from our own. We have a lot to learn from each other if we start from a place of curiosity—wanting to learn from one another and caring about what others have to say—rather than from a place of judgment, or wanting to be right, and thus not taking the time to learn from others. The reason my research team and I were able to hear the thick stories of boys and young men is that we wanted to know what we could learn from them about being a boy and about being human in a culture that tells thin stories about them and everyone else. We have to be curious, in other words, to learn thick stories.

The second and third insights that the boys and young men in my studies and in my classrooms provide are that all of us, regardless of our social identities, want close friendships, *and* we are all born with the cognitive, emotional, and relational skills to have them. The reason there is such variation in "deep secret" friendship patterns and in "soft" skills is not because of our nature but because of our culture, which doesn't value such friendships and doesn't nourish such skills.

And the final insight, the boys and young men in this book remind us—as do our poets, including the Lebanese American poet Kahlil Gibran—that "reason and passion" are equally necessary: one without the other makes many of us unbalanced, alienated, and lonely, and some of us suicidal and/or homicidal. To get where we want to go, which is a society in which all children and adults are able to survive and thrive, we need to start from these four insights and remember that we knew them when we were young, so it's just a matter of remembering them rather starting all over again.

While these insights help us create a culture that better aligns with our nature, we need to take additional steps to make the changes stick. Primary among such changes is to stop sharing thin stories that turn culture into nature and that treat consequences of our culture as if they are *the* problem rather than merely symptoms of a culture blind to itself. We also have to stop blaming social media for our problems. Social media simply reifies our "boy" culture and makes the values of it louder by being designed in such a way that falsely equates being "liked" and having many followers with being meaningfully connected to those followers. Because we are obsessed with the me, me, me, we have designed a technology that is self-oriented and that confuses getting likes with being likable. We can, however, easily create a social media that is in fact *social* and that fosters our natural curiosity and our capacity to build connections with one another. Social connection 1.0 reflects all social media apps available now that bring people together digitally but don't actually foster meaningful connection. Social connection 2.0 entails asking questions, such as those in "36 Questions That Lead to Love," but not follow-up questions. We now need Social Connection 3.0, which involves asking follow-up questions as part of the app experience, such as is done in our Listening Project and in Shari Foos's Narrative Method, and not giving up until we understand how another person sees the world. With Social Connection 3.0, which can easily be done digitally (just as we did on the telephone back in the day), we learn about ourselves and each other and we begin to see the hierarchy of humanness and human qualities for what it is, which is not natural, and forms a major barrier to forging meaningful connection.[4]

When students ask me why we continue to tell thin stories that are hurting us and, in some cases, killing us, I respond by saying that we stopped listening to ourselves a long time ago and began to have fights about who is to blame, who should be at the top, and who is suffering more. While those questions have answers—mostly the people placed at the top; no one; the people placed at the bottom—the answer to the question of how we got here in the first place implicates all of us, but to different degrees depending on where we are in the hierarchy or the power structure.

Creating the necessary cultural change, however, is less daunting when we consider the extent to which we have already done so in the past and continue to do so. With the legalization of same-sex marriage, the #MeToo movement, the Black Lives Matter movement, and the fact that democratic socialism is increasingly accepted in the United States, we know that change that recognizes a common humanity can happen when we listen with curiosity to one another and begin to care and take responsibility for one another. Other examples of cultural change include my students who increasingly identify with "they" as their pronoun of choice and who are becoming more flexible in their sexual identities. They have had enough of our gendered and sexualized straitjackets and want the freedom to think and feel and love whomever and however they want. We are also now more open to the idea that boys and men feel and want close friendships as much as everyone else, as indicated by the increase in articles, books, and movies making that precise point. We are also more open to the idea that girls and women think, as suggested in the growth of STEM opportunities for them.

Friendships are now being valued, especially after COVID, with books coming out with titles such as *Friendship: The Evolution, Biology, and Extraordinary Power of Life's Fundamental Bond*; *Friendship in the Age of Loneliness*; and *Platonic: How the Science of Attachment Can Help You Make—and Keep—Friends.* The French philosopher Geoffroy de Lagasnerie argues that we need to restructure our entire society so that the focus is exclusively on building and maintaining friendships: "Building your life around close friendships rather than family or romance is a joyous and necessary act of rebellion, and governments should put in place 'friendship ministries' to radically rethink the way society is organized."[5] He and his two best friends speak many times daily and make sure they prioritize "meeting up for long chats."[6] They want "to make friendship a space of counterculture against [our] institutional norms."[7]

I SPENT THE LAST four years of my father's life taking care of him in Paris, France, where he'd lived for the last thirty years of his life. He had Parkinson's disease, which made his movement difficult and eventually his spine severely curved. I went with him when I visited Paris to the hospital for poor people, as he was indigent. I also visited him at his rent-controlled apartment in which he was getting home care. The nurses and doctors were gentle with my cantankerous father; and the home care included a caretaker, Imen, who came to check on him three times a day and made his meals and cleaned the kitchen. He also received a once-a-week massage from a professional masseuse in the comfort of his own home. He wanted to die at home, and because of the support provided by the French government, and of course by all the people who took care of him, he was able to do just that and do it in a dignified way. The bottom line is my father wouldn't have lived as long or as well if he hadn't received those benefits or that care.

What I was reminded of from this experience is the urgency of creating not only cultural but also structural and institutional changes, including creating towns and cities that have social infrastructure embedded in them, such as parks and funded libraries where people can gather.[8] I live in a city in which a homeless person has lived across the street from me for eighteen years. My children have normalized the situation and simply call her "the lady who lives across the street." In a country as rich as the United States, it is reprehensible that it is no longer shocking to see people living permanently on the street. Solutions must entail giving everyone the opportunity to be employed at jobs with decent pay and benefits and to have housing, food, clean water, healthcare, and the capacity to care for and be cared by their loved ones. But if we continue to think the problem is our biology rather than our culture, large-scale structural change is impossible, as we don't think it will create the change that *we* want, including the boys and men who are committing acts of violence. A culture that listens with curiosity, takes responsibility, and cares creates the internal change necessary for large-scale and significant structural, institutional, and community changes.

Jean Piaget, one of the patriarchs in the field of developmental psychology, defined the concept of collective dialogue as "listening to and being responsive to one another."[9] We need to have a collective dialogue that draws from the insights of both the rebels in this book and young people of all identities in our schools, workplaces, and homes. Years ago, a fifteen-year-old boy asked me for whom I wrote my previous book about friendships. When I told him that I wrote it for parents and teachers, he looked at me quizzically and asked, “Why not for us, as it would make us feel less alone?” This book is for all the rebels who remind us of who we are as humans: what it means to care, to value our friendships, and to honor both sides of ourselves—the yin and the yang that make us whole and that offer us the possibility of surviving *and* thriving.

All I am saying is simply this: that all [human]kind is tied together; all life is interrelated, and we are all caught in an inescapable network of mutuality, tied in a single garment of identity.

—MARTIN LUTHER KING JR., COMMENCEMENT SPEECH AT OBERLIN COLLEGE, 1965

Acknowledgments

I would be remiss not to start with the obvious. Had it not been for the hundreds of boys and young men who participated in my longitudinal and mixed-method research studies and those in my classrooms over the past few decades, this book would never have happened. The fact that the boys and young men in my research studies are mostly boys of color from poor and working-class communities and are Black, Brown, and Asian American makes their contribution even more significant, as they prove that all humans have something to say about being human and how to solve our own problems. They also confirm what bell hooks said about marginality, that it "nourishes one's capacity to resist. It offers the possibility from which to see and create, to imagine alternative new worlds."[1] They have helped us do just that. Thank you.

This book would also not have been possible without the undergraduate and graduate students who have been part of my research teams since I began as a professor at New York University in 1995. Thank you for your willingness to listen with curiosity to the children and teenagers in our studies. The data I present in this book are the product of your ability to get their thick stories. I also want to thank the funders who made my research possible, including the William T. Grant Foundation, which supported me in my very first study of friendships, the National Science Foundation, the Spencer Foundation, the Einhorn Collaborative, the Novo Foundation, the Rockefeller Foundation, the Chan Zuckerberg Initiative, and, of course, my home base, New York University. Thank you for being at the forefront of what matters and for funding studies that help us solve the public health crises of our time.

Thank you to Leslie Meredith, my literary agent, who reached out to me in 2019 to see if I might be interested in writing another book. Without her support and determination to get my proposal into the hands of editors who she thought would be good for the book, I wouldn't have ended up with Stephen Morrow, who was at Dutton and who immediately saw the importance of this book and was an enthusiastic and helpful editor. Thank you as well to the editor Jill Schwartzman and to her assistant Charlotte Peters at Dutton, who carefully and lovingly got the book to the finish line. Thank you to the copy editor, Nancy Inglis, for her stellar work that significantly improved the book. And thank you to Sofia Encheva, who was my editorial assistant throughout the writing of this book. Your attention to the details and your passion for the topic made the book much better and so much more enjoyable to write.

This book also grew out of a lifetime of thick love. The type of love that makes you feel seen and heard. The type that makes your brain crackle with insights and allows you to see others in the way they want to be seen. My thick love story starts with my mom, my first *and* my second dad, Henzo, and continues with my family, including my siblings and their partners, my children, my godmother and her husband, my ex-husband, uncles and aunts, nieces and nephews, cousins, and my glorious grandmother Rhoda Elizabeth Biden Way, who instilled in me from an early age an "Oh no you won't" attitude. It also includes mentors, friends, colleagues, and current and former students who have nurtured my curiosity and thus my resistance; I have learned much from all of them.

Among those gorgeous humans in my friend community, there are those who shaped this book directly, including my graduate school mentor and now BFF Carol Gilligan, who started a revolution in psychology in 1982 by pointing out that girls and women are human too, and that relationships matter not just for those with two X chromosomes but for all of us, as discussed in her new book *In a Human Voice*. Ann Morning, my CFF (curiosity friend forever), has also been critical in the writing of this book. Our almost daily conversations filled with thick analyses of ourselves, our relationships, and the world around us have made me a deeper thinker and feeler and have been the source of many of the insights in this book. Thank you, love.

Then there are my other friends who shaped this book indirectly and who inspire me daily, including Hiro Yoshikawa, Jennifer Hill, Tai Pleasanton (who is also my cousin), Jean Rhodes, Carol Brandt, Lisa Arrastia, Lisa Williams, Leslie Davol, Mary Margaret Jones, Billie Tsien, Pam Quinn, Dana Burde (spelled correctly), and all the women in my "awesome mothers" group whose children went to the same school as mine (Negi, Fe, Mary, Jyoti, Lydie, Makiko, Nadia, Trish, Roya, and Sonam). My friendship network also includes colleagues whose work has greatly influenced mine, such as Deborah Tolman, Lyn Mikel Brown, Judy Chu, Janie Ward, Michael Cunningham,

Diane Hughes, Cathie Tamis-LeMonda, Sumie Okazaki, Margarita Azmitia, Xinyin Chen, Jennifer Hoos Rothberg, Jennifer Siebel Newsom, Megan Ryan, John Botti, Gina Voskov, Shari Foos, Marc Brackett, Robin Stern, Gary Barker, Mark Greene, Mark Grayson, Saliha Bava, Jeff Wetzler (who just came out with *Ask,* a book that is a perfect companion to mine), and Lukas Dhont, who made his sublime Grand Prix–winning and Oscar-nominated movie, *Close,* which was inspired by my previous book on boys' friendships. I also want to give a special shout-out to Tim Shriver, who gave me the name of the podcast I want to do with one of my best friends in the future. It will be called *How to Act like a Five-Year-Old,* and we will interview interesting people, including five-year-olds, using the method I describe in this book.

My former doctoral students, who are now leading scholars or practitioners in their own right, have also influenced my thinking and feeling along the way and include Joseph Nelson, Onnie Rogers, Taveeshi Gupta, Rui Yang, Dana Edell, Anna Smith, Kerstin Pahl, Erika Niwa, Carlos Santos, Lisa Silverman, Rachel Gingold, Susan Rosenbloom, Yueming Jia, Preetika Mukherjee, Monique Jethwani, Angelica Puzio, Esther Sin, Anna Bennet, Rachel Taffe, and Yufei Gu. And of course, I must thank my Listening Project team at NYU, whose incredible work is described in this book. Thank you to Dr. Crystal A. Clarke, Holly Van Hare, Dr. Jinjoo Han, Sean Small, Dr. Laura Peynado, who is the principal at one of our middle schools, our program officer Marc Chun at the Chan Zuckerberg Initiative, and the dozens of NYU students who help us teach the Listening Project in middle and high schools across NYC each week.

I also want to thank the influencers in my life—most of whom I have never met—who have made me who I am and are the rebels I most admire outside of my family, friends, and former and current students. They include the first rebel I became aware of as a high school student: Richard Wright, the author of *Native Son,* who revealed through his fiction the devastating impact on Black families of a "boy" culture that doesn't care, listen, or take responsibility. The rebels also include anthropologist Margaret Mead, who proved through her cross-cultural studies in the 1930s that gender (and adolescence) is a social construct and not a biological one. Then there is Black feminist scholar bell hooks, with her intersectional ways of seeing the world and her reminder that "if we are only committed to an improvement in that politic of domination that we feel leads directly to our individual exploitation or oppression, we not only remain attached to the status quo but act in complicity with it, nurturing and maintaining those very systems of domination. Until we are all able to accept the interlocking, interdependent nature of systems of domination and recognize specific ways each system is maintained, we will continue to act in ways that undermine our individual quest for freedom and collective liberation struggle. The ability to acknowledge blind spots can emerge only as we expand our concern about politics of domination and our capacity to care about the oppression and exploitation of others. A love ethic makes this expansion possible."[2] And radical educator Paulo Freire, whose recognition of our common humanity, demand for collective responsibility, and insistence on not flipping the hierarchy inspired large parts of this book. My influencers also include Michelle Fine, a social psychologist at City University of New York, who embodies rebellion in her research and underscores our natural capacity for it; fiction and nonfiction writer Chimamanda Ngozi Adichie, whom I am indebted to for exposing the way single stories dehumanize but also the way stories can bring back our dignity and self-respect. My gratitude extends as well to *New York Times* columnist David Brooks, who has been fighting the good fight for the softer sides of ourselves for more than a decade.

Finally, I want to express my appreciation to my children, Raphael and Chiara, who are my brilliant angels shining the light on the truth and who care deeply about their family and friends and the world around them. They are the rebels in my household who regularly remind me that speaking truth to power is not only possible but necessary and that nothing matters more than friendships, including within one's own family. Thank you for your thick love, my kookamongas, and for showing me how to "be water, my friend," as martial artist Bruce Lee famously said.

Notes

Epigraph

1. Michael Carlson, "Carl Oglesby: Political Activist and Campaigner Against the Vietnam War," *The Independent,* September 29, 2011, https://www.independent.co.uk/news/obituaries/carl-oglesby-political-activist-and-campaigner-against-the-vietnam-war-2362928.html.

Thin and Thick Stories

1. I draw from Clifford Geertz's discussion of thin and thick interpretation in *The Interpretation of Cultures: Selected Essays* (New York: Basic Books, 1973) in my constructs of thin and thick stories. However, my constructs are not simply about the literal and symbolic meanings of the stories. I am also addressing how our thin stories ignore the power structure that drives them and how our thick stories recognize the hierarchy of humans and human qualities embedded in "boy" culture.
2. Chimamanda Ngozi Adichie, "The Danger of a Single Story," Facing History & Ourselves, August 2, 2016, https://www.facinghistory.org/resource-library/danger-single-story.
3. Nicholas Ray, director, *Rebel Without a Cause,* Warner Bros., 1955.
4. *Rebel Without a Cause,* 01:02:00–01:02:54.
5. While we may think that European philosophers who lived many centuries ago have little relevance to our lives now, one need only read about or listen to any reflection on the state of the world to see evidence of

their thinking. As I write this chapter, Hobbes's description of life outside society as "solitary, poor, nasty, brutish, and short" is invoked in an article that describes the state of mind of voters in a particular region of India. See Supriy Ranjan and Pankaj Kumar, "Stress on Safety, Security: Hobbesian Fear Primary Driver of BJP's UP Poll Campaign," *New Indian Express*, February 26, 2022. The phrase "Hobbesian jungle" is regularly used in mainstream media, and John Locke's primacy of individual autonomy over the common good and Descartes's separation of rationality from emotionality continue to drive political argument and the education of our children.

6. The individual focus of our culture benefits the corporations that sell products to alleviate mental health problems and thus is all part of a culture that privileges money over people.
7. See Lydia Denworth, *Friendship: The Evolution, Biology, and Extraordinary Power of Life's Fundamental Bond* (New York: W. W. Norton, 2020).
8. Bobbi J. Carothers and Harry T. Reis, "Men and Women Are from Earth: Examining the Latent Structure of Gender," *Journal of Personality and Social Psychology* 104, no. 2 (2013): 385–407, doi: 10.1037/a0030437.
9. Lise Eliot, *Pink Brain, Blue Brain: How Small Differences Grow into Troublesome Gaps—and What We Can Do About It* (Boston: Mariner Books, 2010), front flap.
10. Eliot, *Pink Brain, Blue Brain*, 14–15.
11. Minda Belete wrote his senior thesis at NYU Abu Dhabi about the pink tax and first introduced me to the phenomenon. See also "From Cradle to Cane: The Cost of Being a Female Consumer; A Study of Gender Pricing in New York City," New York City Department of Consumer Affairs, December 2015, https://www1.nyc.gov/assets/dca/downloads/pdf/partners/Study-of-Gender-Pricing-in-NYC.pdf; Stephanie Gonzalez Guittar, Liz Grauerholz, Erin N. Kidder, Shameika D. Daye, and Megan McLaughlin, "Beyond the Pink Tax: Gender-Based Pricing and Differentiation of Personal Care Products," *Gender Issues* 39, no. 1 (2022): 1–23, doi: 10.1007/s12147-021-09280-9.
12. Lloyd B. Lueptow, Lori Garovich-Szabo, and Margaret B. Lueptow, "Social Change and the Persistence of Sex Typing: 1974–1997," *Social Forces* 80, no. 1 (2001): 1–36, http://www.jstor.org/stable/2675530.
13. Max Dickins, "When It Comes to Banter, Men Are in Their Element. But That Is No Foundation for Lasting Friendship," *The Guardian*, July 9, 2022, https://www.theguardian.com/lifeandstyle/2022/jul/09/when-it-comes

-to-banter-men-are-in-their-element-but-that-is-no-foundation-for-lasting-friendship.

14. Anna Louie Sussman, "Why Aren't More People Marrying? Ask Women What Dating Is Like," *New York Times*, November 11, 2023, https://www.nytimes.com/ 2023/ 11/ 11/ opinion/ marriage-women-men-dating.html.
15. Kaamil Ahmed, "Nine out of 10 People Are Biased Against Women, Says 'Alarming' UN Report," *The Guardian*, June 12, 2023, https://www.theguardian.com/global-development/2023/jun/12/nine-out-of-10-people-are-biased-against-women-says-alarming-un-report.
16. Alexandra Alter, "How a Debut Graphic Memoir Became the Most Banned Book in the Country," *New York Times*, May 1, 2022, https://www.nytimes.com/2022/05/01/books/maia-kobabe-gender-queer-book-ban.html.
17. William Shakespeare, *Hamlet, Prince of Denmark*, ed. Philip Edwards and Heather Anne Hirschfeld, 3rd ed. (Cambridge: Cambridge University Press, 2019), act 1, scene 2, lines 147–52.
18. Ovid, *The Metamorphoses*, trans. Ian Johnston, 2012, http://johnstoniatexts.x10host.com/ovid/ovid6html.html, book 6, lines 170–73, 201–2.
19. "The Equal Rights Amendment," Richard Nixon Presidential Library and Museum, March 10, 2022, https://www.nixonlibrary.gov/news/equal-rights-amendment.
20. R. Sam Garrett, *The Voting Rights Act: Historical Development and Policy Background*, Congressional Research Service, April 25, 2023, https://sgp.fas.org/crs/misc/R47520.pdf.
21. Daniel McGraw, "Gibson's Bakery v. Oberlin College: A Case on Being Adults, Not Fighting Discrimination," *Ohio Capital Journal*, April 8, 2022, https://ohiocapitaljournal.com/2022/04/08/gibsons-bakery-v-oberlin-a-case-on-being-adults-not-fighting-discrimination/.
22. For a review of the data regarding gender differences, see Cordelia Fine, *Delusions of Gender: How Our Minds, Society, and Neurosexism Create Difference* (New York: W. W. Norton, 2010).
23. Carol Gilligan, *In a Human Voice* (Medford, MA: Polity Press, 2023).
24. Gilligan, *In a Human Voice*, 173.
25. Margaret Beale Spencer, "Privilege and Critical Race Perspectives' Intersectional Contributions to a Systems Theory of Human Development," in Nancy Budwig et al., eds., *New Perspectives on Human Development* (Cambridge: Cambridge University Press, 2017), 287–312; Cynthia García Coll, Gontran Lamberty, Renee Jenkins, et al., "An Integrative Model for

the Study of Developmental Competencies in Minority Children," *Child Development* 67, no. 5 (1996): 1891–914, doi: 10.2307/1131600.

26. Margaret Mead, *Sex and Temperament in Three Primitive Societies* (New York: Harper Perennial, 2001), 30.
27. Mead, *Sex and Temperament*, 33.
28. Niobe Way, Alisha Ali, Carol Gilligan, and Pedro Noguera, eds., *The Crisis of Connection: Roots, Consequences, and Solutions* (New York: New York University Press, 2018), 13.
29. Way et al., eds., *The Crisis of Connection*, 14.
30. Niobe Way, *Deep Secrets: Boys' Friendships and the Crisis of Connection* (Cambridge, MA: Harvard University Press, 2011), 20.
31. Caroline Criado Perez, *Invisible Women: Data Bias in a World Designed for Men* (London: Chatto & Windus, 2019).

Part One: Boys' Nature

1. bell hooks, *The Will to Change: Men, Masculinity, and Love* (New York: Washington Square Press, 2004), 4.

Chapter 1: Human Nature

1. A story told to me by Kimmi Berlin.
2. See Judy Dunn, *The Beginnings of Social Understanding* (Cambridge, MA: Harvard University Press, 2014).
3. "Darwin's Observations on His Children," Darwin Correspondence Project, June 25, 2015, https://www.darwinproject.ac.uk/people/about-darwin/family-life/darwin-s-observations-his-children.
4. "Darwin's Observations on His Children," Darwin Correspondence Project.
5. Judy Y. Chu, *When Boys Become Boys: Development, Relationships, and Masculinity* (New York: New York University Press, 2014).
6. Chu, *When Boys Become Boys*, 187.
7. Chu, *When Boys Become Boys*, 187.
8. Tara Kuther, *Lifespan Development: Lives in Context,* 3rd ed. (Los Angeles: Sage Publications, 2022).
9. Carol Gilligan, *In a Different Voice: Psychological Theory and Women's Development* (Cambridge, MA: Harvard University Press, 1982).
10. John Bowlby, *Maternal Care and Mental Health* (Geneva: World Health Organization, 1951), 13; see also John Bowlby, *Attachment and Loss*, vol. 1,

Attachment (London: Hogarth Press and the Institute of Psycho-Analysis, 1969).

11. James Robertson, *A Two-Year-Old Goes to Hospital,* Robertson Films, 1952, www.robertsonfilms.info/2_year_old.htm.
12. Bruce D. Lindsay, "'A 2-Year-Old Goes to Hospital': A 50th Anniversary Reappraisal of the Impact of James Robertson's Film," *Journal of Child Health Care* 7, no. 1 (2003): 17–26, doi: 10.1177/1367493503007001672.
13. Mary S. Ainsworth and John Bowlby, "An Ethological Approach to Personality Development," *American Psychologist* 46, no. 4 (1991): 333–41, doi: 10.1037/0003-066X.46.4.333.
14. See, for example, Anouk Spruit, Linda Goos, Nikki Weenink, et al., "The Relation Between Attachment and Depression in Children and Adolescents: A Multilevel Meta-Analysis," *Clinical Child and Family Psychology Review* 23, no. 1 (2019): 54–69, doi: 10.1007/s10567-019-00299-9; Jude Cassidy and Phillip R. Shaver, eds., *Handbook of Attachment: Theory, Research, and Clinical Applications,* 2nd ed. (New York: Guilford Press, 2008).
15. David Graeber and David Wengrow, *The Dawn of Everything: A New History of Humanity* (New York: Farrar, Straus and Giroux, 2021).
16. See Inge Bretherton and Kristine A. Munholland, "Internal Working Models in Attachment Relationships: Elaborating a Central Construct in Attachment Theory," in Cassidy and Shaver, eds., *Handbook of Attachment,* 102–27.
17. Bretherton and Munholland, "Internal Working Models in Attachment Relationships"; see also Marlene M. Moretti and Maya Peled, "Adolescent-Parent Attachment: Bonds That Support Healthy Development," *Paediatrics & Child Health* 9, no. 8 (2004): 551–55, doi: 10.1093/pch/9.8.551.
18. See Cassidy and Shaver, eds., *Handbook of Attachment,* 419–35; see also R. Chris Fraley and Phillip R. Shaver, "Adult Romantic Attachment: Theoretical Developments, Emerging Controversies, and Unanswered Questions," *Review of General Psychology* 4, no. 2 (2000): 132–54, doi: 10.1037/1089-2680.4.2.132; Elena Delgado, Cristina Serna, Isabel Martínez, and Edie Cruise, "Parental Attachment and Peer Relationships in Adolescence: A Systematic Review," *International Journal of Environmental Research and Public Health* 19, no. 3 (2022): 1064, doi: 10.3390/ijerph19031064; Joseph P. Allen, "The Attachment System in Adolescence," in Cassidy and Shaver, eds., *Handbook of Attachment,* 419–35; Joseph P. Allen, "Experience, Development, and Resilience: The Legacy of Stuart

Hauser's Explorations of the Transition from Adolescence into Early Adulthood," *Research in Human Development* 7, no. 4 (2010): 241–56, doi: 10.1080/15427609.2010.526516; Joseph P. Allen, Maryfrances Porter, Christy McFarland, et al., "The Relation of Attachment Security to Adolescents' Paternal and Peer Relationships, Depression, and Externalizing Behavior," *Child Development* 78, no. 4 (2007): 1222–39, http://www.jstor.org/stable/4620699.

19. See Beatrice Beebe, Joseph Jaffe, Sara Markese, et al., "The Origins of 12-Month Attachment: A Microanalysis of 4-Month Mother–Infant Interaction," *Attachment & Human Development* 12, no. 1–2 (2010): 3–141, doi: 10.1080/14616730903338985.
20. See *Still Face Experiment—Dr. Edward Tronick*, Zero to Three, 2007, https://www.youtube.com/watch?v=YTTSXc6sARg; "The Research: The Still Face Experiment," Gottman Institute, December 29, 2020, https://www.gottman.com/blog/research-still-face-experiment/; Ed Tronick and Marjorie Beeghly, "Infants' Meaning-Making and the Development of Mental Health Problems," *American Psychologist* 66, no. 2 (2011): 107–19, doi: 10.1037/a0021631.
21. Tracy Dennis-Tiwary, "Screens Are Keeping Us Connected Now—but They're Still Disruptive to In-Person Communication," April 18, 2020, https://www.drtracyphd.com/press/screens-are-keeping-us-connected-now-but-theyre-still-disruptive-to-in-person-communication.
22. Harry Stack Sullivan, *The Interpersonal Theory of Psychiatry* (New York: W. W. Norton, 1953), 245.
23. Sullivan, *The Interpersonal Theory of Psychiatry*, 245.
24. See, for example, Karen A. Hacker, Shakira F. Suglia, Lise E. Fried, et al., "Developmental Differences in Risk Factors for Suicide Attempts Between Ninth and Eleventh Graders," *Suicide and Life-Threatening Behavior* 36, no. 2 (2006): 154–66, doi: 10.1521/suli.2006.36.2.154; Beverley Fehr and Cheryl Harasymchuk, "The Role of Friendships in Well-Being," in James E. Maddux, ed., *Subjective Well-Being and Life Satisfaction* (New York: Routledge/Taylor & Francis Group, 2018), 103–28.
25. Emily L. Loeb, Alida A. Davis, Meghan A. Costello, and Joseph P. Allen, "Autonomy and Relatedness in Early Adolescent Friendships as Predictors of Short- and Long-Term Academic Success," *Social Development* 29, no. 3 (2020): 818–36, doi: 10.1111/sode.12424.
26. Sherry E. Jones, Kathleen A. Ethier, Marci Hertz, et al., "Mental Health, Suicidality, and Connectedness Among High School Students During the

COVID-19 Pandemic—Adolescent Behaviors and Experiences Survey, United States, January–June 2021," *Morbidity and Mortality Weekly Report (MMWR)* 71, no. 3 (2022): 16–21, https://www.cdc.gov/mmwr/volumes/71/su/su7103a3.htm.

27. See Lydia Denworth, *Friendship: The Evolution, Biology, and Extraordinary Power of Life's Fundamental Bond* (New York: W. W. Norton, 2020).
28. George C. Williams, *Adaptation and Natural Selection: A Critique of Some Current Evolutionary Thought* (Princeton, NJ: Princeton University Press, 1966), 94.
29. Yang Claire Yang, Courtney Boen, Karen Gerken, et al., "Social Relationships and Physiological Determinants of Longevity Across the Human Life Span," *Proceedings of the National Academy of Sciences* 113, no. 3 (2016): 578–83, doi: 10.1073/pnas.1511085112.
30. William J. Chopik, "Associations Among Relational Values, Support, Health, and Well-Being Across the Adult Lifespan," *Personal Relationships* 24, no. 2 (2017): 408–22, doi: 10.1111/pere.12187.
31. Simone Schnall, Kent D. Harber, Jeanine K. Stefanucci, and Dennis R. Proffitt, "Social Support and the Perception of Geographical Slant," *Journal of Experimental Social Psychology* 44, no. 5 (2008): 1246–55, doi: 10.1016/j.jesp.2008.04.011.
32. Schnall et al., "Social Support and the Perception of Geographical Slant."
33. Harvard Study of Adult Development, Massachusetts General Hospital & Harvard Medical School, Harvard Second Generation Study, 2015, https://www.adultdevelopmentstudy.org/.
34. Joshua Wolf Shenk, "What Makes Us Happy?," *The Atlantic*, June 2009, www.theatlantic.com/magazine/archive/2009/06/what-makes-us-happy/307439.
35. Roy F. Baumeister and Mark R. Leary, "The Need to Belong: Desire for Interpersonal Attachments as a Fundamental Human Motivation," *Psychological Bulletin* 117, no. 3 (1995): 497–529, doi: 10.1037/0033-2909.117.3.497.
36. Michael Tomasello, *Why We Cooperate* (Cambridge, MA: MIT Press, 2009).
37. Antonio R. Damasio, *The Feeling of What Happens: Body and Emotion in the Making of Consciousness* (New York: Mariner Books, 2000).
38. Matthew D. Lieberman, *Social: Why Our Brains Are Wired to Connect* (New York: Crown, 2013), ix, 5.
39. Lieberman, *Social*, 283.

40. Lieberman, *Social*, 20.
41. Lieberman, *Social*, 65.
42. Frans B. M. de Waal, *The Age of Empathy: Nature's Lessons for a Kinder Society* (New York: Harmony Books, 2009), 5.
43. Waal, *The Age of Empathy*, 48, 60.
44. Sarah Blaffer Hrdy, *Mothers and Others: The Evolutionary Origins of Mutual Understanding* (Cambridge, MA: Belknap Press of Harvard University Press, 2009), 4.
45. Hrdy, *Mothers and Others.*
46. Hrdy, *Mothers and Others*, 14.
47. Hrdy, *Mothers and Others*, 15.
48. Hrdy, *Mothers and Others*, 28.
49. Malcolm Gladwell, *Outliers: The Story of Success* (New York: Penguin Books, 2009).
50. Eric Klinenberg, *Palaces for the People: How Social Infrastructure Can Help Fight Inequality, Polarization, and the Decline of Civic Life* (New York: Crown, 2018), 3.
51. Klinenberg, *Palaces for the People*, 3.
52. Klinenberg, *Palaces for the People*, 3.
53. See Urie Bronfenbrenner, *The Ecology of Human Development: Experiments by Nature and Design* (Cambridge, MA: Harvard University Press, 1979).
54. Bronfenbrenner, *The Ecology of Human Development.*
55. Lyn Mikel Brown and Carol Gilligan, *Meeting at the Crossroads: Women's Psychology and Girls' Development* (Cambridge, MA: Harvard University Press, 1992).
56. Michael Cunningham, Dena Phillips Swanson, Joseph Youngblood, et al., "Spencer's Phenomenological Variant of Ecological Systems Theory (PVEST): Charting Its Origin and Impact," *American Psychologist* 78, no. 4 (2023): 524–34, doi: 10.1037/amp0001051; Margaret Beale Spencer, "Old Issues and New Theorizing for Health, Achievement, Neighborhood, Growth, and About African-American Youth: A Phenomenological Variant of Ecological Systems Theory," in *Black Youth: Perspectives on Their Status in the United States* (1995): 37–69; Margaret Beale Spencer, "Phenomenology and Ecological Systems Theory: Development of Diverse Groups," in William Damon and Richard M. Lerner, eds., *Child and Adolescent Development: An Advanced Course* (Hoboken, NJ: Wiley, 2008), 696–735.

57. Cynthia García Coll, Gontran Lamberty, Renee Jenkins, et al., "An Integrative Model for the Study of Developmental Competencies in Minority Children," *Child Development* 67, no. 5 (1996): 1891–914, doi: 10.2307/1131600.
58. Coll et al., "An Integrative Model for the Study of Developmental Competencies in Minority Children," 1901.
59. Richard V. Reeves, *Of Boys and Men: Why the Modern Male Is Struggling, Why It Matters, and What to Do About It* (Washington, DC: Brookings Institution Press, 2022).
60. John Gray, *Men Are from Mars, Women Are from Venus: The Classic Guide to Understanding the Opposite Sex* (New York: HarperCollins, 2004).
61. Philippa Perry, "I've Fallen Out with All My Friends and Colleagues—Why?," *The Guardian*, November 26, 2023, https://www.theguardian.com/lifeandstyle/2023/nov/26/i-have-fallen-out-with-friends-and-colleagues-why-philippa-perry; Anna Louie Sussman, "Why Aren't More People Marrying? Ask Women What Dating Is Like," *New York Times*, November 11, 2023, https://www.nytimes.com/2023/11/11/opinion/marriage-women-men-dating.html.

Chapter 2: Boys' Friendships

1. This chapter draws extensively from my book *Deep Secrets: Boys' Friendships and the Crisis of Connection* (Cambridge, MA: Harvard University Press, 2011).
2. All the names of the boys in my studies are pseudonyms in this chapter.
3. Way, *Deep Secrets*, 2.
4. Way, *Deep Secrets*, 97.

Chapter 3: The Story of Nick

1. All the quotes from Nick and some of my prose in this chapter are drawn from my book *Deep Secrets: Boys' Friendships and the Crisis of Connection* (Cambridge, MA: Harvard University Press, 2011), 112–80.

Chapter 4: Adherence

1. This chapter draws extensively from Niobe Way, Jessica Cressen, Samuel Bodian, et al., "'It Might Be Nice to Be a Girl . . . Then You Wouldn't Have to Be Emotionless': Boys' Resistance to Norms of Masculinity During Adolescence," *Psychology of Men & Masculinity* 15, no. 3 (2014): 241–52,

https://doi.org/10.1037/a0037262; and from my book *Deep Secrets: Boys' Friendships and the Crisis of Connection* (Cambridge, MA: Harvard University Press, 2011).

2. Kate Stone Lombardi, *The Mama's Boy Myth: Why Keeping Our Sons Close Makes Them Stronger* (New York: Avery, 2012).
3. Thank you to Albina Uvasheva for this insight.
4. See Jeff Wetzler, *Ask: Tap Into the Hidden Wisdom of People Around You for Unexpected Breakthroughs in Leadership and Life* (New York: Hachette Go, 2024); Jinjoo Han, Niobe Way, Hirokazu Yoshikawa, and Crystal Clarke, "Interpersonal Curiosity and Its Association with Social and Emotional Skills and Well-Being During Adolescence," *Journal of Adolescent Research* (April 7, 2023), doi: 10.1177/07435584231162572; Jinjoo Han, Niobe Way, and Hirokazu Yoshikawa, "Addressing the Crisis of Connection in Middle Schools: The Listening Project," forthcoming.
5. Anne-Laure Le Cunff, "The Science of Curiosity: Why We Keep Asking 'Why,'" Ness Labs, https://nesslabs.com/science-of-curiosity.
6. See Joseph A. Durlak, Roger P. Weissberg, Allison B. Dymnicki, et al., "The Impact of Enhancing Students' Social and Emotional Learning: A Meta-Analysis of School-Based Universal Interventions," *Child Development* 82, no. 1 (2011): 405–32, doi: 10.1111/j.1467-8624.2010.01564.x; Susanne A. Denham, "Emotional Competence During Childhood and Adolescence," in Vanessa LoBue, Koraly Pérez-Edgar, and Kristin A. Buss, eds., *Handbook of Emotional Development* (Cham, Switzerland: Springer, 2019), 493–541; Christiana Cipriano, Michael J. Strambler, Lauren Hunter Naples, et al., "The State of Evidence for Social and Emotional Learning: A Contemporary Meta-Analysis of Universal School-Based SEL Interventions," *Child Development* 94, no. 5 (2023): 1181–204, doi: 10.1111/cdev.13968.
7. Richard V. Reeves and Ember Smith, "The Male College Crisis Is Not Just in Enrollment, but Completion," Brookings, October 8, 2021, https://www.brookings.edu/blog/up-front/2021/10/08/the-male-college-crisis-is-not-just-in-enrollment-but-completion/.
8. "Number and Percentage Distribution of Spring 2002 High School Sophomores, by Highest Level of Education Completed, and Socioeconomic Status and Selected Student Characteristics While in High School: 2013," National Center for Education Statistics (NCES), June 2016, https://nces.ed.gov/programs/digest/d20/tables/dt20_104.91.asp.

9. See Jeanna Smialek, "What Social Trends Taught Us About the 2023 Economy," *New York Times,* December 20, 2023, https://www.nytimes.com/2023/12/20/business/economy/social-trends-2023-economy.html?unlocked_article_code=1.Ik0.FIDT.3gFHQc0dmCRm&smid=url-share.
10. Joel Mittleman, "Intersecting the Academic Gender Gap: The Education of Lesbian, Gay, and Bisexual America," *American Sociological Review* 87, no. 2 (2022): 303–35, doi: 10.1177/00031224221075776.
11. Joel Mittleman, "What Gay Men's Stunning Success Might Teach Us About the Academic Gender Gap," *Washington Post,* February 24, 2022, www.washingtonpost.com/opinions/2022/02/24/gay-men-academic-success-gender-gap-lessons.
12. Mittleman, "What Gay Men's Stunning Success Might Teach Us About the Academic Gender Gap."
13. Mittleman, "What Gay Men's Stunning Success Might Teach Us About the Academic Gender Gap."
14. "Lionel Trilling," Contemporary Thinkers: Lionel Trilling, September 2, 2015, https://contemporarythinkers.org/lionel-trilling/; see also Lionel Trilling, *The Liberal Imagination: Essays on Literature and Society* (New York: Viking, 1950), 286.
15. Robert N. Bellah et al., "Democracy in America Today: Preface to the 2007 Edition of 'Habits of the Heart,'" *Sociology of Religion* 68, no. 2 (2007): 213–17, http://www.jstor.org/stable/20453148.
16. Robert N. Bellah et al., *Habits of the Heart: Individualism and Commitment in American Life; With a New Preface* (Berkeley: University of California Press, 2008), 147.
17. Bellah et al., *Habits of the Heart,* 144–47.
18. Bellah et al., *Habits of the Heart,* 146.
19. Bellah et al., *Habits of the Heart,* 17.
20. Bellah et al., *Habits of the Heart,* 19.
21. Bellah et al., *Habits of the Heart,* 20.
22. Richard G. Wilkinson and Kate Pickett, *The Spirit Level: Why Greater Equality Makes Societies Stronger* (New York: Bloomsbury, 2010), 40.
23. See Niobe Way, Alisha Ali, Carol Gilligan, and Pedro Noguera, eds., *The Crisis of Connection: Roots, Consequences, and Solutions* (New York: New York University Press, 2018).
24. It is also a culture that has a game called "Fuck, Marry, or Kill," in which players are given a list of people and the player has to indicate which

one they want to do with that person (see "Fuck, Marry, Kill," Wikipedia, July 20, 2023, https://en.wikipedia.org/wiki/Fuck,_marry,_kill). It is more often played by men referring to women than by women referring to men.

25. See, for example, David Thomas, *Raising Emotionally Strong Boys: Tools Your Son Can Build On for Life* (Minneapolis: Bethany House Publishers, 2022); Michael Reichert and Richard Hawley, *I Can Learn from You: Boys as Relational Learners* (Cambridge, MA: Harvard Education Press, 2014); Michael Reichert, *How to Raise a Boy: The Power of Connection to Build Good Men* (New York: TarcherPerigee, 2019); Judy Y. Chu, *When Boys Become Boys: Development, Relationships, and Masculinity* (New York: New York University Press, 2014); William Pollack, *Real Boys: Rescuing Our Sons from the Myths of Boyhood* (New York: Henry Holt, 1999); Pedro Noguera, *The Trouble with Black Boys: . . . And Other Reflections on Race, Equity, and the Future of Public Education* (San Francisco: Jossey-Bass, 2008); Warren Farrell and John Gray, *The Boy Crisis: Why Our Boys Are Struggling and What We Can Do About It* (Dallas: BenBella Books, 2018); Michael S. Kimmel, *Guyland: The Perilous World Where Boys Become Men* (New York: Harper Perennial, 2009); Laura Griffin, Warwick Hosking, Peter Richard Gill, et al., "The Gender Paradox: Understanding the Role of Masculinity in Suicidal Ideation," *American Journal of Men's Health* 16, no. 5 (2022), doi: 10.1177/15579883221123853; Y. Joel Wong, Jesse Owen, and Munyi Shea, "A Latent Class Regression Analysis of Men's Conformity to Masculine Norms and Psychological Distress," *Journal of Counseling Psychology* 59, no. 1 (2012): 176–83, doi: 10.1037/a0026206.
26. Kimmel, *Guyland*, 462.
27. James Gilligan, *Violence: Reflections on a National Epidemic* (New York: Vintage Books, 1997).
28. Pollack, *Real Boys*, 3.
29. Pollack, *Real Boys*, 3.
30. Michael C. Reichert and Joseph D. Nelson, "I Want to Learn from You: Relational Strategies to Engage Boys in School," in Way et al., eds., *The Crisis of Connection*, 344–58.
31. Margaret E. Greene, Brian Heilman, Gary Barker, and Taveeshi Gupta, *International Men & Gender Equality Survey (Images): A Global Report in 15 Headlines* (New York: UNFPA, 2022).
32. See Mark C. Greene, *Remaking Manhood: The Battle Against Dominance-Based Masculine Culture: Collected Writings from the Healthy Masculinity*

Movement 2017–2023 (New York: ThinkPlay Partners, 2023); Howard C. Stevenson, "Boys in Men's Clothing: Racial Socialization and Neighborhood Safety as Buffers to Hypervulnerability in African American Adolescent Males," in Niobe Way and Judy Y. Chu, eds., *Adolescent Boys: Exploring Diverse Cultures of Boyhood* (New York: New York University Press, 2004), 59–77. See also *Ever Forward,* an organization founded by Ashanti Branch that "mentors underserved youth in middle and high school by providing them with safe, brave communities that build character and transform lives." More information can be found on their website: https://everforwardclub.org/#everforward-overview. Also check out Brothers, founded by Kim Evensen to educate about "the importance of male friendships and the positive effects arising from strong male relationships," at https://www.wearebrothers.org/kim-evensen/.

33. See Mark C. Greene, *The Little #MeToo Book for Men* (New York: ThinkPlay Partners, 2018); Saliha Bava and Mark Greene, *The Relational Book for Parenting: Raising Children to Connect, Collaborate, and Innovate by Growing Our Families' Relationship Superpowers* (New York: ThinkPlay Partners, 2018), and Greene, *Remaking Manhood.*
34. bell hooks, *The Will to Change: Men, Masculinity, and Love* (New York: Washington Square Press, 2004), 12.
35. See Taveeshi Gupta, Niobe Way, Rebecca K. McGill, et al., "Gender-Typed Behaviors in Friendships and Well-Being: A Cross-Cultural Study of Chinese and American Boys," *Journal of Research on Adolescence* 23, no. 1 (2013): 57–68, doi: 10.1111/j.1532-7795.2012.00824.x; James M. O'Neil, "The Psychology of Men," in Elizabeth Altmaier and Jo-Ida Hansen, eds., *The Oxford Handbook of Counseling Psychology* (New York: Oxford University Press, 2012), 375–408.
36. See Judy Chu, Michelle V. Porche, and Deborah L. Tolman, "The Adolescent Masculinity Ideology in Relationships Scale: Development and Validation of a New Measure for Boys," *Men and Masculinities* 8, no. 1 (2005): 93–115, doi: 10.1177/1097184X03257453; Michael Cunningham and Leah Newkirk Meunier, "The Influence of Peer Experiences on Bravado Attitudes Among African American Males," in Way and Chu, eds., *Adolescent Boys,* 219–27; Joseph H. Pleck, Freya L. Sonenstein, and Leighton C. Ku, "Masculinity Ideology: Its Impact on Adolescent Males' Heterosexual Relationships," *Journal of Social Issues* 49, no. 3 (1993): 11–29, doi: 10.1111/j.1540-4560.1993.tb01166.x.

37. See Adam A. Rogers, Kimberly A. Updegraff, Carlos E. Santos, and Carol Lynn Martin, "Masculinity and School Adjustment in Middle School," *Psychology of Men & Masculinity* 18, no. 1 (2017): 50–61, doi: 10.1037/men0000041; Carlos E. Santos, Kathrine Galligan, Erin Pahlke, and Richard A. Fabes, "Gender-Typed Behaviors, Achievement, and Adjustment Among Racially and Ethnically Diverse Boys During Early Adolescence," *American Journal of Orthopsychiatry* 83, nos. 2–3 (2013): 252–64, doi: 10.1111/ajop.12036.
38. Y. Joel Wong, Moon-Ho Ringo Ho, Shu-Yi Wang, and I. S. Keino Miller, "Meta-analyses of the Relationship Between Conformity to Masculine Norms and Mental Health-Related Outcomes," *Journal of Counseling Psychology* 64, no. 1 (2017): 80–93, doi: 10.1037/cou0000176.
39. Wilkinson and Pickett, *The Spirit Level.*
40. Niobe Way, *Deep Secrets: Boys' Friendships and the Crisis of Connection* (Cambridge, MA: Harvard University Press, 2011), 113.
41. Elysia Choi, "Understanding Racial/Ethnic Joking and Its Relations to Developmental Outcomes in Youth of Color," PhD dissertation, New York University, 2023.
42. Way et al., eds., *The Crisis of Connection*, 66–67.
43. C. J. Pascoe, *Dude, You're a Fag: Masculinity and Sexuality in High School* (Berkeley: University of California Press, 2007), 23.
44. See Jean Anyon, "Intersections of Gender and Class: Accommodation and Resistance by Working-Class and Affluent Females to Contradictory Sex Role Ideologies," *Journal of Education* 166, no. 1 (1984): 25–48, https://www.jstor.org/stable/42742035; Lyn Mikel Brown and Carol Gilligan, *Meeting at the Crossroads: Women's Psychology and Girls' Development* (Cambridge, MA: Harvard University Press, 1992); Carol Gilligan, *Joining the Resistance* (Malden, MA: Polity Press, 2011); May Ling Halim, Diane N. Ruble, and David M. Amodio, "From Pink Frilly Dresses to 'One of the Boys': A Social-Cognitive Analysis of Gender Identity Development and Gender Bias," *Social and Personality Psychology Compass* 5, no. 11 (2011): 933–49, doi: 10.1111/j.1751-9004.2011.00399.x; Heather A. Priess, Sara M. Lindberg, and Janet Shibley Hyde, "Adolescent Gender-Role Identity and Mental Health: Gender Intensification Revisited," *Child Development* 80, no. 5 (2009): 1531–44, doi: 10.1111/j.1467-8624.2009.01349.x.
45. Those who study shifting gender patterns in China contend that this new "masculine woman" has become a role model for young girls and women, and a marker of success. While China has a long tradition of a softer

version of masculinity (i.e., the "wen" 文 in Confucianism), it is now a country that focuses only on the harder version (i.e., the "wu" 武 in Confucianism), with schools across China encouraging boys to "man up" in a distinctly American way. In an article on how the Chinese government is imposing a "man up" campaign to encourage "traditional" masculinity, the journalist describes the traumatic experiences of an eleven-year-old boy who was made fun of by his peers for being too "girlie" and for having a high-pitched voice. (See Zixu Wang, Xin Chen, and Caroline Radnofsky, "China Proposes Teaching Masculinity to Boys as State Is Alarmed by Changing Gender Roles," NBC News, March 5, 2021, https://www.nbcnews.com/news/world/china-proposes-teaching-masculinity-boys-state-alarmed-changing-gender-roles-n1258939.) Such gender-based bullying among boys and young men is a recent phenomenon in China. China's Education Ministry plans to "cultivate masculinity" in boys by hiring and training more gym teachers and testing students in physical education. (See Li Pei, "Letter on the Reply to the Proposal No. 4404 [No. 410 for Education] of the Third Meeting of the 13th National Committee of the Chinese People's Political Consultative Conference [Translated from Mandarin]," 中华人民共和国教育部 [Ministry of Education of the People's Republic of China], 2020, http://www.moe.gov.cn/jyb_xxgk/xxgk_jyta/jyta_jiaoshisi/202101/t20210128_511584.html.)

46. Way, *Deep Secrets*, 273–74.
47. Way, *Deep Secrets*, 275.

Chapter 5: Resistance

1. This chapter draws extensively from Niobe Way, Jessica Cressen, Samuel Bodian, et al., "'It Might Be Nice to Be a Girl . . . Then You Wouldn't Have to Be Emotionless': Boys' Resistance to Norms of Masculinity During Adolescence," *Psychology of Men & Masculinity* 15, no. 3 (2014): 241–52, doi: 10.1037/a0037262; and from my book *Deep Secrets: Boys' Friendships and the Crisis of Connection* (Cambridge, MA: Harvard University Press, 2011).
2. Andrew P. Smiler, "'I Wanted to Get to Know Her Better': Adolescent Boys' Dating Motives, Masculinity Ideology, and Sexual Behavior," *Journal of Adolescence* 31, no. 1 (2008): 17–32, doi: 10.1016/j.adolescence.2007.03.006.
3. Amy T. Schalet, *Not Under My Roof: Parents, Teens, and the Culture of Sex* (Chicago: University of Chicago Press, 2011).

4. Judy Y. Chu, *When Boys Become Boys: Development, Relationships, and Masculinity* (New York: New York University Press, 2014); see also Judy Chu, Michelle V. Porche, and Deborah L. Tolman, "The Adolescent Masculinity Ideology in Relationships Scale: Development and Validation of a New Measure for Boys," *Men and Masculinities* 8, no. 1 (2005): 93–115, doi: 10.1177/1097184X03257453.
5. Chu, *When Boys Become Boys*, 33.
6. Way, et al., "'It Might Be Nice to Be a Girl,'" 241–52.
7. Leoandra Onnie Rogers, "The 'Black Box': Identity Development and the Crisis of Connection Among Black Adolescent Boys," in Niobe Way, Alisha Ali, Carol Gilligan, and Pedro Noguera, eds., *The Crisis of Connection: Roots, Consequences, and Solutions* (New York: New York University Press, 2018), 129–43.
8. All the names of the students in this paragraph are pseudonyms.
9. All the names of the students in this paragraph are pseudonyms.
10. All the names of the students in this paragraph are pseudonyms.
11. See, for example, Chu, Porche, and Tolman, "The Adolescent Masculinity Ideology in Relationships Scale"; William S. Pollack, *Real Boys: Rescuing Our Sons from the Myths of Boyhood* (New York: Henry Holt, 1999); Way et al., " 'It Might Be Nice to Be a Girl,'"; Y. Joel Wong, Moon-Ho Ringo Ho, Shu-Yi Wang, and I. S. Keino Miller, "Meta-analyses of the Relationship Between Conformity to Masculine Norms and Mental Health-Related Outcomes," *Journal of Counseling Psychology* 64, no. 1 (2017): 80–93, doi: 10.1037/cou0000176; James R. Mahalik, Benjamin D. Locke, Larry H. Ludlow, et al., "Development of the Conformity to Masculine Norms Inventory," *Psychology of Men & Masculinity* 4, no. 1 (2003): 3–25, doi: 10.1037/1524-9220.4.1.3.
12. Carlos Santos, "The Missing Story: Resistance to Ideals of Masculinity in the Friendships of Middle School Boys," PhD dissertation, New York University, 2010.
13. Taveeshi Gupta, Niobe Way, Rebecca K. McGill, et al., "Gender-Typed Behaviors in Friendships and Well-Being: A Cross-Cultural Study of Chinese and American Boys," *Journal of Research on Adolescence* 23, no. 1 (2013): 57–68, doi: 10.1111/j.1532-7795.2012.00824.x.
14. See Leoandra Onnie Rogers, Rui Yang, Niobe Way, Sharon L. Weinberg, and Anna Bennet, "'We're Supposed to Look like Girls, but Act like Boys': Adolescent Girls' Adherence to Masculinity Norms," *Journal of Research on Adolescence* 30, no. S1 (2020): 270–85, doi: 10.1111/jora.12475.

Chapter 6: The Story of Danny

1. All the quotes in this chapter and some of the prose are drawn from my book *Deep Secrets: Boys' Friendships and the Crisis of Connection* (Cambridge, MA: Harvard University Press, 2011), 106, 143, 184, 229–61.

Part Three: The Nature/Culture Clash

1. Judith Herman, "Complex PTSD: A Syndrome in Survivors of Prolonged and Repeated Trauma," *Journal of Traumatic Stress* 5 (1992): 377–91, doi: 10.1002/jts.2490050305.

Chapter 7: Suicide

1. *Youth Risk Behavior Survey—Data Summary & Trends Report 2009–2019,* Centers for Disease Control and Prevention, 2019, https://www.cdc.gov/healthyyouth/data/yrbs/pdf/YRBSDataSummaryTrendsReport2019-508.pdf. Accessed March 25, 2022.
2. Jan Hoffman, "Young Adults Report Rising Levels of Anxiety and Depression in Pandemic," *New York Times,* August 13, 2020, https://www.nytimes.com/2020/08/13/health/Covid-mental-health-anxiety.html.
3. Jean M. Twenge, "The Age of Anxiety? The Birth Cohort Change in Anxiety and Neuroticism, 1952–1993," *Journal of Personality and Social Psychology* 79, no. 6 (2000): 1007–21, doi: 10.1037/0022-3514.79.6.1007.
4. Erika Edwards, "All Adults Under 65 Should Be Screened for Anxiety, Health Panel Says," NBC News, June 20, 2023, https://www.nbcnews.com/health/health-news/anxiety-screening-recommended-adults-65-panel-says-rcna89803.
5. Loneliness affects not only our minds but also our bodies. A heightened emotional state of always feeling on guard leads us to make unhealthy life choices that lead to hypertension, cardiovascular disease, memory impairment, and difficulty regulating emotions. When a lonely person experiences stress, cholesterol levels rise faster than in a non-lonely one, as does blood pressure. High levels of cortisol also flood the lonely body, creating a fight-or-flight reaction that makes us feel as if we are under physical attack. The effects on the body include chronic inflammation, high blood pressure, high cholesterol, heart disease, stroke, arthritis, Alzheimer's disease, and cancer. Psychologist Julianne Holt-Lunstad's meta-analysis of 148 studies on 308,000 people found that those with weak social relationships had a 50 percent decreased likelihood of survival than those with strong ones. See Julianne Holt-Lunstad, Timothy B. Smith,

and J. Bradley Layton, "Social Relationships and Mortality Risk: A Meta-analytic Review," *PLoS Medicine* 7, no. 7 (2010): e1000316, doi:10.1371/journal.pmed.1000316.

6. "Loneliness Is at Epidemic Levels in America," Cigna Newsroom, 2020, https://newsroom.thecignagroup.com/loneliness-in-america.
7. Vivek H. Murthy, *Our Epidemic of Loneliness and Isolation: The U.S. Surgeon General's Advisory on the Healing Effects of Social Connection and Community*, Office of the U.S. Surgeon General, 2023, https://www.hhs.gov/sites/default/files/surgeon-general-social-connection-advisory.pdf.
8. Sally C. Curtin, "State Suicide Rates Among Adolescents and Young Adults Aged 10–24: United States, 2000–2018," *National Vital Statistics Reports* 69, no. 11 (September 11, 2020), https://doi.org/https://www.cdc.gov/nchs/data/nvsr/nvsr69/nvsr-69-11-508.pdf.
9. Niobe Way, Rick Weissbourd, and Marc Brackett, "The Pandemic Is Fueling a Crisis of Connection. The Next Surgeon General Should Tackle Both," *The Hill*, February 9, 2021, https://thehill.com/changing-america/opinion/537996-the-pandemic-is-fueling-a-crisis-of-connection-in-the-us-the-next/.
10. Yuval Noah Harari, *Homo Deus: A Brief History of Tomorrow* (New York: Harper, 2017), 33.
11. Terry Gross, "After His Son's Suicide and the Jan. 6 Attack, Rep. Jamie Raskin Is Not Giving Up," *Fresh Air*, NPR, January 4, 2022, https://www.npr.org/2022/01/04/1070032923/jamie-raskin-jan-6-capitol-unthinkable.
12. Gross, "After His Son's Suicide and the Jan. 6 Attack, Rep. Jamie Raskin Is Not Giving Up."
13. Thank you, Maya, for sharing your thoughts about your beloved brother.
14. Will H. Moore, "Punched Out," *Will Opines*, April 19, 2017, https://willopines.wordpress.com/2017/04/19/punched-out/.
15. Christian Wickert, "Concept of Anomie (Durkheim)," *SozTheo*, April 12, 2022, https://www.soztheo.de/theories-of-crime/anomie-strain-theories/concept-of-anomie-durkheim/?lang=en.

Chapter 8: Mass Violence

1. A pseudonym was used for each mass shooter described in this chapter. The reason I chose to provide a pseudonym for each mass shooter, even the well-known ones, is to keep the focus on understanding their acts of violence, not on raising their stature in a culture that fetishizes violence by naming the perpetrators.

2. Megan Garvey, "Transcript of the Disturbing Video 'Elliot Rodger's Retribution,'" *Los Angeles Times*, May 24, 2014, www.latimes.com/local/lanow/la-me-ln-transcript-ucsb-shootings-video-20140524-story.html.
3. Audra D. S. Burch, Patricia Mazzei, and Jack Healy, "A 'Mass Shooting Generation' Cries Out for Change," *New York Times*, February 16, 2018, www.nytimes.com/2018/02/16/us/columbine-mass-shootings.html.
4. Mary Kekatos, "As US Reels from Multiple Mass Shootings in California, Can Loneliness Be a Trigger for Violence?," ABC News, January 26, 2023, https://abcnews.go.com/Health/us-reels-multiple-mass-shootings-loneliness-trigger-violence/story?id=96632046.
5. Scott Weich, Paul Bebbington, Dheeraj Rai, et al., "The Population Impact of Common Mental Disorders and Long-Term Physical Conditions on Disability and Hospital Admission," *Psychological Medicine* 43, no. 5 (2013): 921–31, doi: 10.1017/S0033291712001705.
6. Duane M. Rumbaugh, "The Psychology of Harry F. Harlow: A Bridge from Radical to Rational Behaviorism," *Philosophical Psychology* 10, no. 2 (1997): 197–210, doi: 10.1080/09515089708573215.
7. Stephen J. Suomi, "Touch and the Immune System in Rhesus Monkeys," in Tiffany M. Field, ed., *Touch in Early Development* (London: Psychology Press, 1995).
8. Harry F. Harlow, "The Nature of Love," address to the sixty-sixth annual convention of the American Psychological Association, Washington, D.C., August 31, 1958, *Classics in the History of Psychology,* Christopher D. Green, York University, Toronto, March 2000, http://psychclassics.yorku.ca/Harlow/love.htm.
9. Harry F. Harlow, R. O. Dodsworth, and M. K. Harlow, "Total Social Isolation in Monkeys," *Proceedings of the National Academy of Sciences* 54, no. 1 (1965): 90–97, doi: 10.1073/pnas.54.1.90.
10. Graziano Pinna, Erbo Dong, Kinzo Matsumoto, et al., "In Socially Isolated Mice, the Reversal of Brain Allopregnanolone Down-Regulation Mediates the Anti-aggressive Action of Fluoxetine," *Proceedings of the National Academy of Sciences* 100, no. 4 (2003): 2035–40, doi: 10.1073/pnas.0337642100; Noreena Hertz, *The Lonely Century: How to Restore Human Connection in a World That's Pulling Apart* (New York: Currency, 2021); James V. P. Check, Daniel Perlman, and Neil M. Malamuth, "Loneliness and Aggressive Behaviour," *Journal of Social and Personal Relationships* 2, no. 3 (1985): 243–52, doi: 10.1177/0265407585023001; see also Willem H. J.

Martens and George B. Palermo, "Loneliness and Associated Violent Antisocial Behavior: Analysis of the Case Reports of Jeffrey Dahmer and Dennis Nilsen," *International Journal of Offender Therapy and Comparative Criminology* 49, no. 3 (2005): 298–307, doi: 10.1177/0306624x05274898.

11. Check, Perlman, and Malamuth, "Loneliness and Aggressive Behaviour."
12. Margaret K. Cooke and Jeffrey H. Goldstein, "Social Isolation and Violent Behavior," *Forensic Reports* 2, no. 4 (1989): 287–94.
13. Matthew Lysiak, *Newtown: An American Tragedy* (New York: Gallery Books, 2013), 217; see also Kekatos, "As US Reels from Multiple Mass Shootings in California, Can Loneliness Be a Trigger for Violence?"
14. C. Nathan DeWall, Jean M. Twenge, Seth A. Gitter, and Roy F. Baumeister, "It's the Thought That Counts: The Role of Hostile Cognition in Shaping Aggressive Responses to Social Exclusion," *Journal of Personality and Social Psychology* 96, no. 1 (2009): 45–59, doi: 10.1037/a0013196.
15. See Fjolla Arifi, "5 Signs You're in a Constant State of 'Fight or Flight,'" *HuffPost,* June 26, 2023, https://www.huffpost.com/entry/signs-fight-or-flight-mode_l_649307a2e4b06123d83171b4.
16. Amy P. Cohen, Deborah Azrael, and Matthew Miller, "Rate of Mass Shootings Has Tripled Since 2011, New Research from Harvard Shows," *Mother Jones,* October 15, 2014, www.motherjones.com/politics/2014/10/mass-shootings-increasing-harvard-research; see also German Lopez, "America's Gun Problem," *New York Times,* May 26, 2022, https://www.nytimes.com/2022/05/26/briefing/guns-america-shooting-deaths.html.
17. Gun Violence Archive, www.gunviolencearchive.org/past-tolls; see also Larry Buchanan and Lauren Leatherby, "Who Stops a 'Bad Guy with a Gun'?," *New York Times,* June 22, 2022, https://www.nytimes.com/interactive/2022/06/22/us/shootings-police-response-uvalde-buffalo.html.
18. Saeed Ahmed, "America Has Seen at Least 601 Mass Shootings So Far in 2022," NPR, November 20, 2022, www.npr.org/2022/05/15/1099008586/mass-shootings-us-2022-tally-number; see also Adam Housley et al., "Las Vegas Shooting: At Least 59 Dead in Massacre Trump Calls 'Act of Pure Evil,'" Fox News, October 2, 2017, https://www.foxnews.com/us/las-vegas-shooting-at-least-59-dead-in-massacre-trump-calls-act-of-pure-evil.
19. Thank you to Ann Morning for this insight.
20. Brian Whitney, ed., *Exit Plan: The Writings of Mass Shooters* (Two Fools Press, 2021), 6.
21. Michael S. Kimmel, *Angry White Men: American Masculinity at the End of an Era* (New York: Nation Books, 2017).

22. Bill Chappell, "The Tsarnaev Brothers: What We Know About the Boston Bombing Suspects," NPR, April 20, 2013, https://www.npr.org/sections/thetwo-way/2013/04/20/178112198/the-tsarnaev-brothers-what-we-know-about-the-boston-bombing-suspects.
23. Hannah Arendt, *The Origins of Totalitarianism* (New York: Harcourt Brace Jovanovich, 1973), 475.
24. Whitney, ed., *Exit Plan: The Writings of Mass Shooters.*
25. Research underscores that introverts and socially awkward people, including those on the spectrum, want meaningful friendships as much as all other humans. See Catherine Pearson, "9 Ways to Improve Your Relationships in 2024," *New York Times,* December 28, 2023, https://www.nytimes.com/2023/12/28/well/family/family-relationships-dating-mindfulness-sex.html.
26. Carol Marbin Miller and Kyra Gurney, "Parkland Shooter Always in Trouble, Never Expelled. Could School System Have Done More?," *Miami Herald,* February 20, 2018, https://www.miamiherald.com/news/local/article201216104.html.
27. "Emotional or Behavioral Disability," *Wikipedia,* accessed July 23, 2022, https://en.wikipedia.org/wiki/Emotional_or_behavioral_disability.
28. See Kyra Gurney et al., "'Many' Dead, Former Student in Custody After School Shooting at Stoneman Douglas High in Broward," *Miami Herald,* February 14, 2018 (archived from the original on February 14, 2018), https://web.archive.org/web/20180214223127/http://www.miamiherald.com/news/local/education/article200094039.html; Kelli Kennedy, "Here's What We Know About Nikolas Cruz, the Florida School Shooting Suspect," Boston.com, February 14, 2018, https://www.boston.com/news/national-news/2018/02/14/nikolas-cruz-parkland-florida-school-shooting-suspect/; Lisa de Moraes, "Sen. Bill Nelson: Florida School Shooter Wore Gas Mask, Launched Smoke Grenades, Pulled Fire Alarm—Update," *Deadline,* February 14, 2018, https://deadline.com/2018/02/parkland-florida-high-school-shooting-gunman-tv-networks-video-1202288652/.
29. Thank you, Ann Morning, for this insight.
30. Peter Langman, "Two Notes by Evan Ramsey," SchoolShooters.info—Resources on School Shootings, Perpetrators, and Prevention, October 16, 2015, https://schoolshooters.info/sites/default/files/ramsey_notes_1.0.pdf.
31. "Facebook Post by Chardon Ohio High School Shooting Suspect T. J. Lane," *Daily Beast,* April 24, 2017, https://www.thedailybeast.com/facebook-post-by-chardon-ohio-high-school-shooting-suspect-tj-lane.

32. Peter Langman, compiler, "Luke Woodham's Writings," SchoolShooters .info—Resources on School Shootings, Perpetrators, and Prevention, June 27, 2016, https://schoolshooters.info/sites/default/files/woodham_writings _1.0.pdf.
33. Valery Fabrikant, "Am I Sorry?," SchoolShooters.info—Resources on School Shootings, Perpetrators, and Prevention, 2002, https:// schoolshooters.info/sites/default/files/Fabrikant_Am_I_Sorry.pdf.
34. Peter Langman, compiler, "Themes in the Writings of Eric Harris," School Shooters.info—Resources on School Shootings, Perpetrators, and Prevention, November 14, 2014, https://schoolshooters.info/sites/default /files/harris_themes_1.6.pdf.
35. Cultofdreams, "Bastian Bosse's Suicide Note," Tumblr, March 27, 2018, cultofdreams.tumblr.com/post/172317671296/russiaoniichan-bastian -bosse-s-suicide-note-on/amp.
36. Jonathan Shay, *Achilles in Vietnam: Combat Trauma and the Undoing of Character* (New York: Simon & Schuster, 1995), 3.
37. Shay, *Achilles in Vietnam*, xiii.
38. Shay, *Achilles in Vietnam*, xx.
39. Shay, *Achilles in Vietnam*, xx.
40. Shay, *Achilles in Vietnam*, xx–xxi.
41. Shay, *Achilles in Vietnam*, 21.
42. Shay, *Achilles in Vietnam*, 21.
43. Shay, *Achilles in Vietnam*, 23.
44. Elliot Rodger, "My Twisted World: The Story of Elliot Rodger," DocumentCloud, 2014, https://s3.documentcloud.org/documents/1173808 /elliot-rodger-manifesto.pdf, 135.
45. Shay, *Achilles in Vietnam*, 178.
46. Shay, *Achilles in Vietnam*, xxi.
47. Shay, *Achilles in Vietnam*, 79.
48. Shay, *Achilles in Vietnam*, 79.
49. Shay, *Achilles in Vietnam*, 6.
50. Shay, *Achilles in Vietnam*, 4.

Chapter 9: The Story of Troy

1. This is a pseudonym of a mass shooter.
2. Elliot Rodger, "My Twisted World: The Story of Elliot Rodger," DocumentCloud, 2014, https://s3.documentcloud.org/documents/1173808

/elliot-rodger-manifesto.pdf. Page numbers in the text refer to the page in the online manifesto.

3. Jonathan Shay, *Achilles in Vietnam: Combat Trauma and the Undoing of Character* (New York: Simon & Schuster, 1995).
4. bell hooks, *The Will to Change: Men, Masculinity, and Love* (New York: Washington Square Press, 2004), 139–140.

Part Four: Solutions

1. Benedictus de Spinoza, *Spinoza: Ethics,* trans. W. H. White (Ware, Hertfordshire, UK: Wordsworth Editions, 2001), 131.

Chapter 10: Joining Their Cause

1. See Michelle M. Chouinard, P. L. Harris, and Michael P. Maratsos, "Children's Questions: A Mechanism for Cognitive Development," *Monographs of the Society for Research in Child Development* 72, no. 1 (2007), doi: 10.1111/j.1540-5834.2007.00412.x; and Jamie Jirout, Virginia Vitello, and Sharon Zumbrunn, "Curiosity in Schools," in Goren Gordon, ed., *The New Science of Curiosity* (Hauppauge, NY: Nova Science Publishers, 2018), 243–66, available at https://www.researchgate.net/publication/329569586_CURIOSITY_IN_SCHOOLS; Susan Engel, *The Hungry Mind: The Origins of Curiosity in Childhood* (Cambridge, MA: Harvard University Press, 2015); Judy Dunn, *The Beginnings of Social Understanding* (Cambridge, MA: Harvard University Press, 1988); Jinjoo Han, Niobe Way, Hirokazu Yoshikawa, and Crystal Clarke, "Interpersonal Curiosity and Its Association with Social and Emotional Skills and Well-Being During Adolescence," *Journal of Adolescent Research* (April 7, 2023), doi: 10.1177/07435584231162572.
2. Books that focus on or discuss interpersonal curiosity include Jeff Wetzler, *Ask: Tap Into the Hidden Wisdom of People Around You for Unexpected Breakthroughs in Leadership and Life* (New York: Hachette Go, 2024); and Susan Engel, *The Hungry Mind: The Origins of Curiosity in Childhood* (Cambridge, MA: Harvard University Press, 2015), respectively.
3. Catherine Pearson, "9 Ways to Improve Your Relationships in 2024," *New York Times,* December 28, 2023, https://www.nytimes.com/2023/12/28/well/family/family-relationships-dating-mindfulness-sex.html.
4. Émile Durkheim, *On Suicide* (New York: Penguin Classics Translation, 2007).

5. Kristen M. Santullo, "Newspaper Strike of 1899," *History of New York City*, November 7, 2017, https://blogs.shu.edu/nyc-history/2017/11/07/newspaper-strike-of-1900.
6. Walter J. Nicholls, *The DREAMers: How the Undocumented Youth Movement Transformed the Immigrant Rights Debate* (Stanford, CA: Stanford University Press, 2013).
7. Masood Farivar, "Florida Shooting Unleashes Youth Crusade for Stricter Gun Laws," *VOA*, February 22, 2018, https://www.voanews.com/a/florida-shooting-unleashes-childrens-crusade-stricter-gun-laws/4265435.html.
8. Farivar, "Florida Shooting Unleashes Youth Crusade for Stricter Gun Laws."
9. Farivar, "Florida Shooting Unleashes Youth Crusade for Stricter Gun Laws."
10. Farivar, "Florida Shooting Unleashes Youth Crusade for Stricter Gun Laws."
11. Matt Vasilogambros, "After Parkland, States Pass 50 New Gun-Control Laws," *Stateline*, August 2, 2018, https://stateline.org/2018/08/02/after-parkland-states-pass-50-new-gun-control-laws/.
12. Suyin Haynes, "Students from 1,600 Cities Just Walked Out of School to Protest Climate Change. It Could Be Greta Thunberg's Biggest Strike Yet," *Time*, May 24, 2019, https://time.com/5595365/global-climate-strikes-greta-thunberg/.
13. "Public Concern About Climate Change Remains at Record High," Yale School of the Environment, May 19, 2020, https://environment.yale.edu/news/article/public-concern-about-climate-change-remains-at-record-highs.
14. António Guterres, "The Climate Strikers Should Inspire Us All to Act at the Next UN Summit," *The Guardian*, March 15, 2019, https://www.theguardian.com/commentisfree/2019/mar/15/climate-strikers-urgency-un-summit-world-leaders.
15. Jason Walls, "UN Secretary-General Antonio Guterres Says His Generation Should Have Done More on Climate Change," *NZ Herald*, May 13, 2019, https://www.nzherald.co.nz/nz/un-secretary-general-antonio-guterres-says-his-generation-should-have-done-more-on-climate-change/2GX43F4A ECJN2QWJQ4AMSDCTNI/.
16. Walls, "UN Secretary-General Antonio Guterres Says His Generation Should Have Done More on Climate Change."
17. See Niobe Way, Alisha Ali, Carol Gilligan, and Pedro Noguera, eds., *The Crisis of Connection: Roots, Consequences, and Solutions* (New York: New York University Press, 2018).

Chapter 11: Schools

1. See Niobe Way, *The Science of Human Connection and Disconnection: A Five-Part Story* (Cambridge, MA: Harvard University Press, forthcoming); see also Niobe Way, Alisha Ali, Carol Gilligan, and Pedro Noguera, eds., introduction to *The Crisis of Connection: Roots, Consequences, and Solutions* (New York: New York University Press, 2018).
2. See Frans B. M. de Waal, *The Age of Empathy: Nature's Lessons for a Kinder Society* (New York: Harmony Books, 2009).
3. Way et al., eds., *The Crisis of Connection.*
4. I received permission from Wyatt Alpert, who wrote the email, to publish its content.
5. Wyatt Alpert, personal communication, 2021.
6. The Listening Project was created in close collaboration with colleagues, teachers, team members, and students over the past eight years. The primary collaborators include Drs. Joseph Nelson, Crystal Clarke, Jinjoo Han, and Hiro Yoshikawa, Laura Peynado, as well as Holly Van Hare, Sean Small, Gina Voskov, and dozens of others in the schools in which we have worked.
7. The Listening Guide is a method for analyzing narrative data that stems from the work that Lyn Mikel Brown and Carol Gilligan did together as part of a larger Harvard collaborative on fostering the healthy development of girls and women: see, for example, Lyn Mikel Brown and Carol Gilligan, *Meeting at the Crossroads: Women's Psychology and Girls' Development* (Cambridge, MA: Harvard University Press, 1992); see also Carol Gilligan and Jessica Eddy, "The Listening Guide: Replacing Judgment with Curiosity," *Qualitative Psychology* 8, no. 2 (2021): 141–51, doi: 10.1037/qup0000213.
8. See Michelle M. Chouinard, P. L. Harris, and Michael P. Maratsos, "Children's Questions: A Mechanism for Cognitive Development," *Monographs of the Society for Research in Child Development* 72, no. 1 (2007), doi: 10.1111/j.1540-5834.2007.00412.x; and Jamie Jirout, Virginia Vitello, and Sharon Zumbrunn, "Curiosity in Schools," in Goren Gordon, ed., *The New Science of Curiosity* (Hauppauge, NY: Nova Science Publishers, 2018), 243–66, available at https://www.researchgate.net/publication/329569586_CURIOSITY_IN_SCHOOLS.
9. See David Brooks, *How to Know a Person: The Art of Seeing Others Deeply and Being Deeply Seen* (New York: Random House, 2023).

10. See Jeff Wetzler, *Ask: Tap Into the Hidden Wisdom of People Around You for Unexpected Breakthroughs in Leadership and Life* (New York: Hachette Go, 2024), for a discussion of this cultural norm.
11. See Bonnie J. Ross Leadbeater and Niobe Way, *Growing Up Fast: Transitions to Early Adulthood of Inner-City Adolescent Mothers* (Mahwah, NJ: Lawrence Erlbaum, 2001).
12. Kate Murphy, *You're Not Listening: What You're Missing and Why It Matters* (New York: Celadon Books, 2020), 221. See also Wetzler, *Ask*.
13. Deborah Tolman, "Echoes of Sexual Objectification: Listening for One Girl's Erotic Voice," in Deborah L. Tolman and Mary Brydon-Miller, eds., *From Subjects to Subjectivities: A Handbook of Interpretive and Participatory Methods* (New York: New York University Press, 2001), 130–44.
14. The Listening Project team includes or included Dr. Crystal Clarke, Holly Van Hare, Dr. Jinjoo Han, Sean Small, Dr. Joseph Nelson, Dr. Hiro Yoshikawa, Dr. Laura Peynado, and many undergraduate and graduate students over the past eight years.
15. Jinjoo Han, Niobe Way, and Hirokazu Yoshikawa, "Addressing the Crisis of Connection in Middle Schools: The Listening Project," forthcoming.
16. This first practice comes from my graduate school mentor at Harvard, who always asked us to start with a real question or a question that we truly want to know the answer to rather than one that we think we already know the answer to. See Carol Gilligan, *In a Human Voice* (Medford, MA: Polity Press, 2023).
17. Michael Kardas, Amit Kumar, and Nicholas Epley, "Overly Shallow? Miscalibrated Expectations Create a Barrier to Deeper Conversation," *Journal of Personality and Social Psychology* 122, no. 3 (2022): 367–98, doi: 10.1037/pspa0000281.
18. Carol Gilligan, *The Birth of Pleasure: A New Map of Love* (New York: Vintage, 2003).
19. "The Art of the Open-Ended Question," North Carolina Department of Health and Human Services, https://files.nc.gov/ncdhhs/documents/files/dss/training/Open-Ended-Questions-.pdf.
20. See The Narrative Method (TNM), "TNM: DIY Human Deck 2," n.d., https://www.thenarrativemethod.org/product-page/tnm-diy-human-deck-2.
21. Daniel Jones, "The 36 Questions That Lead to Love," *New York Times*, January 9, 2015, https://www.nytimes.com/2015/01/09/style/no-37-big-wedding-or-small.html.

22. For more information about the Listening Project and its curriculum, please contact nyu.pach@gmail.com.
23. One of the likely reasons why the practice of transformative interviewing is harder for older people than for younger ones has to do with the decline in curiosity as we get older. The decline, however, is cultural and not natural, and thus we can bring it back to its original state, as when we were five years old. See Jon Carroll, "The Decline of Curiosity," *SFGate,* June 6, 2001, https://www.sfgate.com/entertainment/carroll/article/The-decline-of-curiosity-3315070.php.
24. Jinjoo Han, Niobe Way, Hirokazu Yoshikawa, and Crystal Clarke, "Interpersonal Curiosity and Its Association with Social and Emotional Skills and Well-Being During Adolescence," *Journal of Adolescent Research* (April 7, 2023), doi: 10.1177/ 07435584231162572.
25. Matthew D. Lieberman, *Social: Why Our Brains Are Wired to Connect* (New York: Crown, 2013), 242.
26. Lieberman, *Social,* 283.

Chapter 12: Workplaces and Homes

1. Ellen Rosen, "In an Uncertain Job Market, How Can Companies Retain Workers?," *New York Times,* February 13, 2023, https://www.nytimes.com/2023/02/13/business/employee-retention-quitting-companies.html.
2. I am part of the New Pluralist Group, which is a network of changemakers who are committed to bridging divides; see Farah Stockman, "This Group Has $100 Million and a Big Goal: To Fix America," *New York Times,* November 5, 2022, https://www.nytimes.com/2022/11/05/opinion/polarization-democrats-republicans-pluralism.html.
3. Rosen, "In an Uncertain Job Market, How Can Companies Retain Workers?"
4. "The Surgeon General's Framework for Workplace Mental Health and Well-Being," Office of the U.S. Surgeon General, 2022, https://www.hhs.gov/surgeongeneral/priorities/workplace-well-being/index.html.
5. "The Surgeon General's Framework for Workplace Mental Health and Well-Being," Office of the U.S. Surgeon General.
6. Blair Miller, "Social Skills Revolution: The Rise of Outsider Talent," *The Hill,* June 6, 2023, https://thehill.com/opinion/finance/3802103-social-skills-revolution-the-rise-of-outsider-talent/.
7. Matthew D. Lieberman, *Social: Why Our Brains Are Wired to Connect* (New York: Crown, 2013), 270.

8. Lieberman, *Social*, 273–74.
9. Shayna Joubert, "The 5 Qualities All Successful Leaders Have in Common," *Northeastern University Graduate Programs*, January 24, 2019, https://www.northeastern.edu/graduate/blog/top-5-leadership-qualities/.
10. The exception is found in the Yale Center for Emotional Intelligence (YCEI); see "Yale Center for Emotional Intelligence (YCEI)," Child Study Center, https://medicine.yale.edu/childstudy/services/community-and-schools-programs/center-for-emotional-intelligence/. Marc Brackett, the founding director and author of *Permission to Feel: Unlocking the Power of Emotions to Help Our Kids, Ourselves, and Our Society Thrive* (New York: Celadon Books, 2019), created a method called RULER to foster emotional intelligence in schools and workplaces across the country.
11. Kate Murphy, *You're Not Listening: What You're Missing and Why It Matters* (New York: Celadon Books, 2020), 40.
12. Lieberman, *Social*, 104.
13. Murphy, *You're Not Listening*, 41.
14. Murphy, *You're Not Listening*, 78.
15. Saliha Bava and Mark Greene, *The Relational Workplace: How Relational Intelligence Grows Diverse, Equitable, and Inclusive Cultures of Connection* (New York: ThinkPlay Partners, 2023).
16. See Melanie Hamlett, "Men Have No Friends and Women Bear the Burden," *Harper's Bazaar*, May 2, 2019, https://www.harpersbazaar.com/culture/features/a27259689/toxic-masculinity-male-friendships-emotional-labor-men-rely-on-women/.
17. Anna Louie Sussman, "Why Aren't More People Marrying? Ask Women What Dating Is Like," *New York Times*, November 11, 2023, https://www.nytimes.com/2023/11/11/opinion/marriage-women-men-dating.html.
18. Patrick Ryan, "Boys and Men Are Lonelier Than Ever. What Can We Do About It?," *USA Today*, February 3, 2023, https://www.usatoday.com/story/life/health-wellness/2023/02/03/male-friendship-lonely-close-friends-men/11162423002/.
19. Ginia Bellafante, "Mothers Under Pressure," *New York Review of Books*, June 9, 2022, https://www.nybooks.com/articles/2022/06/09/mothers-under-pressure-ginia-bellafante/.
20. Making Caring Common Project (MCC), "The Children We Mean to Raise: The Real Messages Adults Are Sending About Values," July 2014, https://mcc.gse.harvard.edu/reports/children-mean-raise.

21. Saliha Bava and Mark Greene, *The Relational Book for Parenting: Raising Children to Connect, Collaborate, and Innovate by Growing Our Families' Relationship Superpowers* (New York: ThinkPlay Partners, 2018), 5.
22. Bava and Greene, *The Relational Book for Parenting*, 6.
23. This insight was offered by Carol Brandt, my colleague and close friend at NYU Abu Dhabi.
24. Lieberman, *Social*, 160.
25. Judy Y. Chu, *When Boys Become Boys: Development, Relationships, and Masculinity* (New York: New York University Press, 2014), 169.
26. Chu, *When Boys Become Boys*, 171.
27. Chu, *When Boys Become Boys*, 171.
28. Chu, *When Boys Become Boys*, 171–72.
29. Chu, *When Boys Become Boys*, 178.
30. Chu, *When Boys Become Boys*, 182.
31. Chu, *When Boys Become Boys*, 182.
32. Chu, *When Boys Become Boys*, 182.
33. Chu, *When Boys Become Boys*, 183.
34. Chu, *When Boys Become Boys*, 183.
35. Murphy, *You're Not Listening*, 39.
36. Constance Flanagan, "Trust, Identity, and Civic Hope," *Applied Developmental Science* 7, no. 3 (2003): 166–71, doi: 10.1207/S1532480XADS0703_7.
37. Lise Eliot, *Pink Brain, Blue Brain: How Small Differences Grow into Troublesome Gaps—and What We Can Do About It* (Boston: Mariner Books, 2010), 262.

The Story of Us

1. James Baldwin, *I Am Not Your Negro,* Magnolia Pictures, Amazon MGM Studios, 2016.
2. Niobe Way, *Deep Secrets: Boys' Friendships and the Crisis of Connection* (Cambridge, MA: Harvard University Press, 2013), 1.
3. Sarah Hrdy shared this parable in her book *Mothers and Others: The Evolutionary Origins of Mutual Understanding* (Cambridge, MA: Belknap Press of Harvard University Press, 2009).
4. I have cofounded with others across the United States an AI-driven company called agapi.ai that teaches social connection 3.0. and will use AI to enhance human-to-human connection rather than simply replace humans altogether.

5. Angelique Chrisafis, "French Philosopher Urges People to Rebel—by Making Friends," *The Guardian,* March 6, 2023, https://www.theguardian.com/lifeandstyle/2023/mar/06/french-philosopher-geoffroy-de-lagasnerie-friendships#:~:text=He%20described%20the%20friendship%20as,family%20structures%20and%20romantic%20relationships.
6. Chrisafis, "French Philosopher Urges People to Rebel—by Making Friends."
7. Chrisafis, "French Philosopher Urges People to Rebel—by Making Friends."
8. Eric Klinenberg, *Palaces for the People: How Social Infrastructure Can Help Fight Inequality, Polarization, and the Decline of Civic Life* (New York: Crown, 2018).
9. Kate Murphy, *You're Not Listening: What You're Missing and Why It Matters* (New York: Celadon Books, 2020), 222.

Acknowledgments

1. bell hooks, "Marginalization as a Site of Resistance," in Russell Ferguson, Martha Gever, Trinh T. Minh-ha, and Cornel West, eds., *Out There: Marginalization and Contemporary Culture* (Cambridge: MIT Press, 1990), 341.
2. bell hooks, *Outlaw Culture: Resisting Representations* (New York: Routledge, 1994), 290.

Index

About the Author

Dr. Niobe Way is professor of developmental psychology at NYU, the founder of the Project for the Advancement of Our Common Humanity (PACH; pach.org), creative adviser and cofounder of agapi.kids, and the principal investigator on the Listening Project. She was the president of the Society for Research on Adolescence (SRA), received her BA from UC Berkeley and her doctorate from the Graduate School of Education at Harvard University, and was a National Institute of Mental Health postdoctoral fellow at Yale University in the Department of Psychology.

Her work focuses on social and emotional development of adolescents and how cultural ideologies shape families and child development in the United States and China. She has been researching social and emotional development of adolescents for almost four decades, and has authored or coauthored more than one hundred peer-reviewed journal articles and seven single-authored, coauthored, or coedited books.

Her latest coedited book is *The Crisis of Connection: Its Roots, Consequences, and Solutions.* She has also coedited, with Judy Chu, *Adolescent Boys: Exploring Diverse Cultures of Boyhood.* Her last single-authored book is *Deep Secrets: Boys' Friendships and the Crisis of Connection,* which was the inspiration for *Close,* a movie that won the Grand Prix Award at the Cannes Film Festival and was nominated for an Oscar for best foreign film. She is regularly featured in mainstream media, speaking on the topics of boys, friendships, loneliness, teenagers, gender stereotypes, masculinity, and the roots of violence and ways to prevent violence.